POWER AND ABILITIES

Will Pfeifer
Writer

Kano
Artist

Dave Stewart
J.D. Mettler
Colors

Ken Lopez
Letters

John Van Fleet
Cover Artist

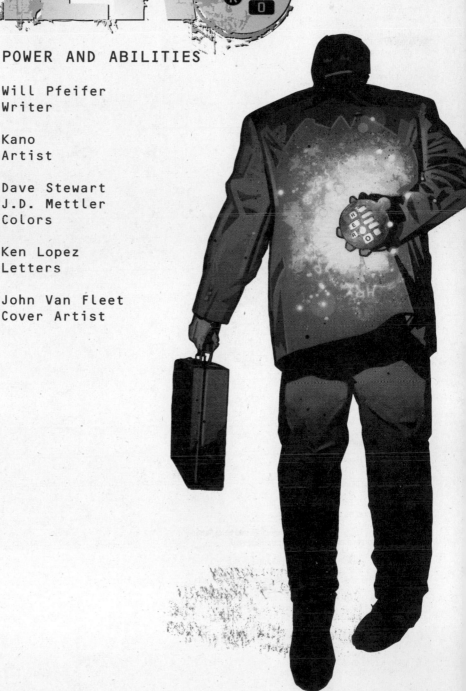

Dan DiDio
VP-Editorial

Peter Tomasi
Mike McAvennie
Editors-original series

Stephen Wacker
Lysa Hawkins
Associate Editors-original series

Valerie D'Orazio
Assistant Editor-original series

Anton Kawasaki
Editor-collected edition

Robbin Brosterman
Senior Art Director

Paul Levitz
President & Publisher

Georg Brewer
VP-Design & Retail Product Development

Richard Bruning
Senior VP-Creative Director

Patrick Caldon
Senior VP-Finance & Operations

Chris Caramalis
VP-Finance

Terri Cunningham
VP-Managing Editor

Alison Gill
VP-Manufacturing

Lillian Laserson
Senior VP & General Counsel

Jim Lee
Editorial Director-WildStorm

David McKillips
VP-Advertising & Custom Publishing

John Nee
VP-Business Development

Cheryl Rubin
VP-Brand Management

Bob Wayne
VP-Sales & Marketing

H-E-R-O: POWERS AND ABILITIES

DC Comics, 1700 Broadway, New York, NY 10019
A Warner Bros. Entertainment Company
Printed in Canada. First Printing.
ISBN: 1-4012-0168-7
Cover illustrations by John Van Fleet.

INTRODUCTION

By Geoff Johns

Will Pfeifer and Kano have given us the many answers to that one question burning in the minds of comics readers everywhere:

"What would you do if you had super-powers?"

DC asked me to write this introduction because of what I said before the first issue of H-E-R-O hit the stands. I told everyone to spread the word – if you bought issue #1 and you didn't like it, I'd buy it back from you. No questions asked.

I gave this book a personal money-back guarantee.

Now, while this might seem hardly out of the ordinary, the thing that got everyone's attention was – I didn't write it. I didn't draw it. I didn't even know the creators behind it. But what I *did* know was that H-E-R-O was going to be one of the best comic book magazines unleashed in 2003.

My brief state of insanity started while I was visiting the DC offices in late 2002. I got a chance to read the black and white copies of issues #1 and 2 of H-E-R-O months before they were printed. I hadn't heard a lot about the book, I hadn't seen a lot of buzz behind it, but after reading the first two issues I hated the idea of H-E-R-O getting lost in the sea of monthly comics. This book was incredibly special. I wanted to read issue #3. I wanted to read issue #15. And the only way I was going to be able to do that

was if the book was a success. So I got on www.thefourthrail.com, a comics review website, and made my money-back offer. Try the book. Don't like it? Send it back to me and I'll buy it back.

The next day my e-mail box was flooded.

One of my editors called me "crazy," many others thought it, and I'm sure a crowd of skeptics laughed at me. Good. That meant they were talking. That meant people were starting to say, "Yeah, Johns is nuts…hey, what exactly *is* H-E-R-O anyway?"

Well, in 1965, DC Comics introduced the concept of DIAL "H" FOR HERO in HOUSE OF MYSTERY #156. It was a feature in the book devoted to a young boy named Robby Reed. Robby had found a strange alien dial that appeared to have letters on it. And when he dialed H-E-R-O, Robby was transformed into a random costumed hero. Robby became known as "The Boy Who Could Change Into 1,000 Super-Heroes!"

He was transformed into guys like Giantboy, Radar-Sonar Man, King Kandy and even Plastic Man. Of course, some heroes (like Super Charge) were incredibly useful, while others (like Balloon Boy) were less than thrilling. But the greatest aspect of it all was the unpredictability. What hero would Robby become, how would he use his powers?

The DIAL "H" FOR HERO feature lasted until HOUSE

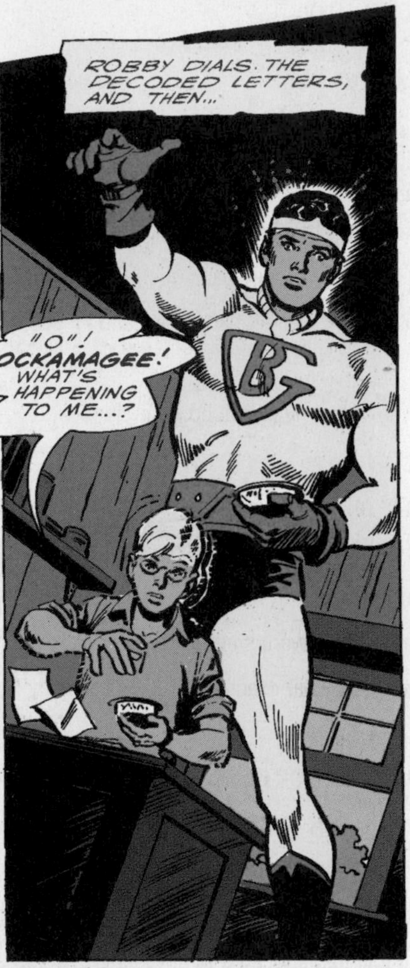
ROBBY DIALS THE DECODED LETTERS, AND THEN...
"O"! SOCKAMAGEE! WHAT'S HAPPENING TO ME...?

OF MYSTERY #173. Robby appeared sporadically, but for the most part he and his H-Dial were forgotten.

About fifteen years later, however, a pair of kids in the small town of Fairfax, Christopher King and Victoria Grant, stumbled upon two new variants of the H-Dial. A wristwatch and a pendant. Together, Chris and Vicki discovered they could become a random super-hero by DIALING "H" FOR HERO. Their feature ran mainly in ADVENTURE COMICS, beginning with issue #479.

The twist was not the fact that it was a pair of teenagers, or that one was a girl, it was that the heroes came from the readers. The heroes Chris and Vicki transformed into were all suggested by the kids buying the book. Mega-Boy, Captain Electron, Phase Master, Gold-girl, Starlet, the Weather Witch and dozens more filled the pages. Nearly every comics reader has made up a super-hero at some point in their lives.

The new DIAL "H" FOR HERO lasted for quite awhile, eventually moving over to THE NEW ADVENTURES OF SUPERBOY before disappearing. The characters even interacted with the TEEN TITANS.

Years later, the H-Dial changed hands again, this time with a young man named Hero Cruz. And then, the concept faded into the background. Waiting for someone to rediscover it again.

Today, the subject of what makes a hero is even more prevalent than ever. And Will Pfeifer obviously knows this. He saw the potential in the concept along with original editor Mike McAvennie. I'm sure one of the questions they asked each other when developing the book was:

"If you could have one super-power, what would it be?"

That's a game every single one of us play. Have you ever dreamed of flying? Of soaring over your home-town, of getting away from it all? Or have you wished to turn invisible? To do whatever you please, to hear what they all say about you when you're not there? What about invulnerability? Or super-strength? Keeping the schoolyard bully at bay. Or have you gotten a little more creative? Maybe elemental transmuting abilities? You turn your old car into solid gold and you won't have to work again for a long, long time.

Super-powers would solve all of your problems, right?

It depends on the type of person you are. And really, that's what H-E-R-O is all about. Will and Kano (and amazing colorists Dave Stewart and J.D. Mettler) have crafted a series that looks at normal everyday people who are transformed into super-heroes and given powers far beyond those of mortal man.

Within this first volume, we're introduced to a down-and-out ice cream counter worker, a successful businessman, and a shy young girl. We get to see how super-powers affect each one of them, and the people around them. It's fascinating stuff.

Months ago, before the first issue of H-E-R-O was released, I saw plenty of people talking about it. Speculating on whether it was really so good that I'd throw my own money on the line. The day it hit the shelves, they found out it was. I received e-mail after e-mail thanking me for the recommendation. I stood my ground, and felt confident that there would be very few issues of H-E-R-O #1 that I would be buying back. Of course, three weeks after it was released, the first issue was going for ten bucks on eBay. In all honesty, I would've loved to get my hands on some copies…

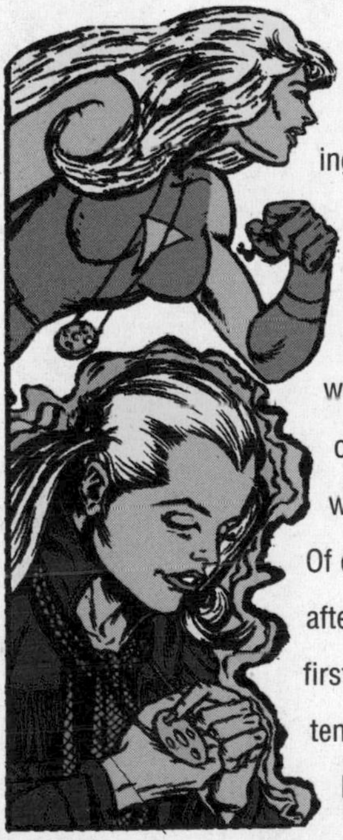

But it never happened.

I didn't buy one single issue back.

I like to think that I helped steer a few people to this book, but honestly, H-E-R-O would've found all of its readers anyway. Will and Kano click like no one else, and the readers obviously picked up on it.

As of today, it's been six months since H-E-R-O debuted. The book gets better and better with every issue. I've seen praise upon praise for each subsequent issue. And now I sit and wait…

Wondering if I'll ever buy H-E-R-O #1…

But knowing I'll be buying issue #15.

Thanks for a great bunch of stories, guys.

— Geoff Johns
July 28, 2003

Geoff Johns writes TEEN TITANS, JSA, THE FLASH and HAWKMAN for DC Comics. He lives with his wife, Anissa, and their dog, Beau, in Sherman Oaks, California. If he could have one power it'd be super-speed, but he'd settle for x-ray vision.

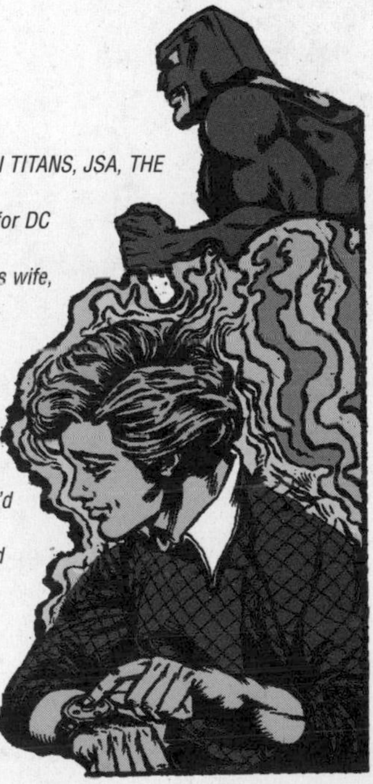

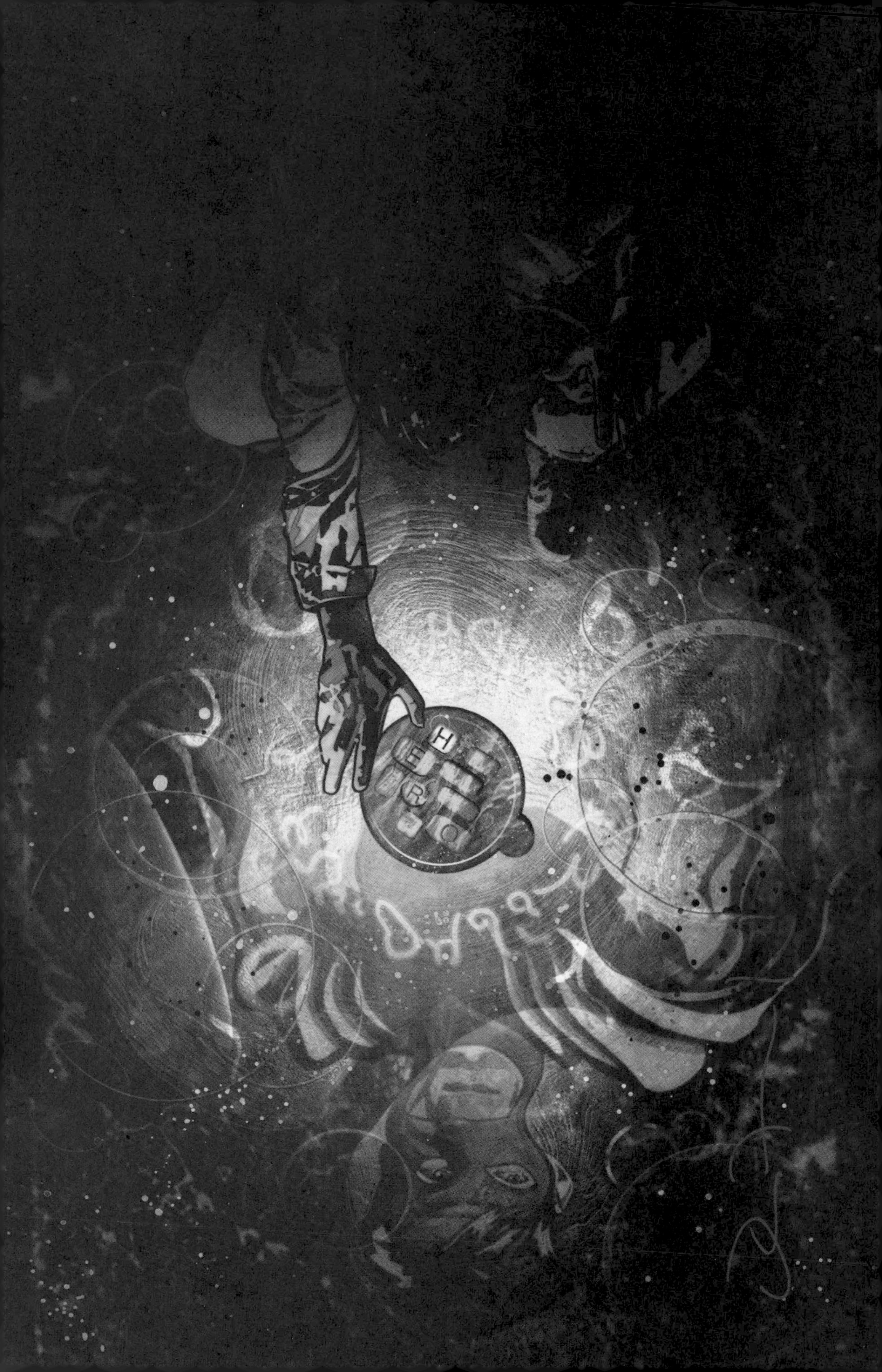
HERO

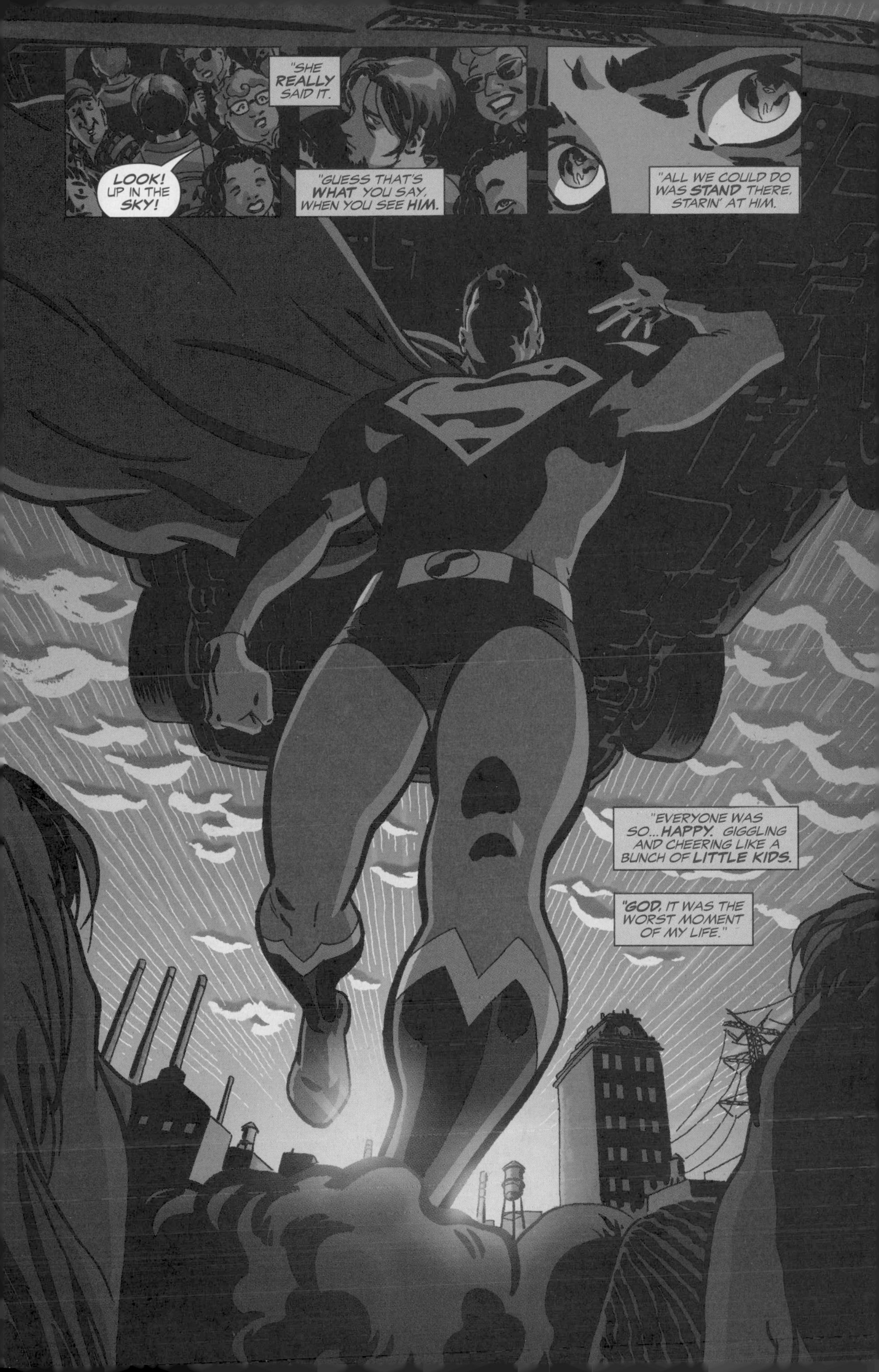
LOOK! UP IN THE SKY!
"SHE REALLY SAID IT.
"GUESS THAT'S WHAT YOU SAY, WHEN YOU SEE HIM.
"ALL WE COULD DO WAS STAND THERE, STARIN' AT HIM.
"EVERYONE WAS SO...HAPPY. GIGGLING AND CHEERING LIKE A BUNCH OF LITTLE KIDS.
"GOD, IT WAS THE WORST MOMENT OF MY LIFE."

IN HEATON
DIAL
555-HERO
MY GOD...
...YOU ACTUALLY SAW SUPERMAN?
A-ARE YOU EVEN LISTENING TO ME?
THAT'S NOT WHAT THIS IS ABOUT!
I DIDN'T CALL TO TALK ABOUT SOME BRUSH WITH GREATNESS!
HELP LINE
WERE NOT HERE TO JUDGE YOU
HELP!
call now HELP PHONE
FOR THE BEST SUBS IN HEATON DIAL 555-HERO
LOST HOPE?
CRISIS HOTLINE
CALL 800-555-HELP TOLL FREE CONFIDENTIAL
CALL
I CALLED 'CAUSE I DON'T SEE ANY POINT!
BECAUSE HE'S EVERYTHING, AND I'M NOTHING!

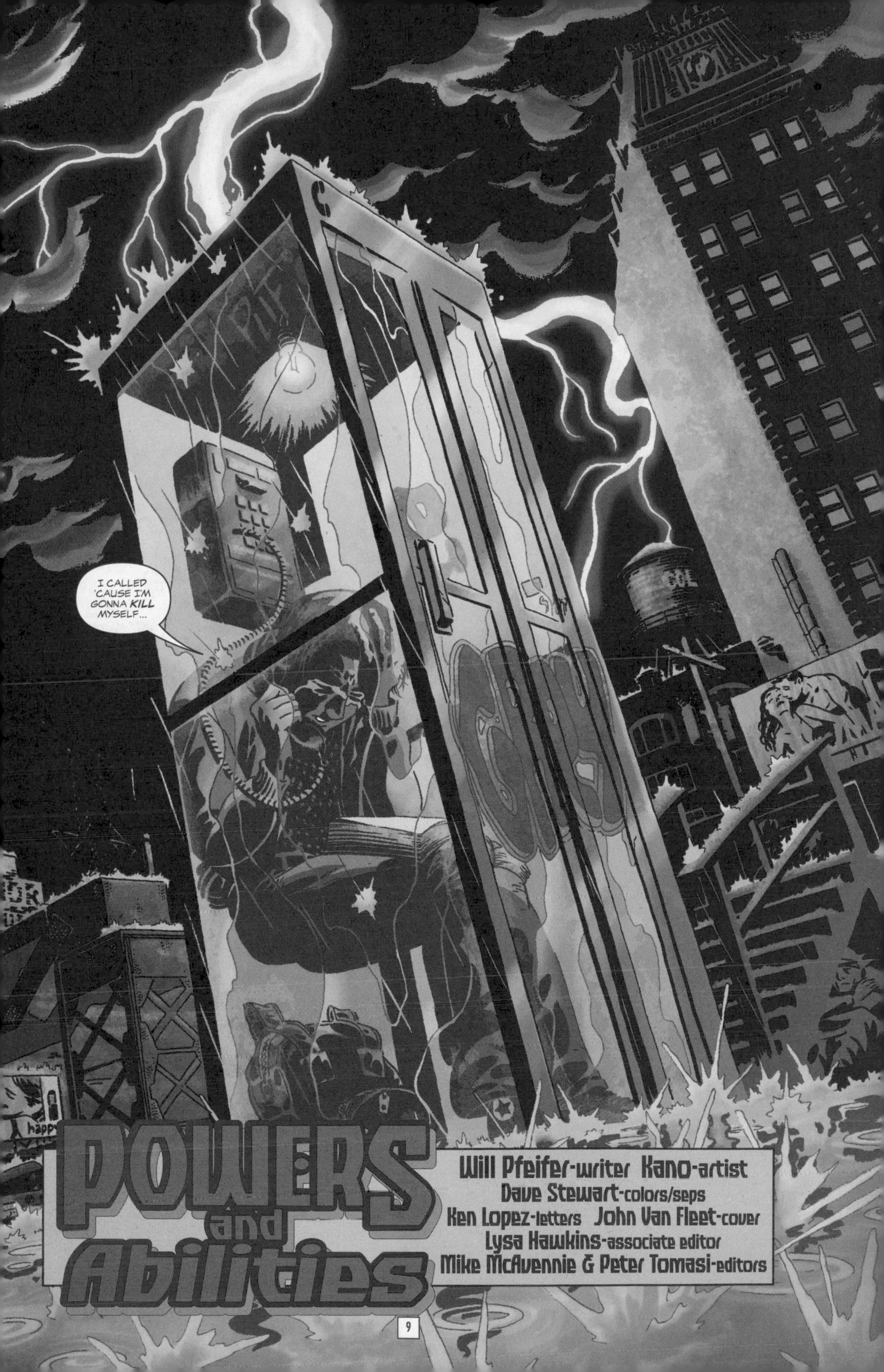
I CALLED 'CAUSE I'M GONNA KILL MYSELF...
POWERS and Abilities
Will Pfeifer-writer Kano-artist
Dave Stewart-colors/seps
Ken Lopez-letters John Van Fleet-cover
Lysa Hawkins-associate editor
Mike McAvennie & Peter Tomasi-editors

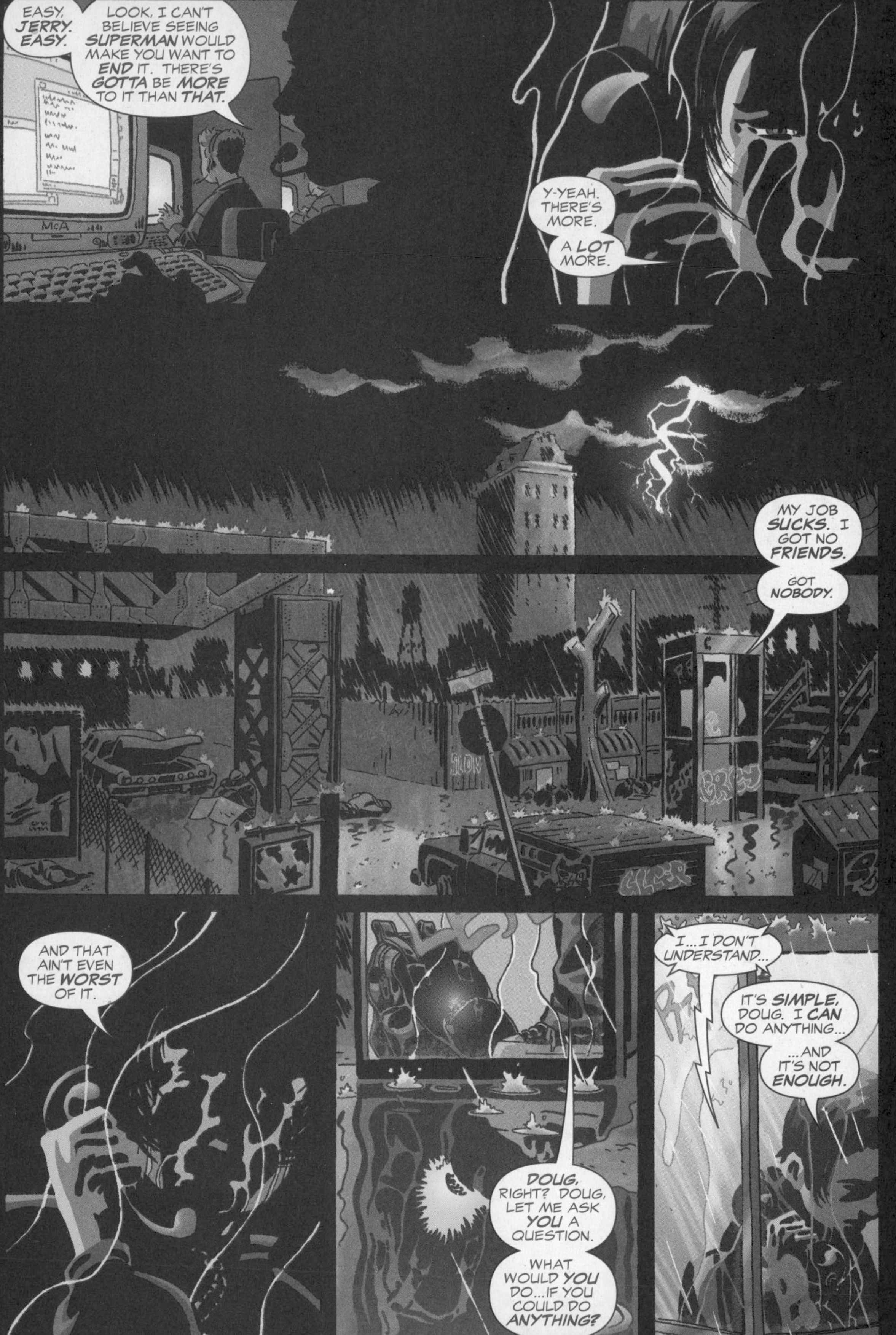
EASY, JERRY. EASY.
LOOK, I CAN'T BELIEVE SEEING SUPERMAN WOULD MAKE YOU WANT TO END IT. THERE'S GOTTA BE MORE TO IT THAN THAT.
Y-YEAH. THERE'S MORE.
A LOT MORE.
MY JOB SUCKS. I GOT NO FRIENDS.
GOT NOBODY.
AND THAT AIN'T EVEN THE WORST OF IT.
DOUG, RIGHT? DOUG, LET ME ASK YOU A QUESTION.
WHAT WOULD YOU DO...IF YOU COULD DO ANYTHING?
I...I DON'T UNDERSTAND...
IT'S SIMPLE, DOUG. I CAN DO ANYTHING...
...AND IT'S NOT ENOUGH.

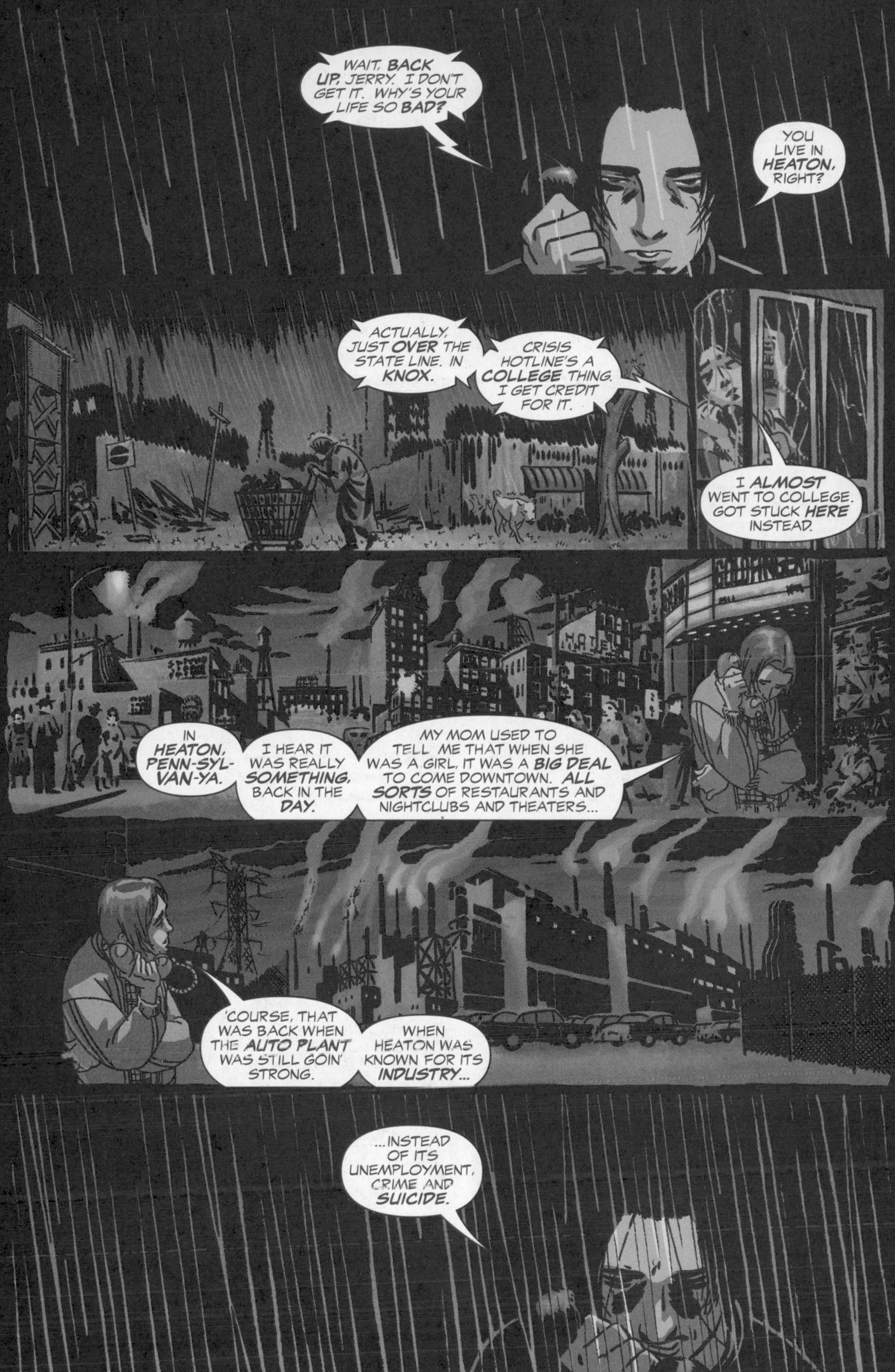
WAIT, BACK UP, JERRY. I DON'T GET IT. WHY'S YOUR LIFE SO BAD?
YOU LIVE IN HEATON, RIGHT?
ACTUALLY, JUST OVER THE STATE LINE. IN KNOX.
CRISIS HOTLINE'S A COLLEGE THING. I GET CREDIT FOR IT.
I ALMOST WENT TO COLLEGE. GOT STUCK HERE INSTEAD.
IN HEATON, PENN-SYL-VAN-YA.
I HEAR IT WAS REALLY SOMETHING, BACK IN THE DAY.
MY MOM USED TO TELL ME THAT WHEN SHE WAS A GIRL, IT WAS A BIG DEAL TO COME DOWNTOWN. ALL SORTS OF RESTAURANTS AND NIGHTCLUBS AND THEATERS...
'COURSE, THAT WAS BACK WHEN THE AUTO PLANT WAS STILL GOIN' STRONG.
WHEN HEATON WAS KNOWN FOR ITS INDUSTRY...
...INSTEAD OF ITS UNEMPLOYMENT, CRIME AND SUICIDE.

"MY LIFE USED TO LOOK EASY--ID GO TO SCHOOL, THEN WORK AT THE **PLANT.** JUST LIKE MOM AND DAD."

"**THEY** WERE HAPPY. WHY WOULDN'T **I** BE?"

"THEN, RIGHT BEFORE I GRADUATED..."

"...THE **PLANT** CLOSED..."

"...DAD **DIED...**

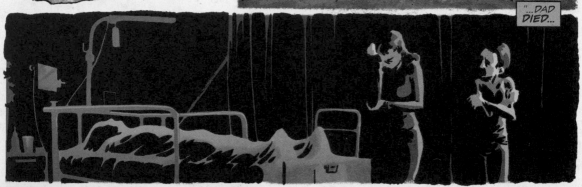

"...AND MOM LEFT. SHE WENT OUT WEST TO FIND **WORK.** 'LEAST, THAT'S WHAT SHE **TOLD** ME."

"**TRUTH** IS, I THINK I REMINDED HER TOO MUCH OF **DAD.**

"I DECIDED TO STICK AROUND. FIGURED THERE **HAD** TO BE A DECENT JOB FOR ME **SOMEWHERE.**

"FIGURED **WRONG.**

"SURE. I GOT DEPRESSED FOR A WHILE. **REALLY** DEPRESSED.

"THEN I HEARD ABOUT A PLACE THAT WAS **HIRING.**

"SO NOW, INSTEAD OF MAKING **CARS** FOR 20 BUCKS AN HOUR...

"...I MAKE **SUNDAES** FOR MINIMUM WAGE."

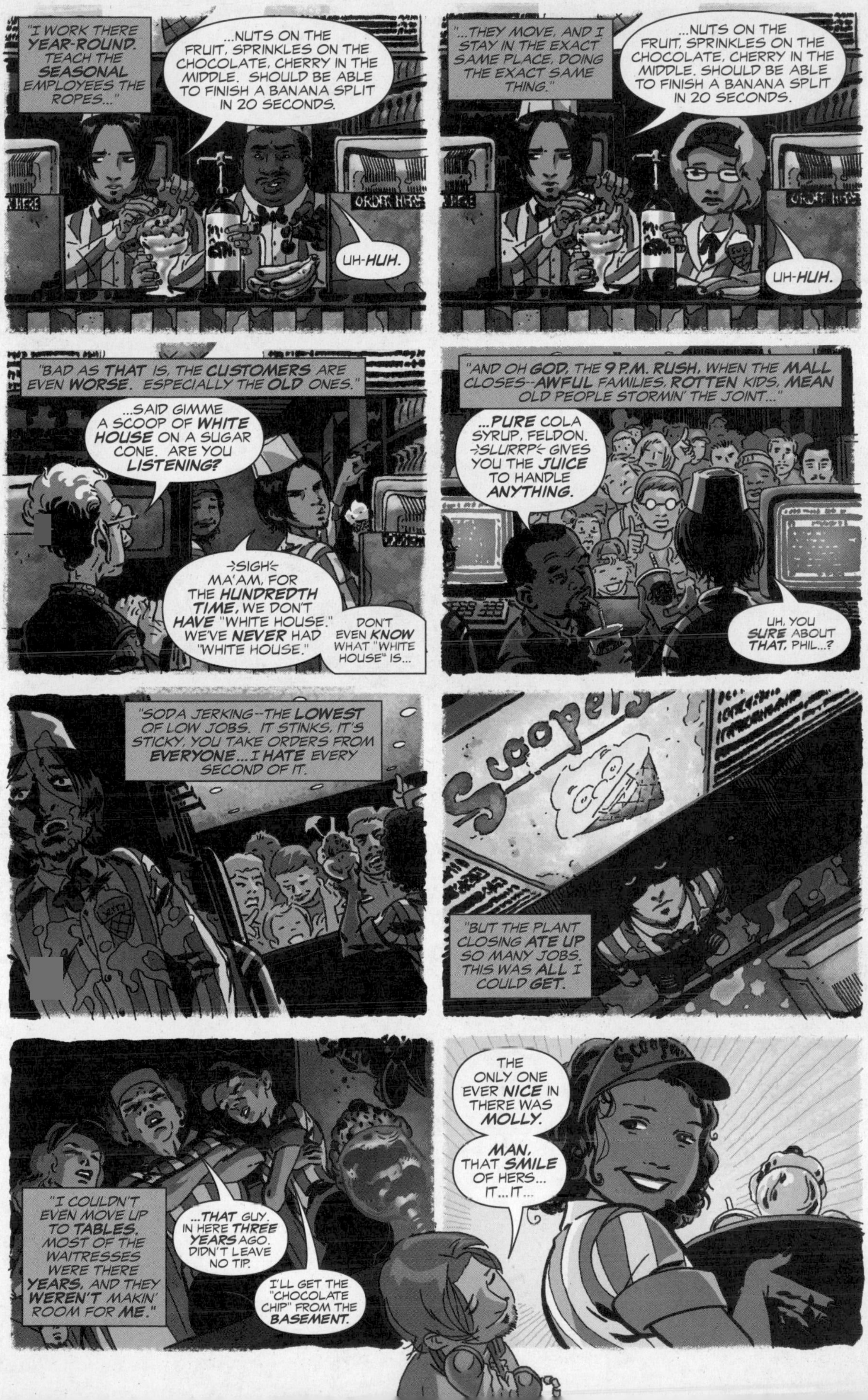
"I WORK THERE YEAR-ROUND. TEACH THE SEASONAL EMPLOYEES THE ROPES..."
...NUTS ON THE FRUIT, SPRINKLES ON THE CHOCOLATE, CHERRY IN THE MIDDLE. SHOULD BE ABLE TO FINISH A BANANA SPLIT IN 20 SECONDS.
ORDER HERE
UH-HUH.
"...THEY MOVE, AND I STAY IN THE EXACT SAME PLACE, DOING THE EXACT SAME THING."
...NUTS ON THE FRUIT, SPRINKLES ON THE CHOCOLATE, CHERRY IN THE MIDDLE. SHOULD BE ABLE TO FINISH A BANANA SPLIT IN 20 SECONDS.
ORDER HERE
UH-HUH.
"BAD AS THAT IS, THE CUSTOMERS ARE EVEN WORSE. ESPECIALLY THE OLD ONES."
...SAID GIMME A SCOOP OF WHITE HOUSE ON A SUGAR CONE. ARE YOU LISTENING?
SIGH MA'AM, FOR THE HUNDREDTH TIME, WE DON'T HAVE "WHITE HOUSE." WE'VE NEVER HAD "WHITE HOUSE."
DON'T EVEN KNOW WHAT "WHITE HOUSE" IS...
"AND OH GOD, THE 9 P.M. RUSH, WHEN THE MALL CLOSES--AWFUL FAMILIES, ROTTEN KIDS, MEAN OLD PEOPLE STORMIN' THE JOINT..."
...PURE COLA SYRUP, FELDON. SLURRP GIVES YOU THE JUICE TO HANDLE ANYTHING.
UH, YOU SURE ABOUT THAT, PHIL...?
"SODA JERKING--THE LOWEST OF LOW JOBS. IT STINKS, IT'S STICKY, YOU TAKE ORDERS FROM EVERYONE...I HATE EVERY SECOND OF IT.
Scoopers
"BUT THE PLANT CLOSING ATE UP SO MANY JOBS. THIS WAS ALL I COULD GET.
"I COULDN'T EVEN MOVE UP TO TABLES. MOST OF THE WAITRESSES WERE THERE YEARS, AND THEY WEREN'T MAKIN' ROOM FOR ME."
...THAT GUY. IN HERE THREE YEARS AGO. DIDN'T LEAVE NO TIP.
I'LL GET THE "CHOCOLATE CHIP" FROM THE BASEMENT.
THE ONLY ONE EVER NICE IN THERE WAS MOLLY.
MAN, THAT SMILE OF HERS... IT...IT...

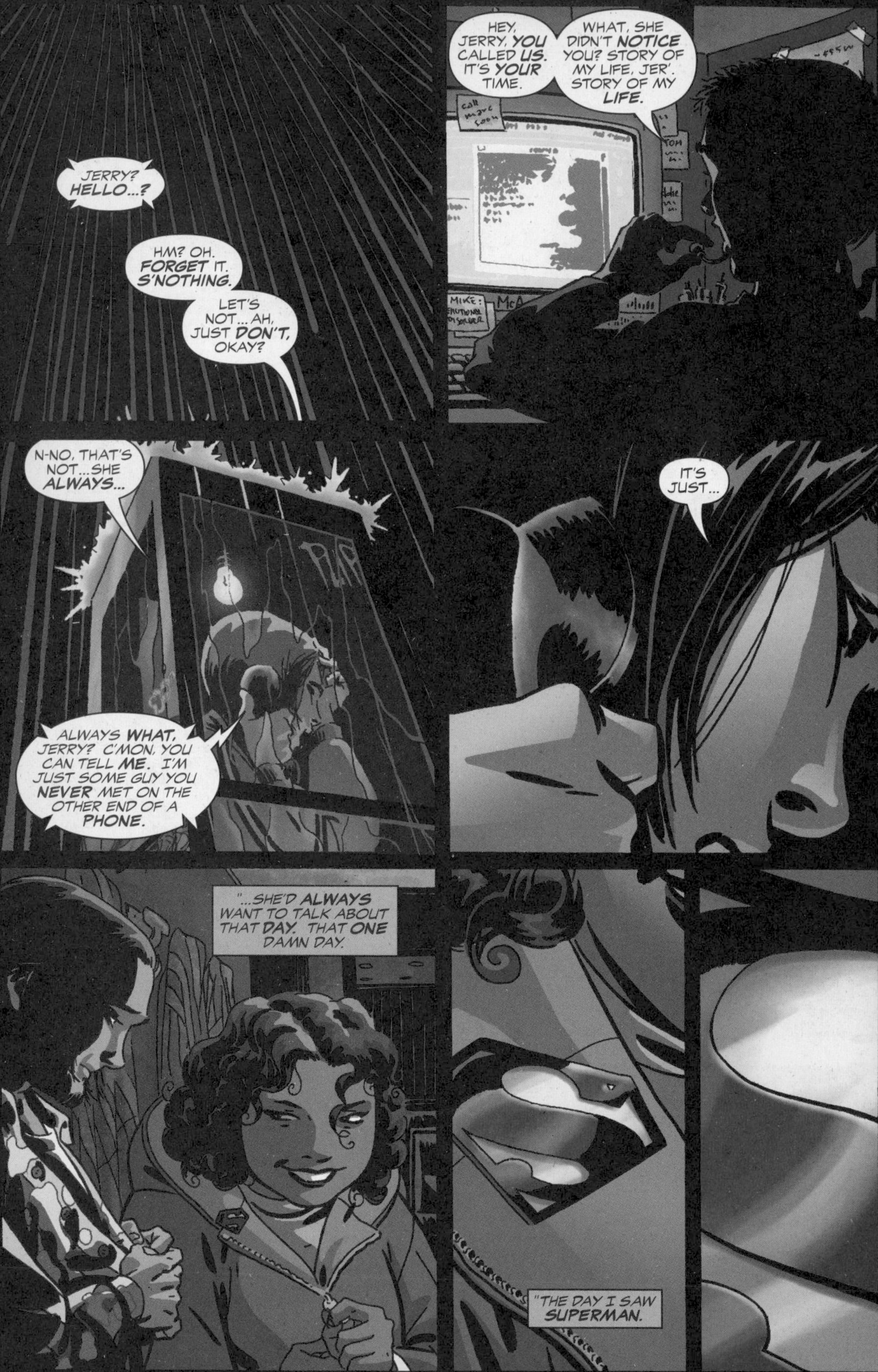

JERRY? HELLO...?
HM? OH. FORGET IT. S'NOTHING.
LET'S NOT...AH, JUST DON'T, OKAY?
HEY, JERRY, YOU CALLED US. IT'S YOUR TIME.
WHAT, SHE DIDN'T NOTICE YOU? STORY OF MY LIFE, JER'. STORY OF MY LIFE.
N-NO, THAT'S NOT...SHE ALWAYS...
ALWAYS WHAT, JERRY? C'MON, YOU CAN TELL ME. I'M JUST SOME GUY YOU NEVER MET ON THE OTHER END OF A PHONE.
IT'S JUST...
"...SHE'D ALWAYS WANT TO TALK ABOUT THAT DAY. THAT ONE DAMN DAY.
"THE DAY I SAW SUPERMAN.

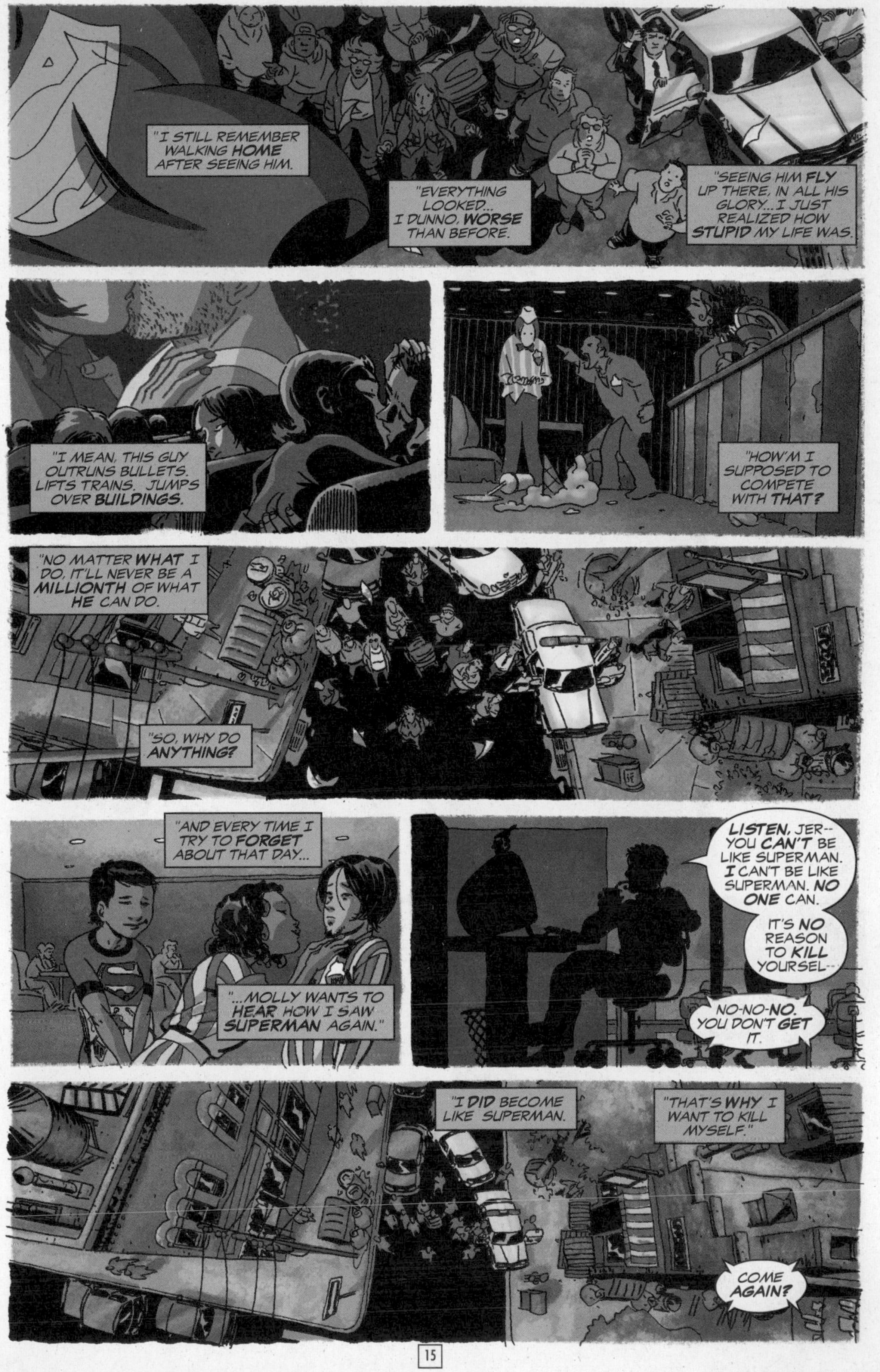
"I STILL REMEMBER WALKING HOME AFTER SEEING HIM.
"EVERYTHING LOOKED... I DUNNO, WORSE THAN BEFORE.
"SEEING HIM FLY UP THERE, IN ALL HIS GLORY... I JUST REALIZED HOW STUPID MY LIFE WAS.
"I MEAN, THIS GUY OUTRUNS BULLETS. LIFTS TRAINS. JUMPS OVER BUILDINGS.
"HOW'M I SUPPOSED TO COMPETE WITH THAT?
"NO MATTER WHAT I DO, IT'LL NEVER BE A MILLIONTH OF WHAT HE CAN DO.
"SO, WHY DO ANYTHING?
"AND EVERY TIME I TRY TO FORGET ABOUT THAT DAY...
"...MOLLY WANTS TO HEAR HOW I SAW SUPERMAN AGAIN."
LISTEN, JER-- YOU CAN'T BE LIKE SUPERMAN. I CAN'T BE LIKE SUPERMAN. NO ONE CAN.
IT'S NO REASON TO KILL YOURSEL--
NO-NO-NO. YOU DON'T GET IT.
"I DID BECOME LIKE SUPERMAN.
"THAT'S WHY I WANT TO KILL MYSELF."
COME AGAIN?

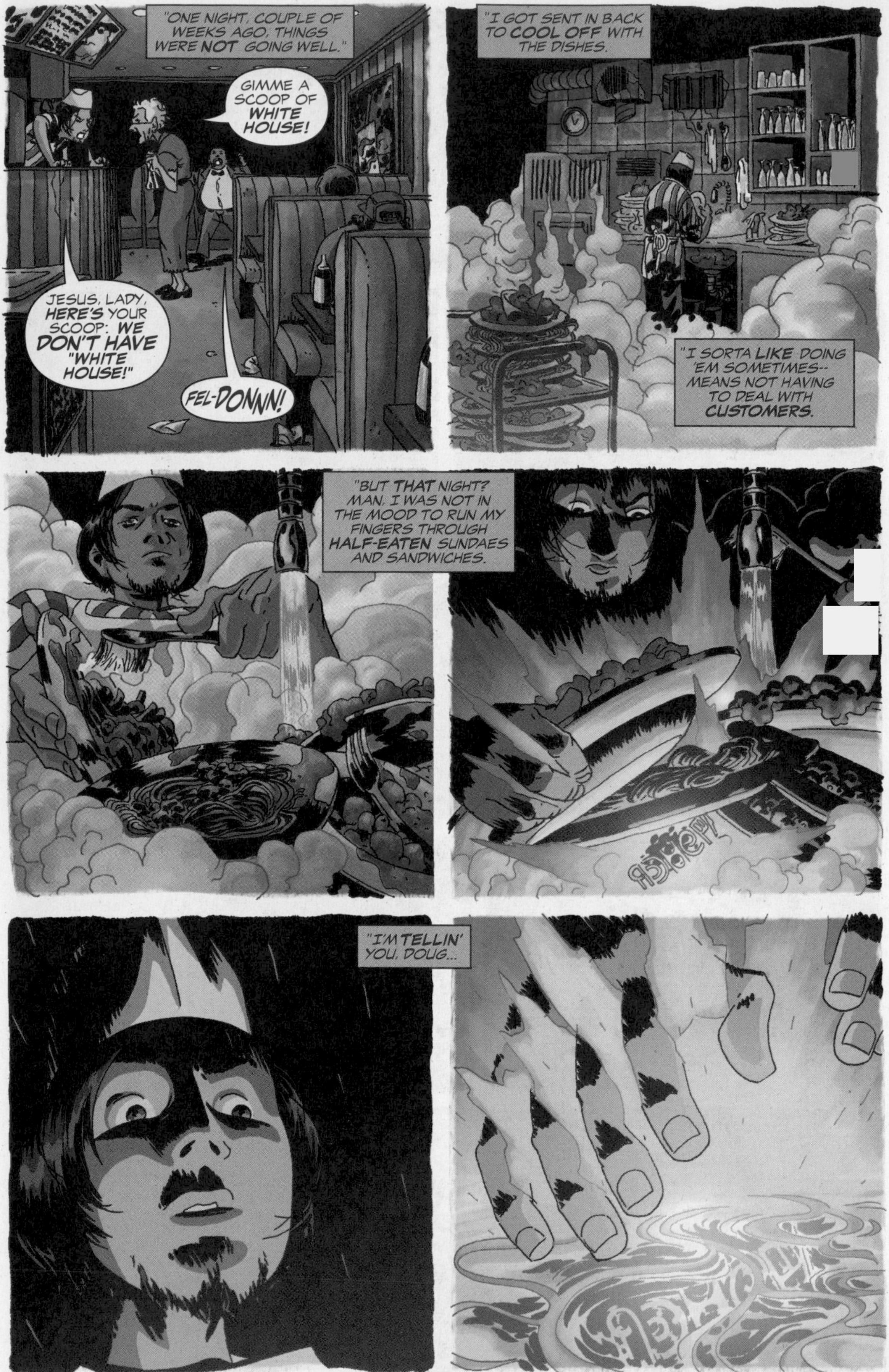
"ONE NIGHT, COUPLE OF WEEKS AGO, THINGS WERE NOT GOING WELL."
GIMME A SCOOP OF WHITE HOUSE!
JESUS, LADY, HERE'S YOUR SCOOP: WE DON'T HAVE "WHITE HOUSE!"
FEL-DONNN!
"I GOT SENT IN BACK TO COOL OFF WITH THE DISHES.
"I SORTA LIKE DOING 'EM SOMETIMES-- MEANS NOT HAVING TO DEAL WITH CUSTOMERS.
"BUT THAT NIGHT? MAN, I WAS NOT IN THE MOOD TO RUN MY FINGERS THROUGH HALF-EATEN SUNDAES AND SANDWICHES.
"I'M TELLIN' YOU, DOUG...

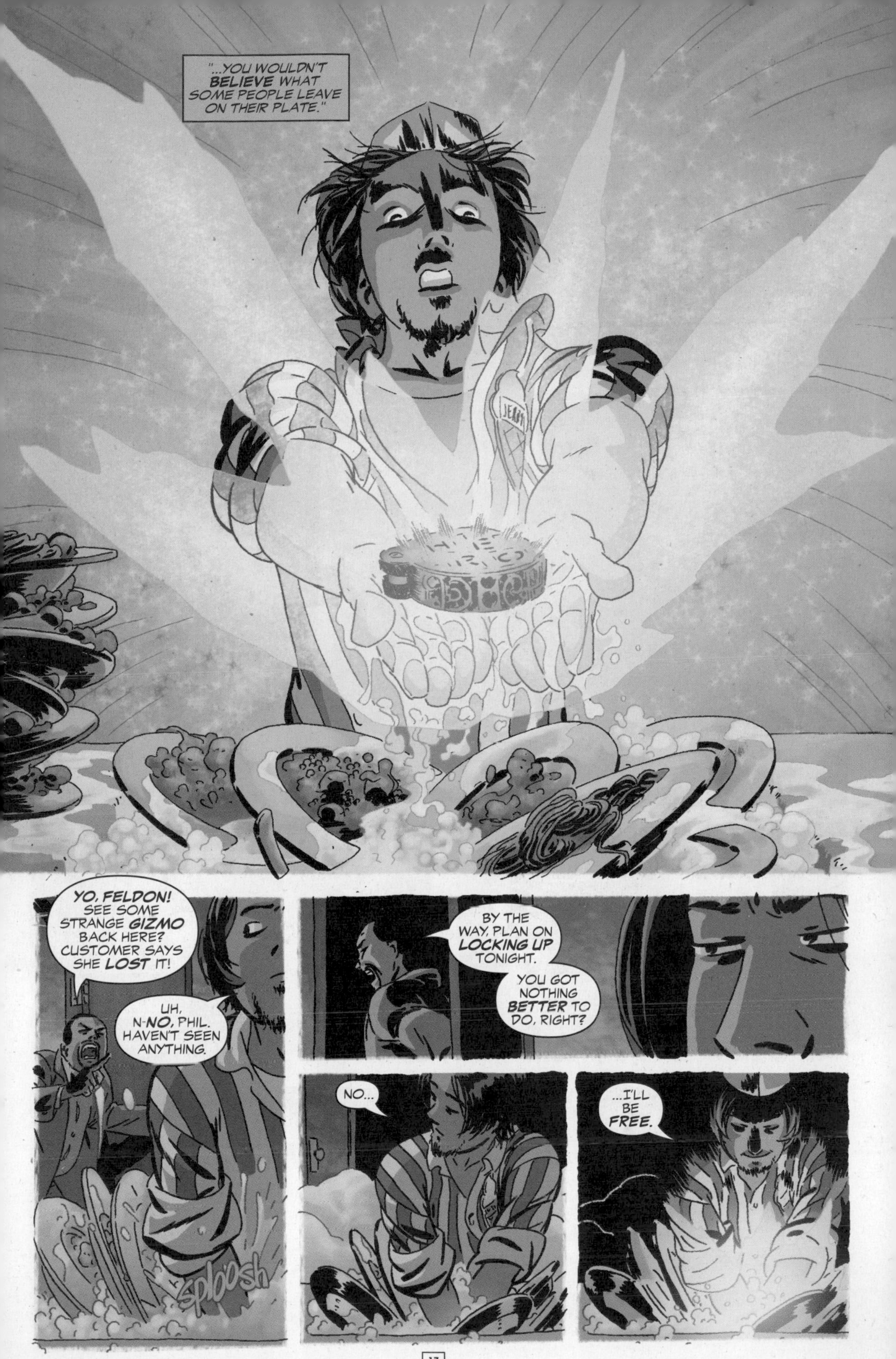
"...YOU WOULDN'T BELIEVE WHAT SOME PEOPLE LEAVE ON THEIR PLATE."
YO, FELDON! SEE SOME STRANGE GIZMO BACK HERE? CUSTOMER SAYS SHE LOST IT!
UH, N-NO, PHIL. HAVEN'T SEEN ANYTHING.
SPLOOSH
BY THE WAY, PLAN ON LOCKING UP TONIGHT.
YOU GOT NOTHING BETTER TO DO, RIGHT?
NO...
...I'LL BE FREE.

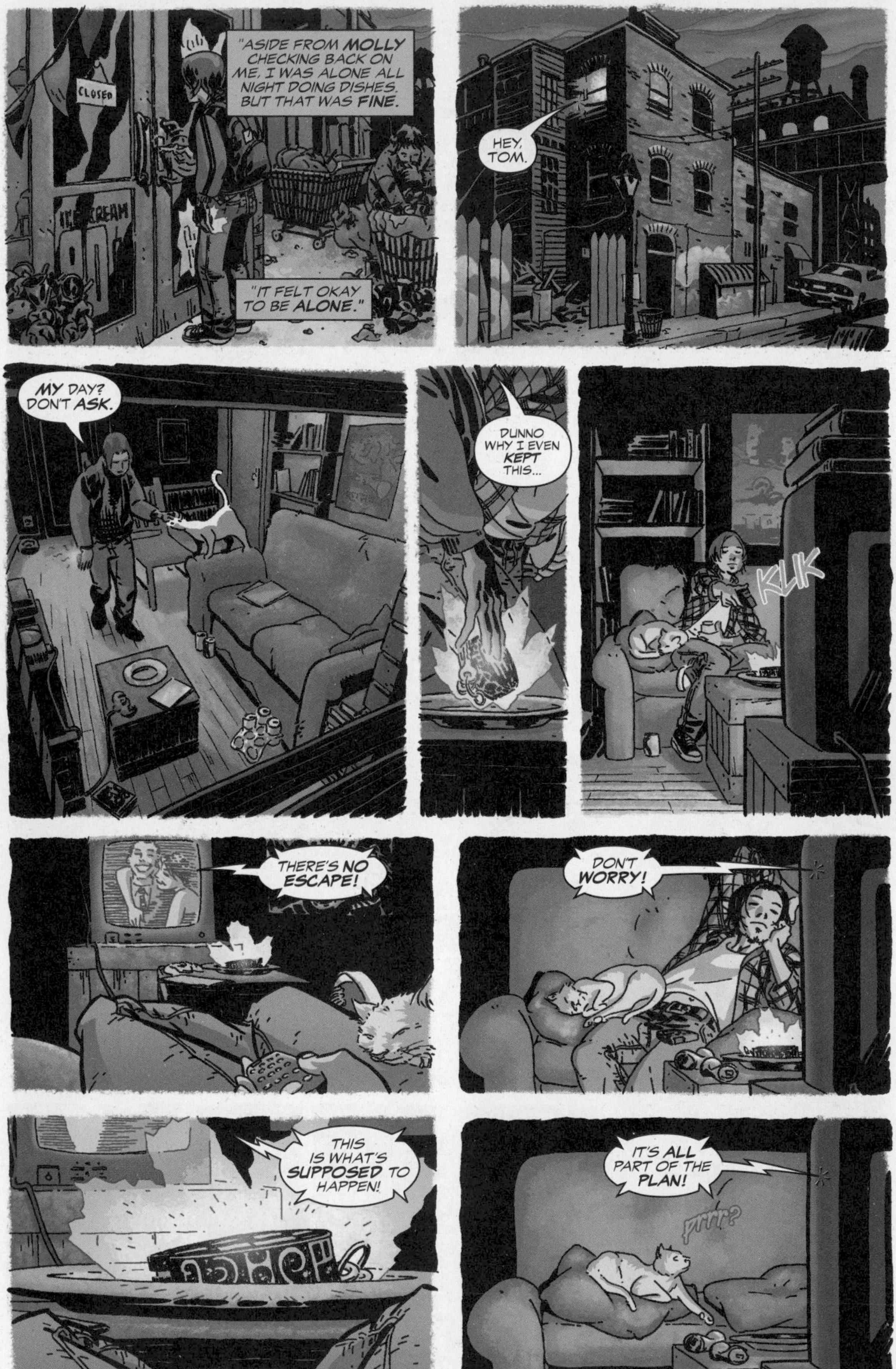

"ASIDE FROM MOLLY CHECKING BACK ON ME, I WAS ALONE ALL NIGHT DOING DISHES. BUT THAT WAS FINE.
CLOSED
ICE CREAM
"IT FELT OKAY TO BE ALONE."
HEY, TOM.
MY DAY? DON'T ASK.
DUNNO WHY I EVEN KEPT THIS...
KLIK
THERE'S NO ESCAPE!
DON'T WORRY!
THIS IS WHAT'S SUPPOSED TO HAPPEN!
IT'S ALL PART OF THE PLAN!
prrr?

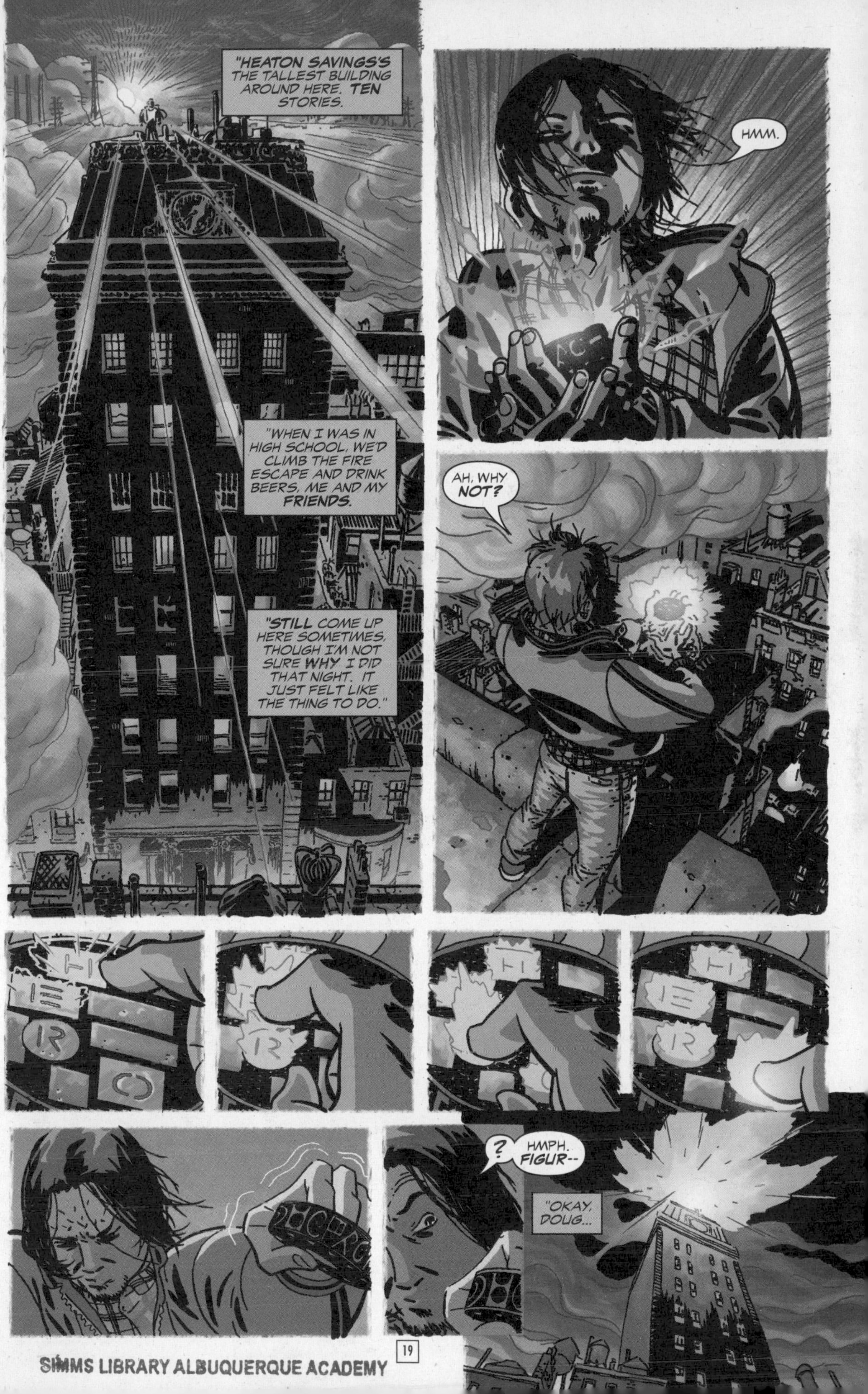
"HEATON SAVINGS'S THE TALLEST BUILDING AROUND HERE. TEN STORIES.
"WHEN I WAS IN HIGH SCHOOL, WE'D CLIMB THE FIRE ESCAPE AND DRINK BEERS, ME AND MY FRIENDS.
"STILL COME UP HERE SOMETIMES, THOUGH I'M NOT SURE WHY I DID THAT NIGHT. IT JUST FELT LIKE THE THING TO DO."
HMM.
AH, WHY NOT?
?
HMPH. FIGUR--
"OKAY, DOUG...

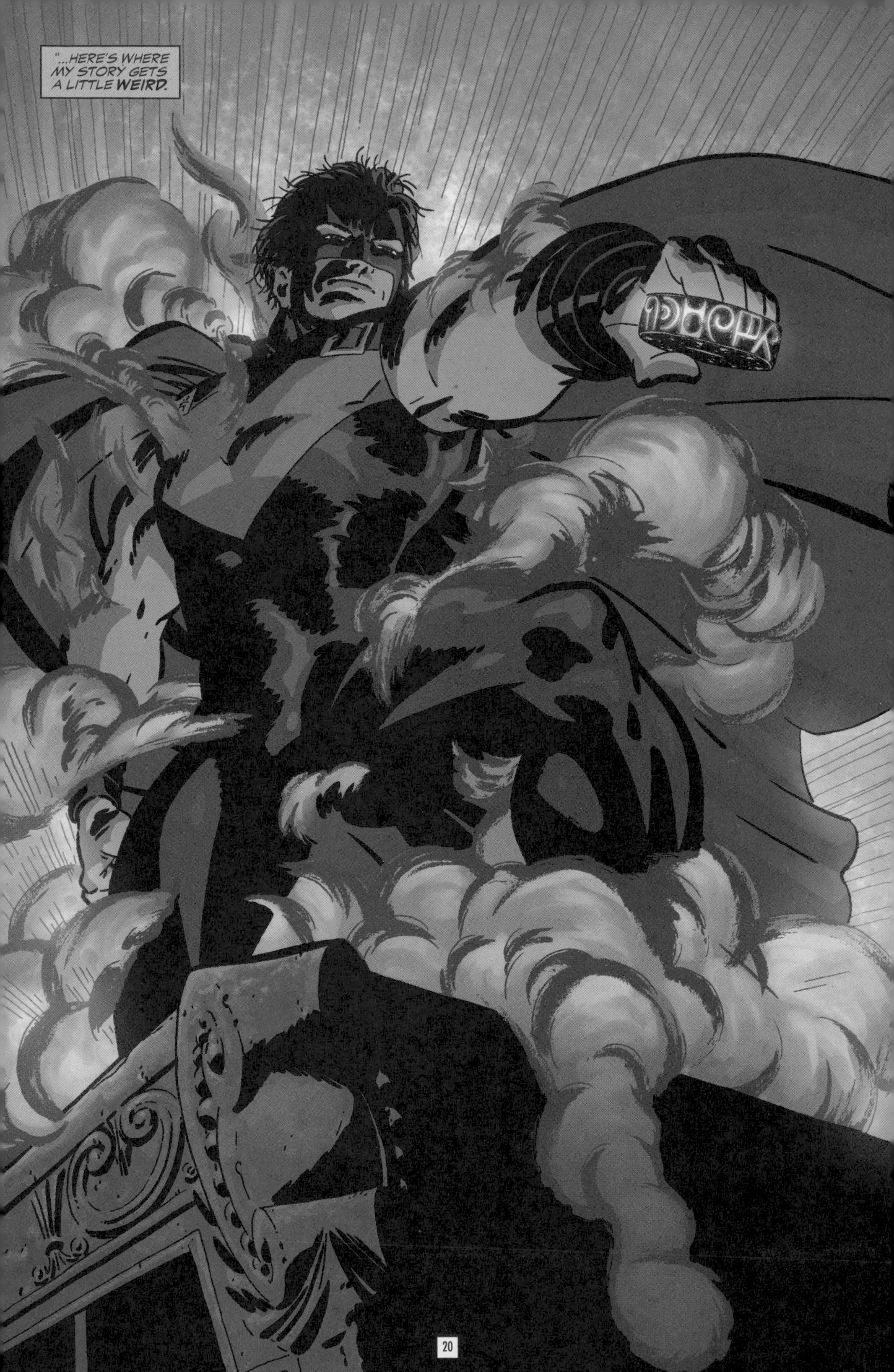
"...HERE'S WHERE MY STORY GETS A LITTLE WEIRD.

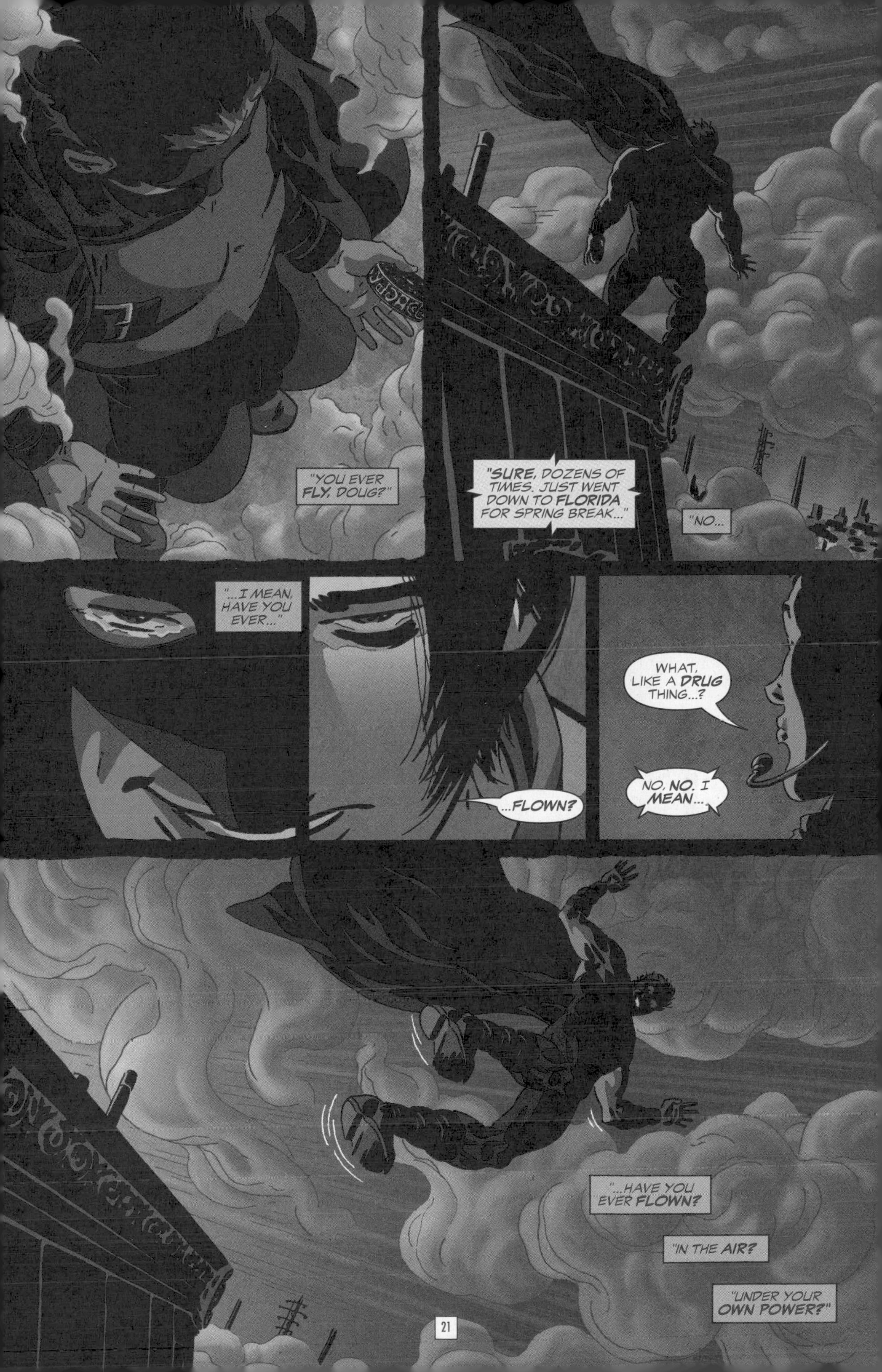
"YOU EVER FLY, DOUG?"
"SURE, DOZENS OF TIMES. JUST WENT DOWN TO FLORIDA FOR SPRING BREAK..."
"NO...
"...I MEAN, HAVE YOU EVER..."
...FLOWN?
WHAT, LIKE A DRUG THING...?
NO, NO. I MEAN...
"...HAVE YOU EVER FLOWN?
"IN THE AIR?
"UNDER YOUR OWN POWER?"

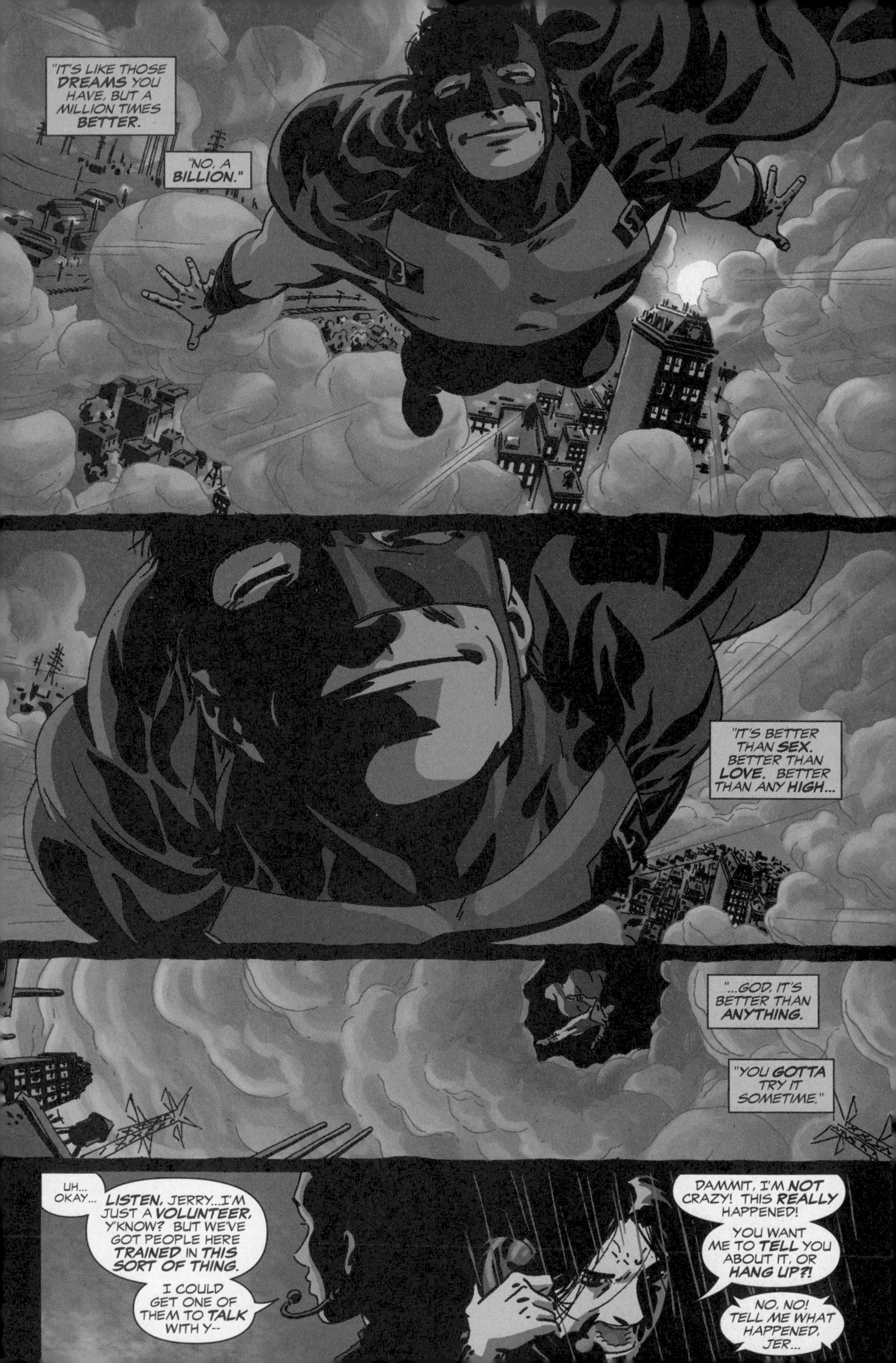
"IT'S LIKE THOSE DREAMS YOU HAVE, BUT A MILLION TIMES BETTER.
"NO, A BILLION."
"IT'S BETTER THAN SEX. BETTER THAN LOVE. BETTER THAN ANY HIGH...
"...GOD, IT'S BETTER THAN ANYTHING.
"YOU GOTTA TRY IT SOMETIME."
UH... OKAY...
LISTEN, JERRY...I'M JUST A VOLUNTEER, Y'KNOW? BUT WE'VE GOT PEOPLE HERE TRAINED IN THIS SORT OF THING.
I COULD GET ONE OF THEM TO TALK WITH Y--
DAMMIT, I'M NOT CRAZY! THIS REALLY HAPPENED!
YOU WANT ME TO TELL YOU ABOUT IT, OR HANG UP?!
NO, NO! TELL ME WHAT HAPPENED, JER...

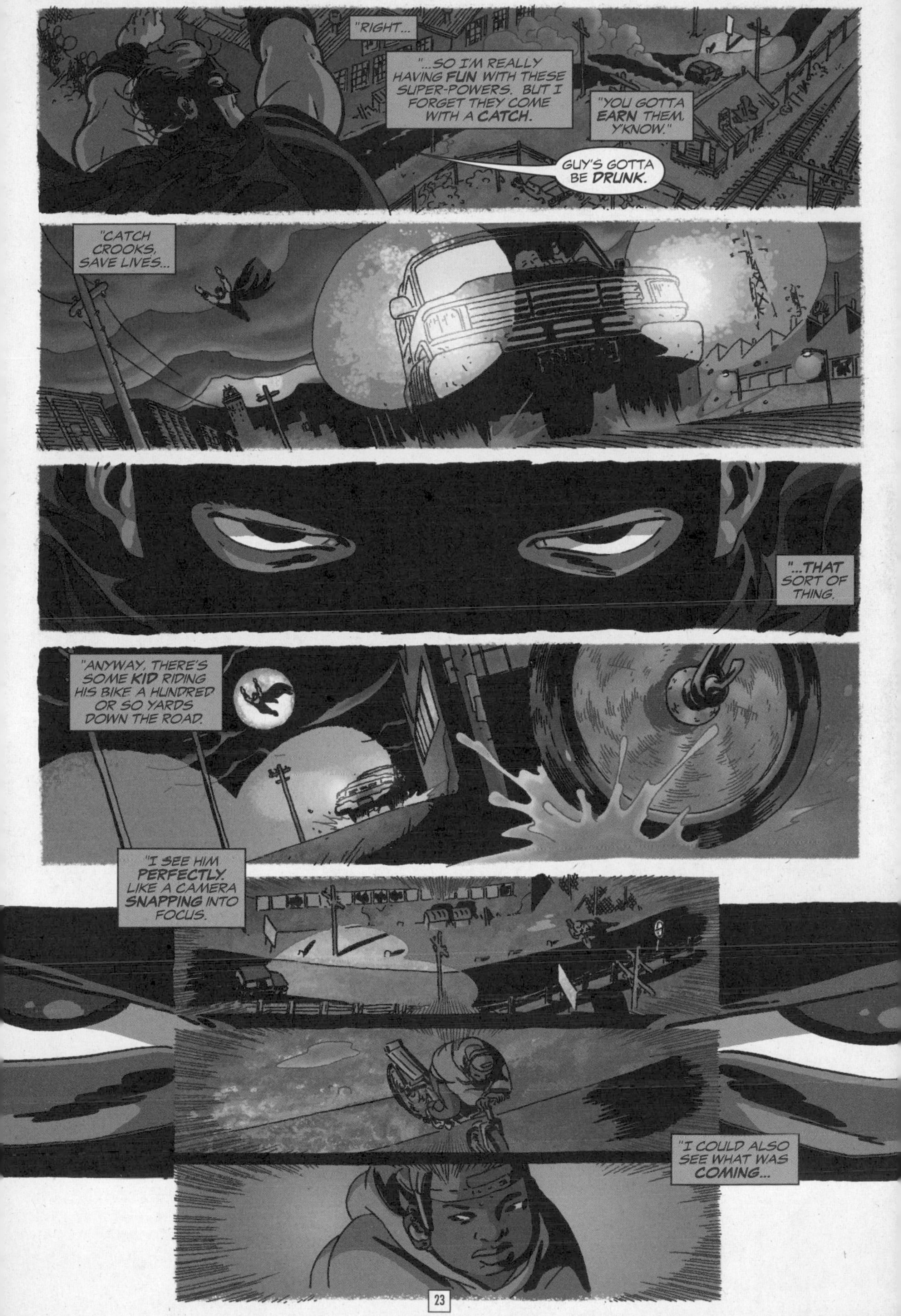
"RIGHT...
"...SO I'M REALLY HAVING FUN WITH THESE SUPER-POWERS. BUT I FORGET THEY COME WITH A CATCH.
"YOU GOTTA EARN THEM, Y'KNOW."
GUY'S GOTTA BE DRUNK.
"CATCH CROOKS, SAVE LIVES...
"...THAT SORT OF THING.
"ANYWAY, THERE'S SOME KID RIDING HIS BIKE A HUNDRED OR SO YARDS DOWN THE ROAD.
"I SEE HIM PERFECTLY, LIKE A CAMERA SNAPPING INTO FOCUS.
"I COULD ALSO SEE WHAT WAS COMING...

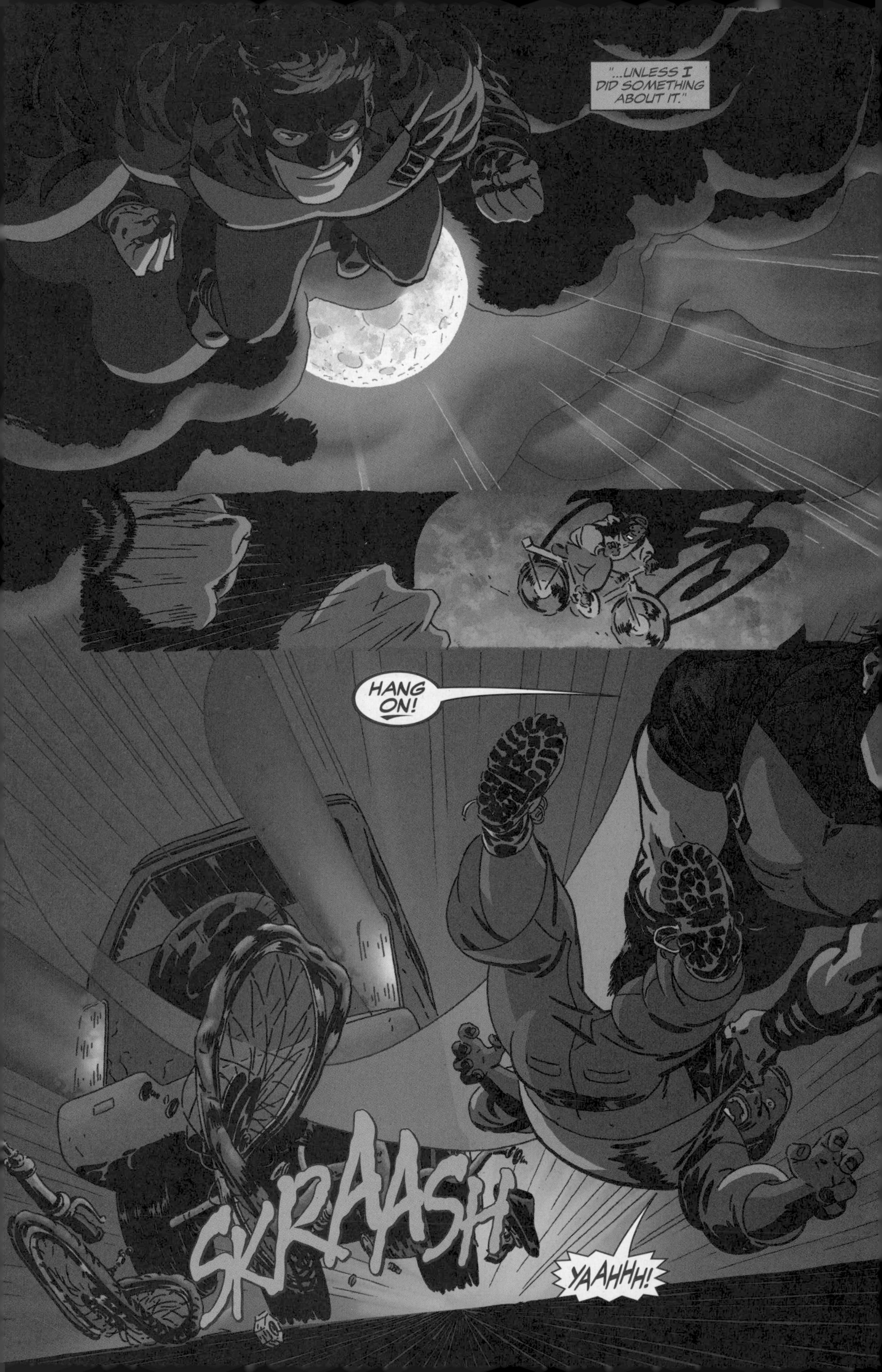
"...UNLESS I DID SOMETHING ABOUT IT."
HANG ON!
SKRAASH
YAAHHH!

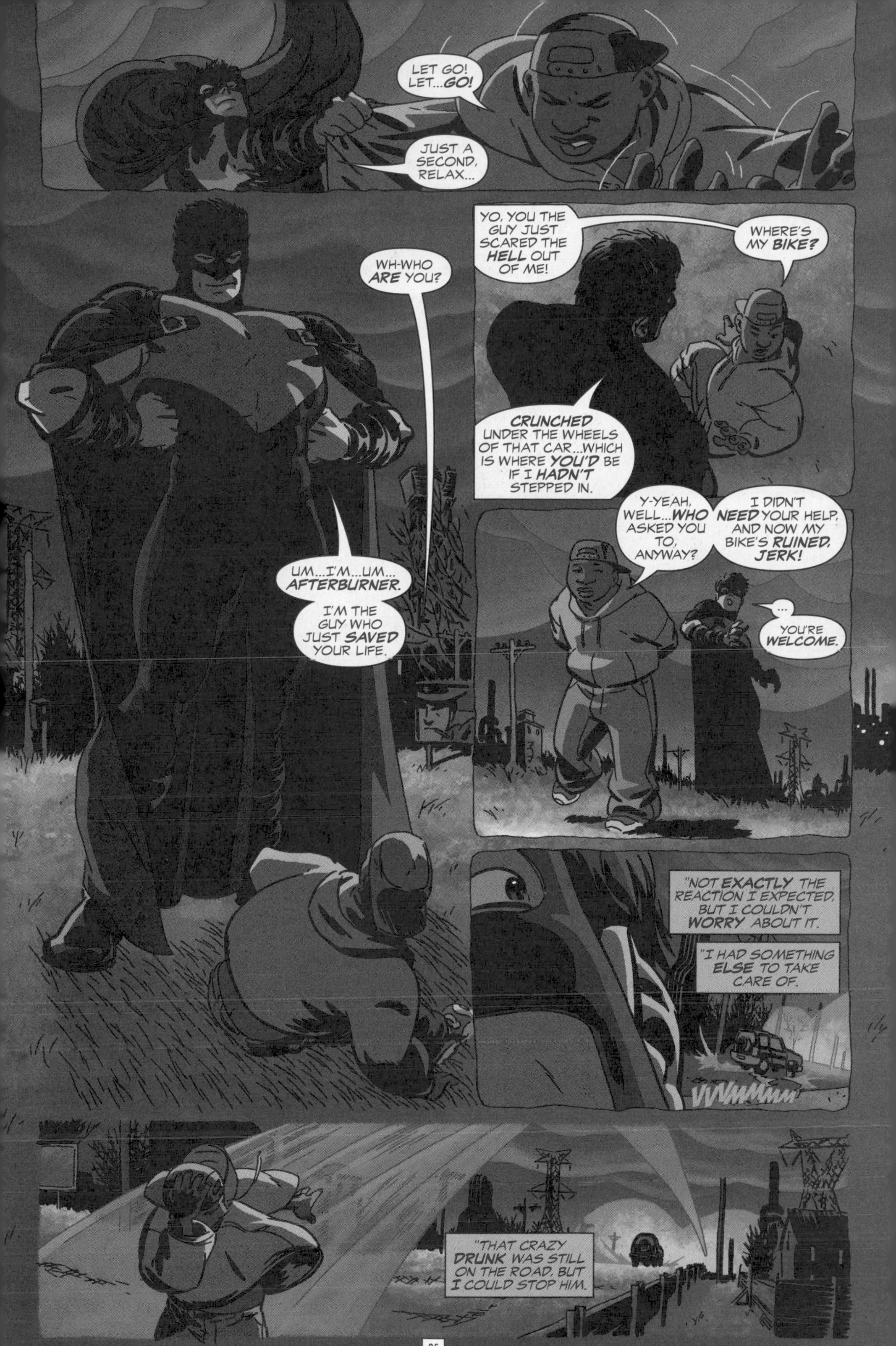

LET GO! LET...GO!
JUST A SECOND, RELAX...
WH-WHO ARE YOU?
UM...I'M...UM... AFTERBURNER.
I'M THE GUY WHO JUST SAVED YOUR LIFE.
YO, YOU THE GUY JUST SCARED THE HELL OUT OF ME!
WHERE'S MY BIKE?
CRUNCHED UNDER THE WHEELS OF THAT CAR...WHICH IS WHERE YOU'D BE IF I HADN'T STEPPED IN.
Y-YEAH, WELL...WHO ASKED YOU TO, ANYWAY?
I DIDN'T NEED YOUR HELP, AND NOW MY BIKE'S RUINED, JERK!
...
YOU'RE WELCOME.
"NOT EXACTLY THE REACTION I EXPECTED, BUT I COULDN'T WORRY ABOUT IT.
"I HAD SOMETHING ELSE TO TAKE CARE OF.
VVVVMMMM
"THAT CRAZY DRUNK WAS STILL ON THE ROAD, BUT I COULD STOP HIM.

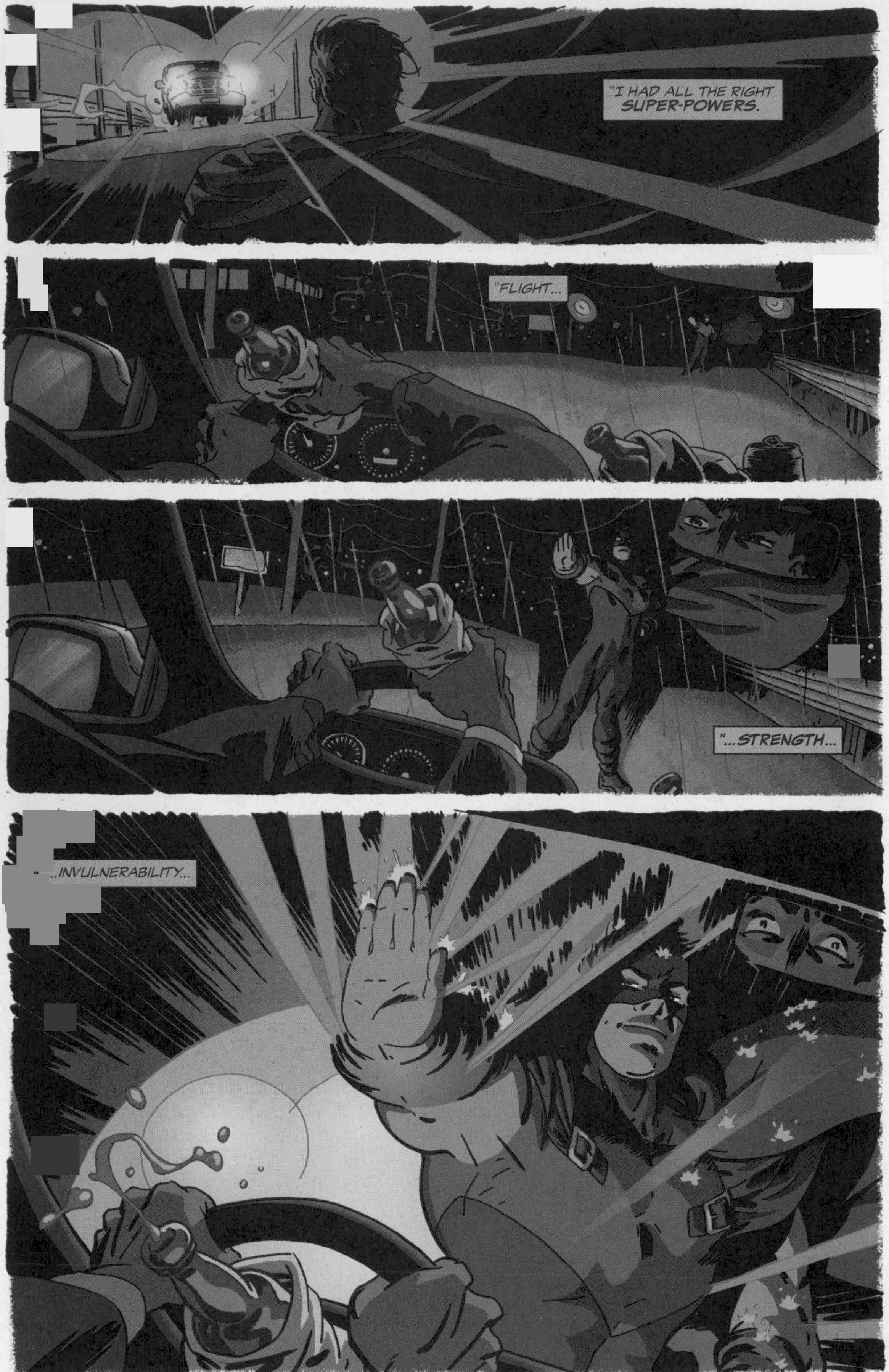
"I HAD ALL THE RIGHT SUPER-POWERS.
"FLIGHT...
"...STRENGTH...
"...INVULNERABILITY...

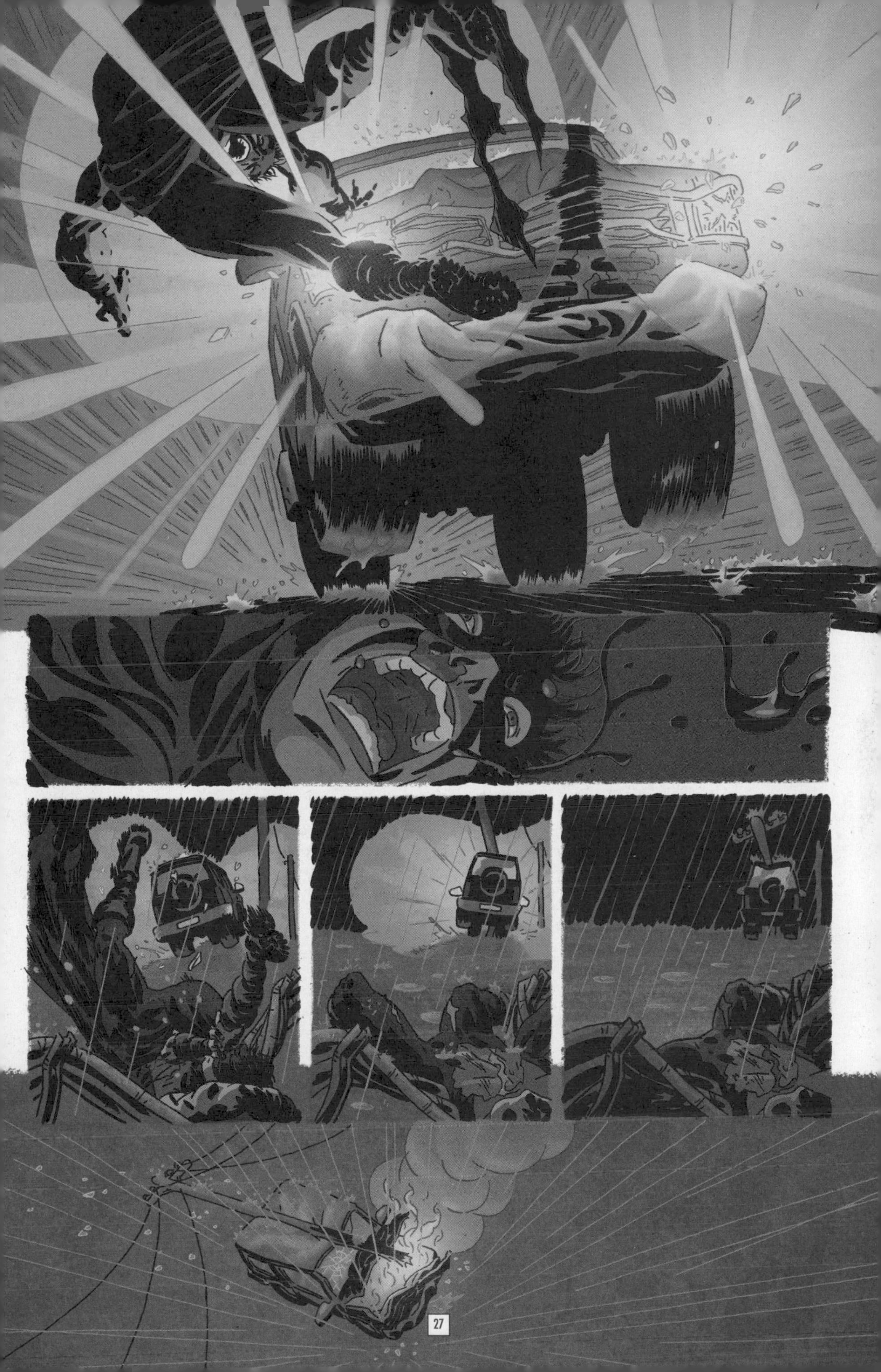

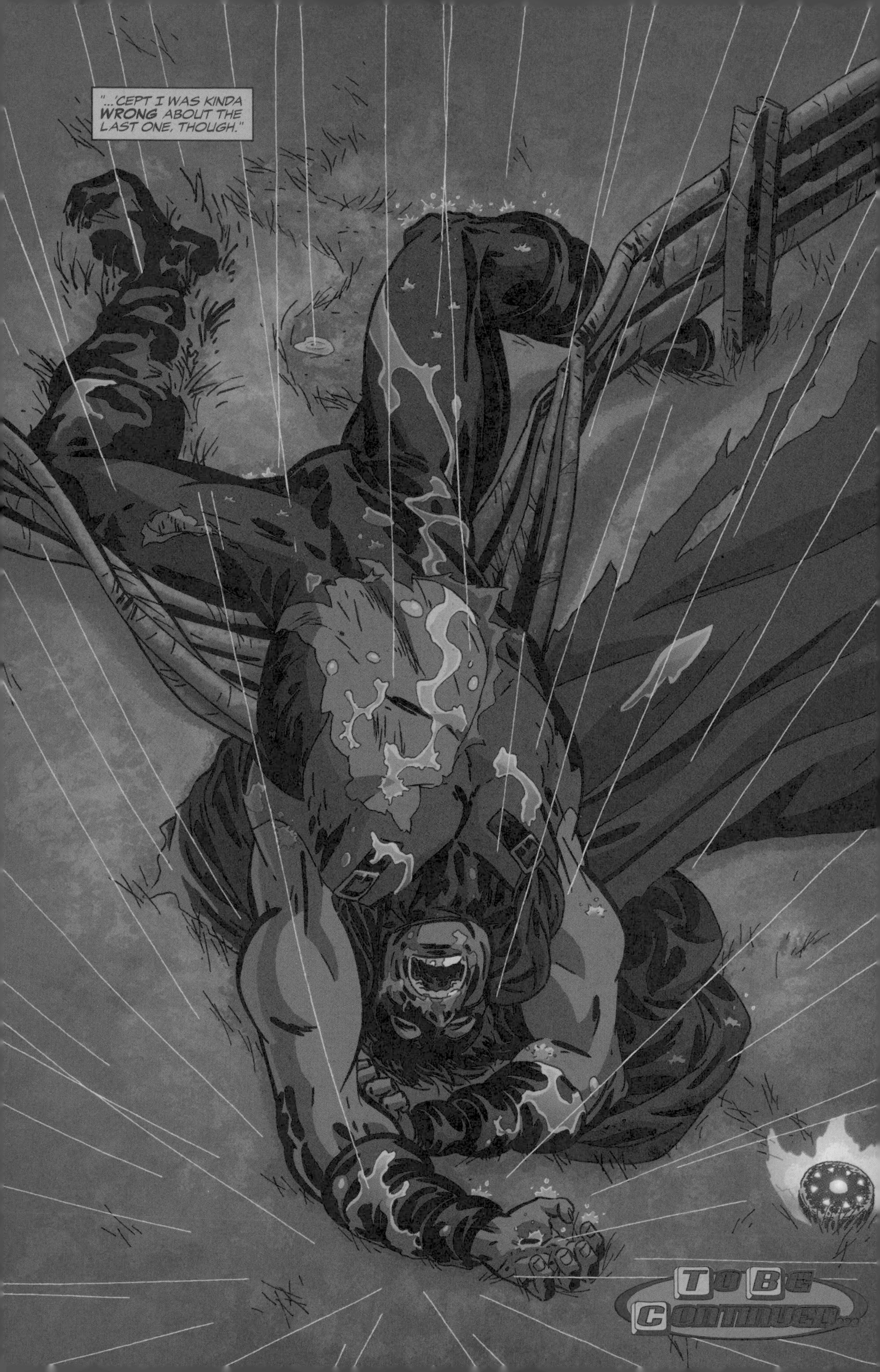
"...'CEPT I WAS KINDA WRONG ABOUT THE LAST ONE, THOUGH."
TO BE CONTINUED...

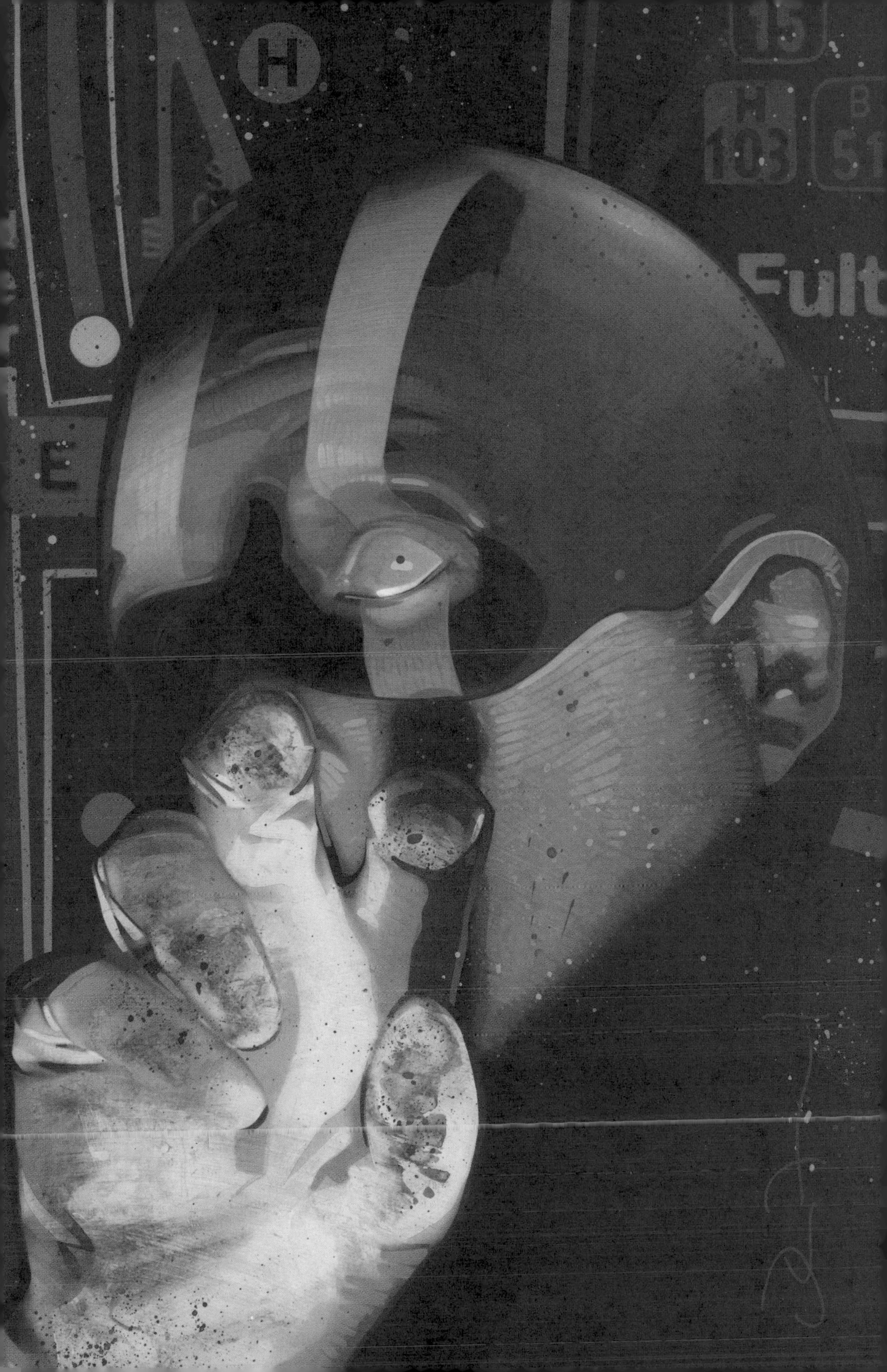
H
15
H
103
E

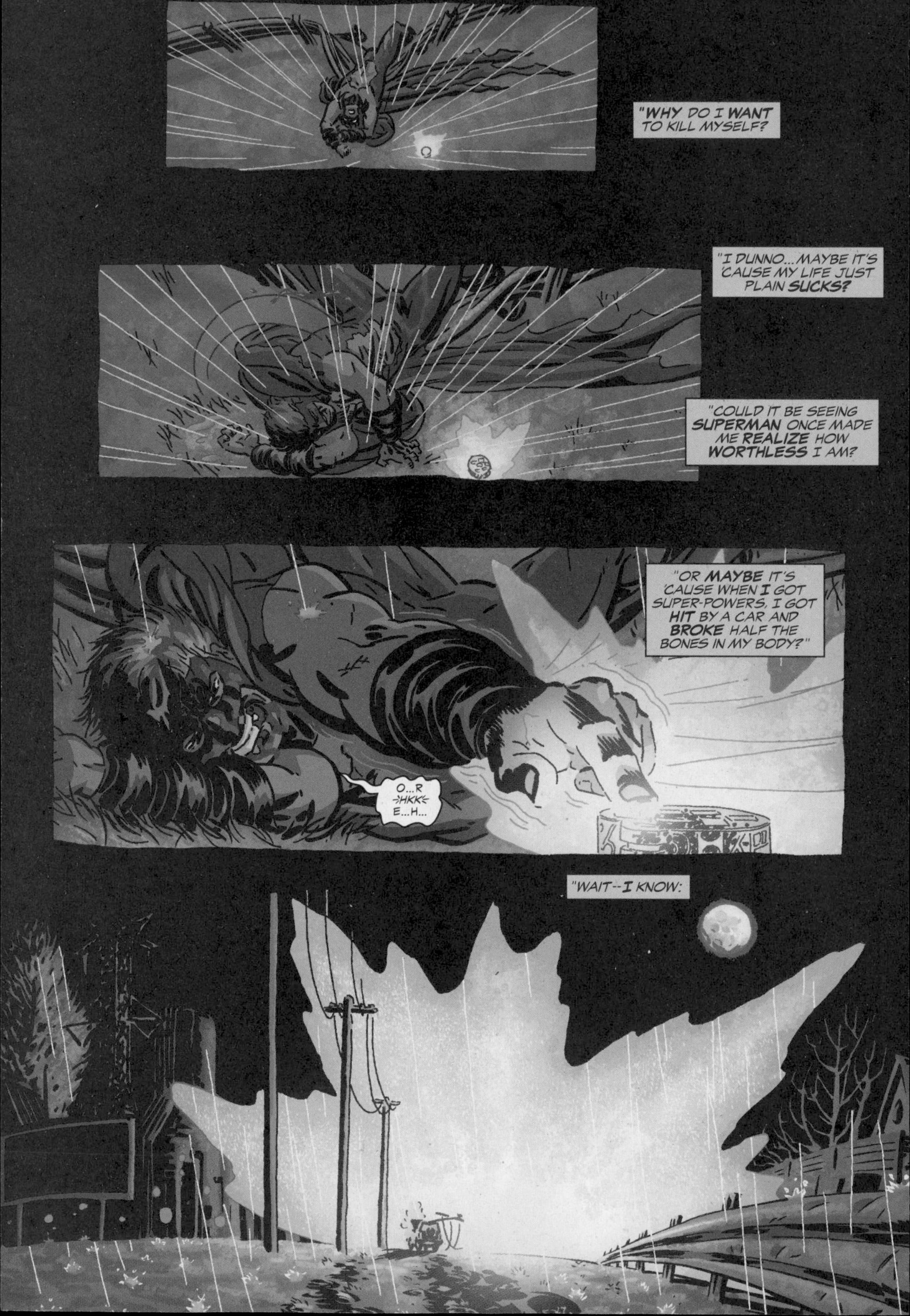
"WHY DO I WANT TO KILL MYSELF?
"I DUNNO...MAYBE IT'S 'CAUSE MY LIFE JUST PLAIN SUCKS?
"COULD IT BE SEEING SUPERMAN ONCE MADE ME REALIZE HOW WORTHLESS I AM?
"OR MAYBE IT'S 'CAUSE WHEN I GOT SUPER-POWERS, I GOT HIT BY A CAR AND BROKE HALF THE BONES IN MY BODY?"
O...R HKK E...H...
"WAIT--I KNOW:

"TRY ALL OF THE ABOVE!"

POWERS and Abilities Part TWO

WILL PFEIFER | KANO | KEN LOPEZ | DAVE STEWART | JOHN VAN FLEET | MIKE McAVENNIE and PETER TOMASI
WRITER | ARTIST | LETTERS | COLORS/SEPS | COVER | EDITORS

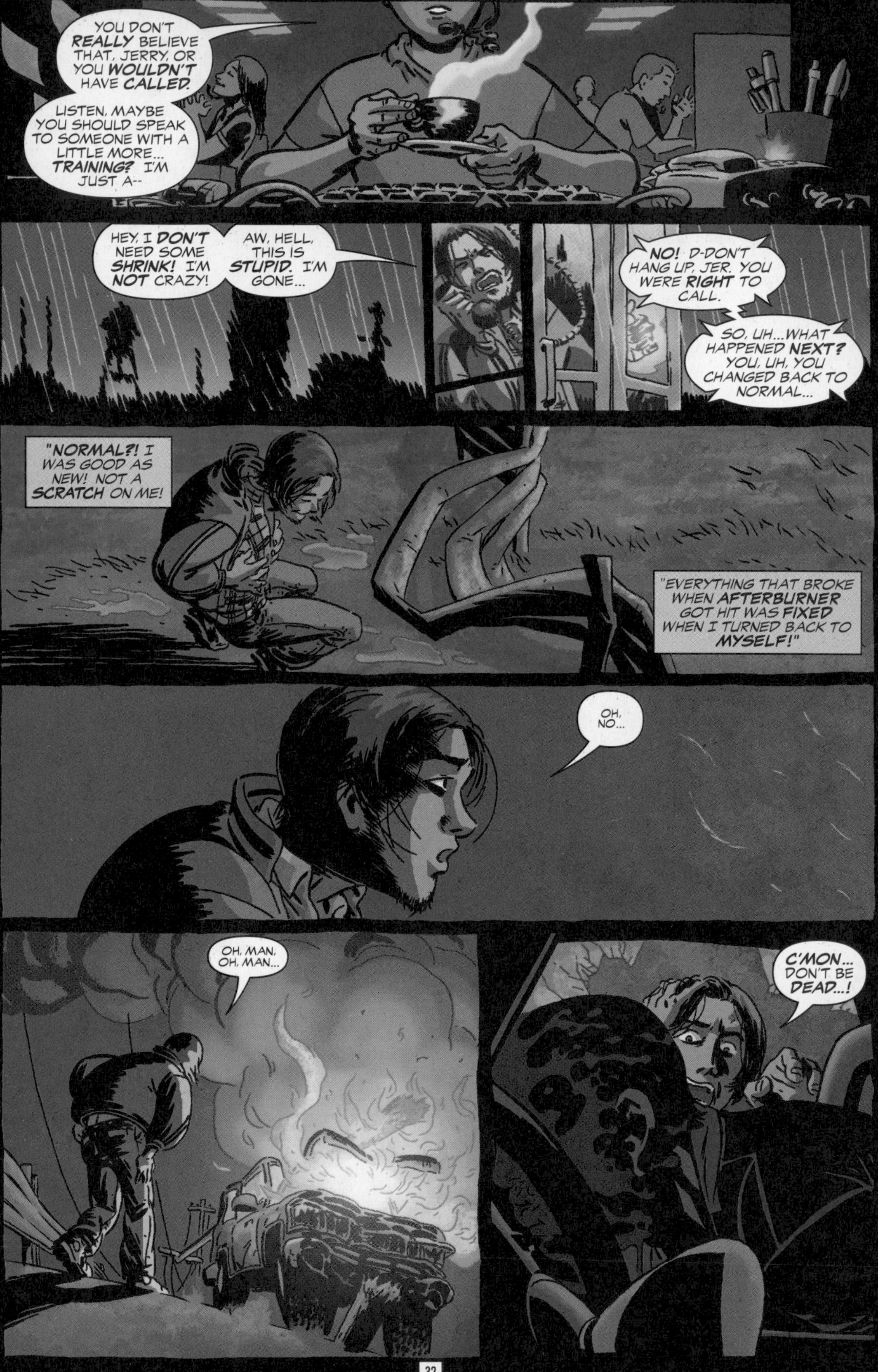

YOU DON'T REALLY BELIEVE THAT, JERRY, OR YOU WOULDN'T HAVE CALLED.
LISTEN, MAYBE YOU SHOULD SPEAK TO SOMEONE WITH A LITTLE MORE... TRAINING? I'M JUST A--
HEY, I DON'T NEED SOME SHRINK! I'M NOT CRAZY!
AW, HELL, THIS IS STUPID. I'M GONE...
NO! D-DON'T HANG UP, JER. YOU WERE RIGHT TO CALL.
SO, UH...WHAT HAPPENED NEXT? YOU, UH, YOU CHANGED BACK TO NORMAL...
"NORMAL?! I WAS GOOD AS NEW! NOT A SCRATCH ON ME!
"EVERYTHING THAT BROKE WHEN AFTERBURNER GOT HIT WAS FIXED WHEN I TURNED BACK TO MYSELF!"
OH, NO...
OH, MAN, OH, MAN...
C'MON... DON'T BE DEAD...!

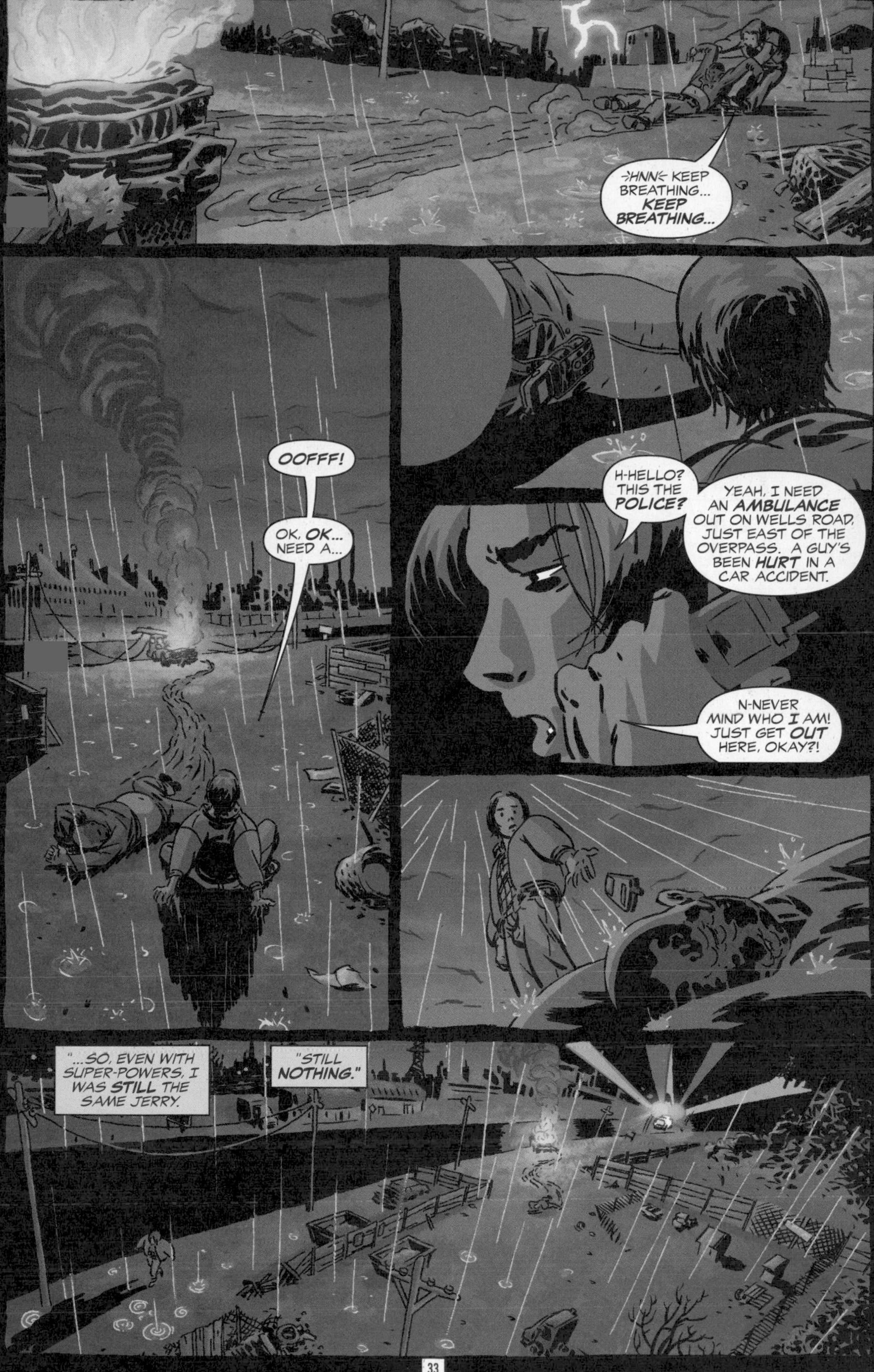
-HNN- KEEP BREATHING... KEEP BREATHING...
OOFFF!
OK, OK... NEED A...
H-HELLO? THIS THE POLICE?
YEAH, I NEED AN AMBULANCE OUT ON WELLS ROAD, JUST EAST OF THE OVERPASS. A GUY'S BEEN HURT IN A CAR ACCIDENT.
N-NEVER MIND WHO I AM! JUST GET OUT HERE, OKAY?!
"...SO, EVEN WITH SUPER-POWERS, I WAS STILL THE SAME JERRY.
"STILL NOTHING."

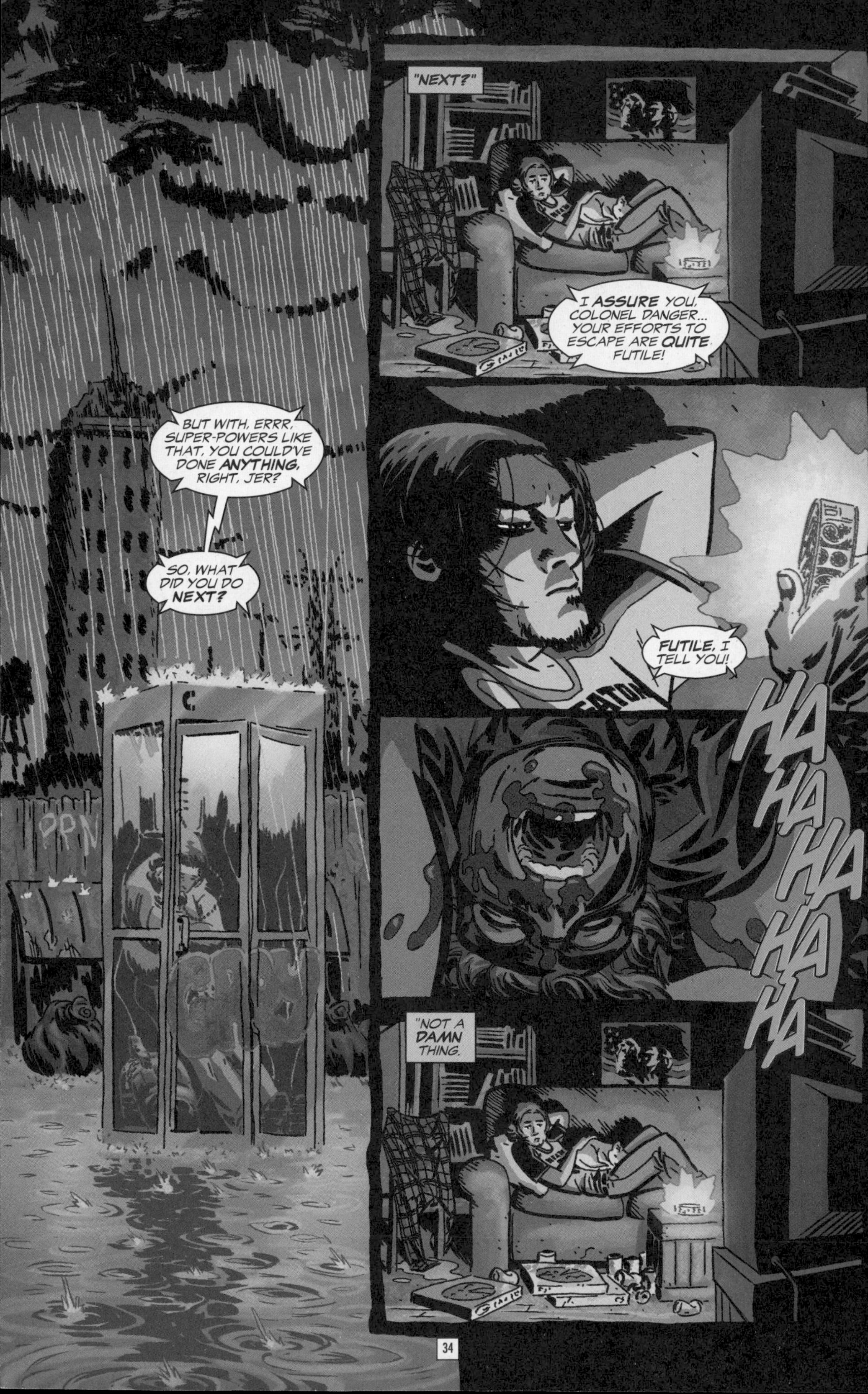
BUT WITH, ERRR, SUPER-POWERS LIKE THAT, YOU COULD'VE DONE ANYTHING, RIGHT, JER?
SO, WHAT DID YOU DO NEXT?
"NEXT?"
I ASSURE YOU, COLONEL DANGER... YOUR EFFORTS TO ESCAPE ARE QUITE FUTILE!
FUTILE, I TELL YOU!
HA HA HA HA HA HA HA
"NOT A DAMN THING.

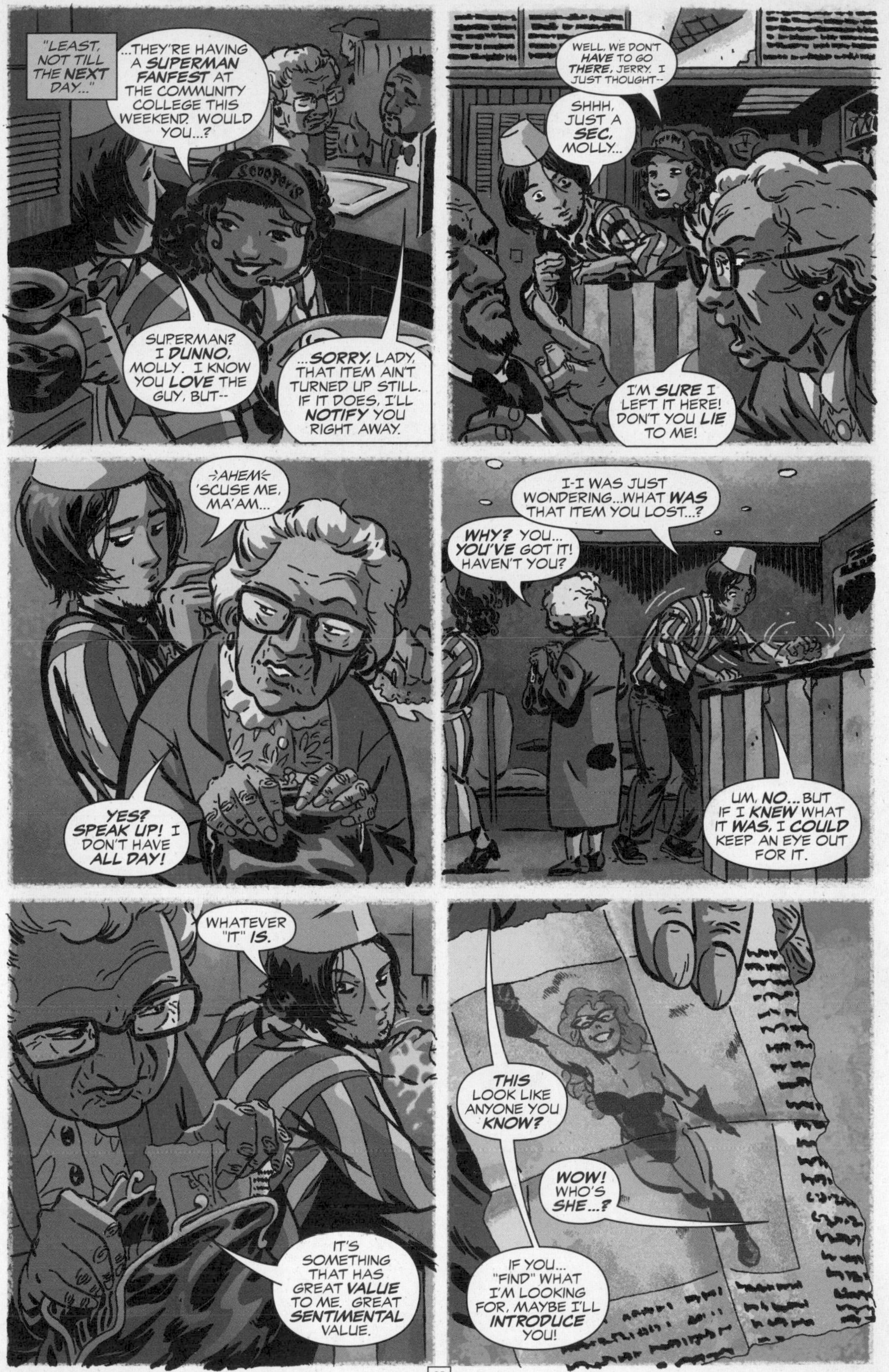
"LEAST, NOT TILL THE NEXT DAY..."
...THEY'RE HAVING A SUPERMAN FANFEST AT THE COMMUNITY COLLEGE THIS WEEKEND. WOULD YOU...?
SUPERMAN? I DUNNO, MOLLY. I KNOW YOU LOVE THE GUY, BUT--
...SORRY, LADY, THAT ITEM AIN'T TURNED UP STILL. IF IT DOES, I'LL NOTIFY YOU RIGHT AWAY.
WELL, WE DON'T HAVE TO GO THERE, JERRY. I JUST THOUGHT--
SHHH, JUST A SEC, MOLLY...
I'M SURE I LEFT IT HERE! DON'T YOU LIE TO ME!
AHEM 'SCUSE ME, MA'AM...
YES? SPEAK UP! I DON'T HAVE ALL DAY!
I-I WAS JUST WONDERING...WHAT WAS THAT ITEM YOU LOST...?
WHY? YOU... YOU'VE GOT IT! HAVEN'T YOU?
UM, NO... BUT IF I KNEW WHAT IT WAS, I COULD KEEP AN EYE OUT FOR IT.
WHATEVER "IT" IS.
IT'S SOMETHING THAT HAS GREAT VALUE TO ME. GREAT SENTIMENTAL VALUE.
THIS LOOK LIKE ANYONE YOU KNOW?
WOW! WHO'S SHE...?
IF YOU... "FIND" WHAT I'M LOOKING FOR, MAYBE I'LL INTRODUCE YOU!

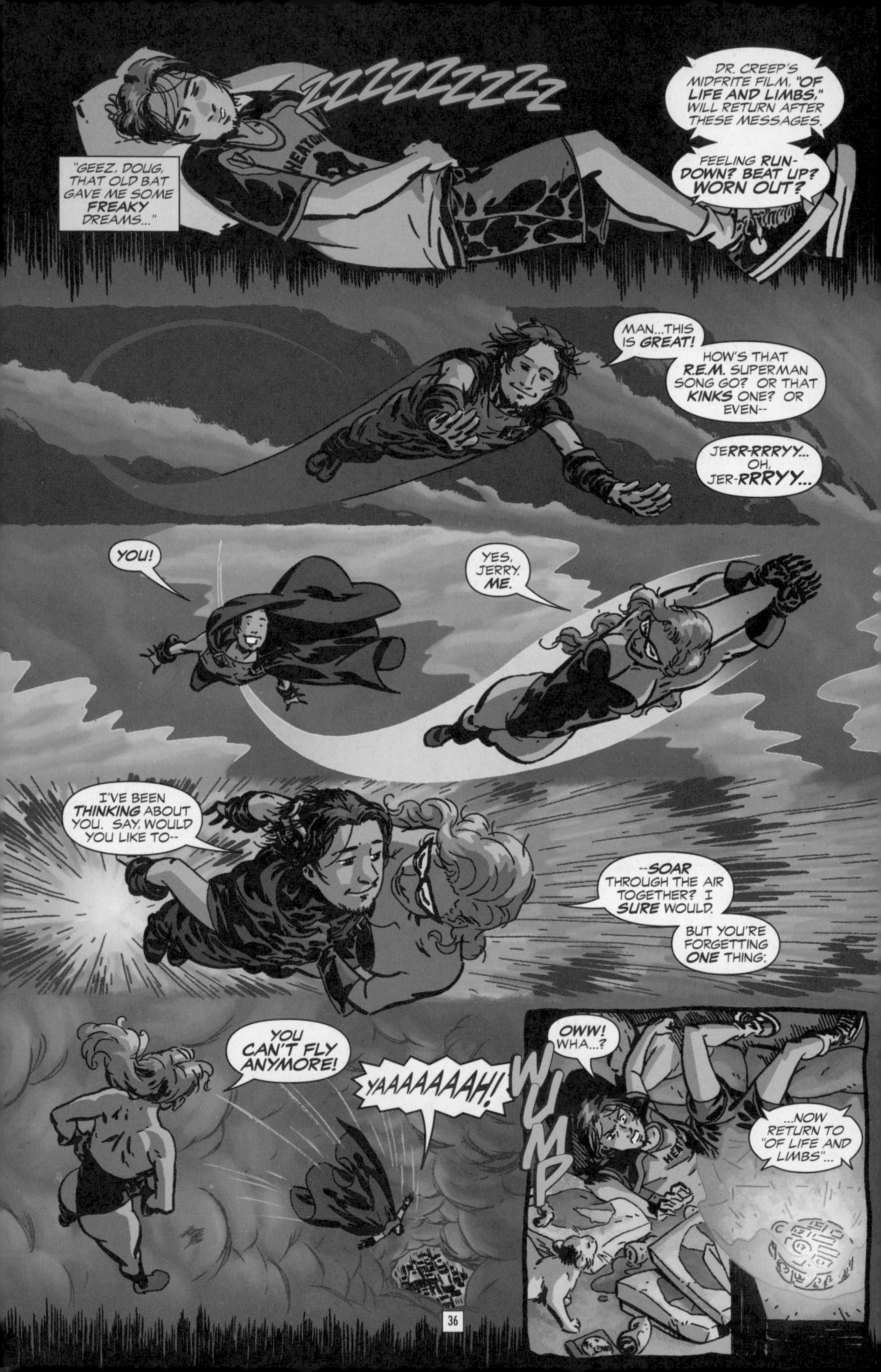

ZZZZZZZZZZz
"GEEZ, DOUG, THAT OLD BAT GAVE ME SOME FREAKY DREAMS..."
DR. CREEP'S MIDFRITE FILM, "OF LIFE AND LIMBS," WILL RETURN AFTER THESE MESSAGES.
FEELING RUN-DOWN? BEAT UP? WORN OUT?
MAN...THIS IS GREAT!
HOW'S THAT R.E.M. SUPERMAN SONG GO? OR THAT KINKS ONE? OR EVEN--
JERR-RRRYY... OH, JER-RRRYY...
YOU!
YES, JERRY. ME.
I'VE BEEN THINKING ABOUT YOU. SAY, WOULD YOU LIKE TO--
--SOAR THROUGH THE AIR TOGETHER? I SURE WOULD.
BUT YOU'RE FORGETTING ONE THING:
YOU CAN'T FLY ANYMORE!
YAAAAAAAH!
WUMP
OWW! WHA...?
...NOW RETURN TO "OF LIFE AND LIMBS"...

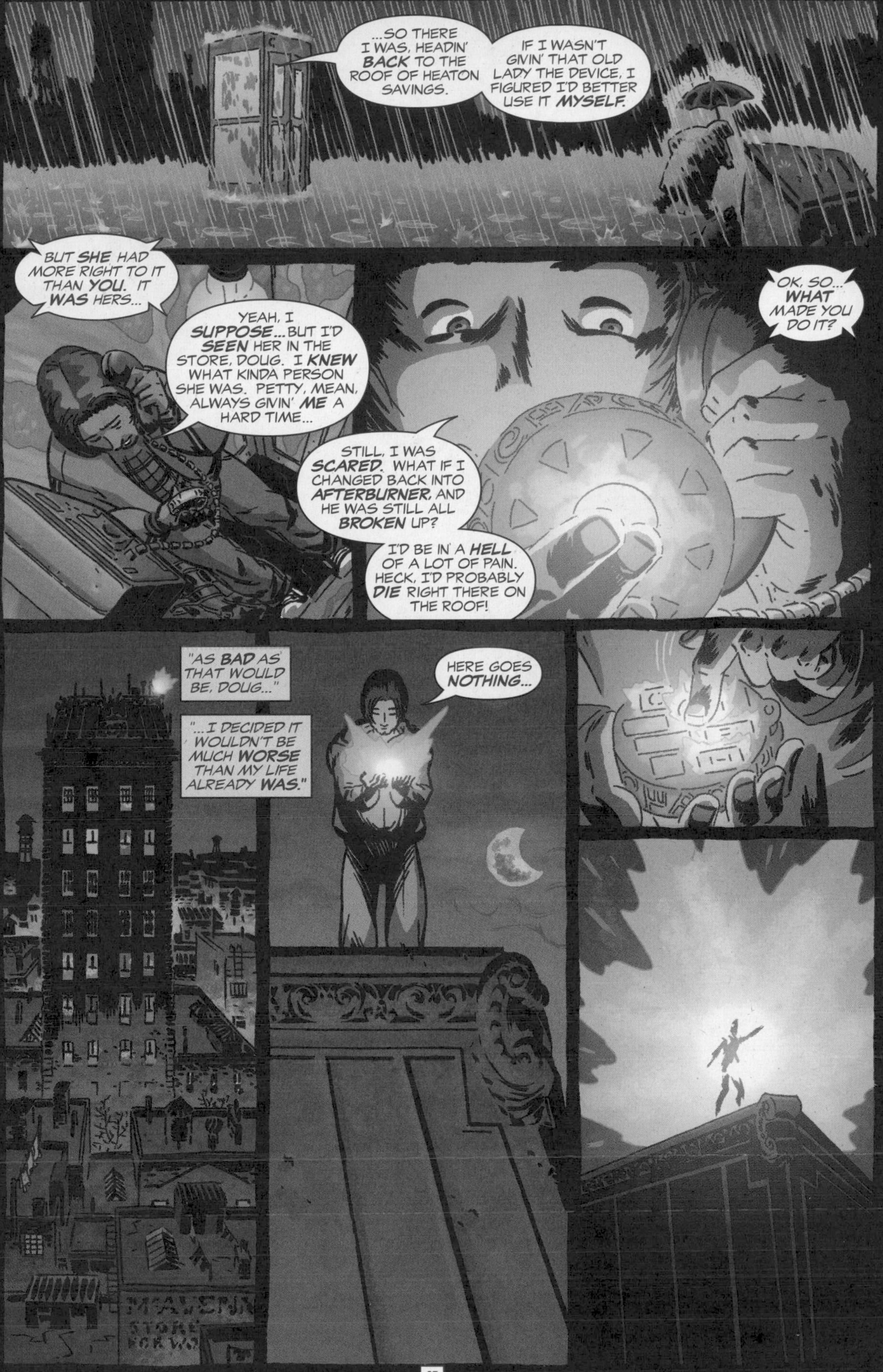
...SO THERE I WAS, HEADIN' BACK TO THE ROOF OF HEATON SAVINGS.
IF I WASN'T GIVIN' THAT OLD LADY THE DEVICE, I FIGURED I'D BETTER USE IT MYSELF.
BUT SHE HAD MORE RIGHT TO IT THAN YOU. IT WAS HERS...
YEAH, I SUPPOSE...BUT I'D SEEN HER IN THE STORE, DOUG. I KNEW WHAT KINDA PERSON SHE WAS. PETTY, MEAN, ALWAYS GIVIN' ME A HARD TIME...
OK, SO... WHAT MADE YOU DO IT?
STILL, I WAS SCARED. WHAT IF I CHANGED BACK INTO AFTERBURNER, AND HE WAS STILL ALL BROKEN UP?
I'D BE IN A HELL OF A LOT OF PAIN. HECK, I'D PROBABLY DIE RIGHT THERE ON THE ROOF!
"AS BAD AS THAT WOULD BE, DOUG..."
"...I DECIDED IT WOULDN'T BE MUCH WORSE THAN MY LIFE ALREADY WAS."
HERE GOES NOTHING...

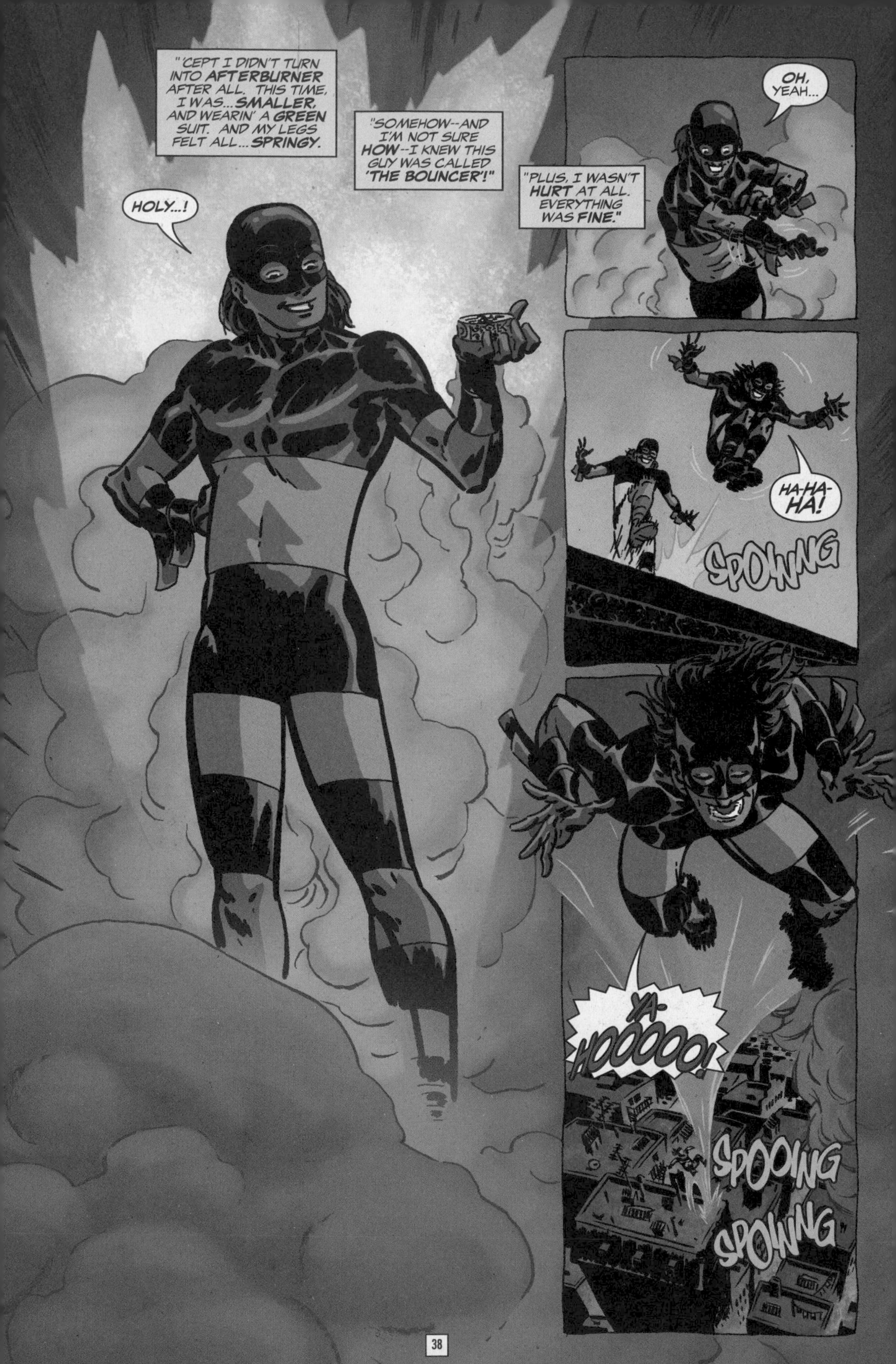
"'CEPT I DIDN'T TURN INTO AFTERBURNER AFTER ALL. THIS TIME, I WAS...SMALLER, AND WEARIN' A GREEN SUIT. AND MY LEGS FELT ALL...SPRINGY.
"SOMEHOW--AND I'M NOT SURE HOW--I KNEW THIS GUY WAS CALLED 'THE BOUNCER'!"
HOLY...!
"PLUS, I WASN'T HURT AT ALL. EVERYTHING WAS FINE."
OH, YEAH...
HA-HA-HA!
SPOINNG
YA-HOOOOO!
SPOOING
SPOINNG

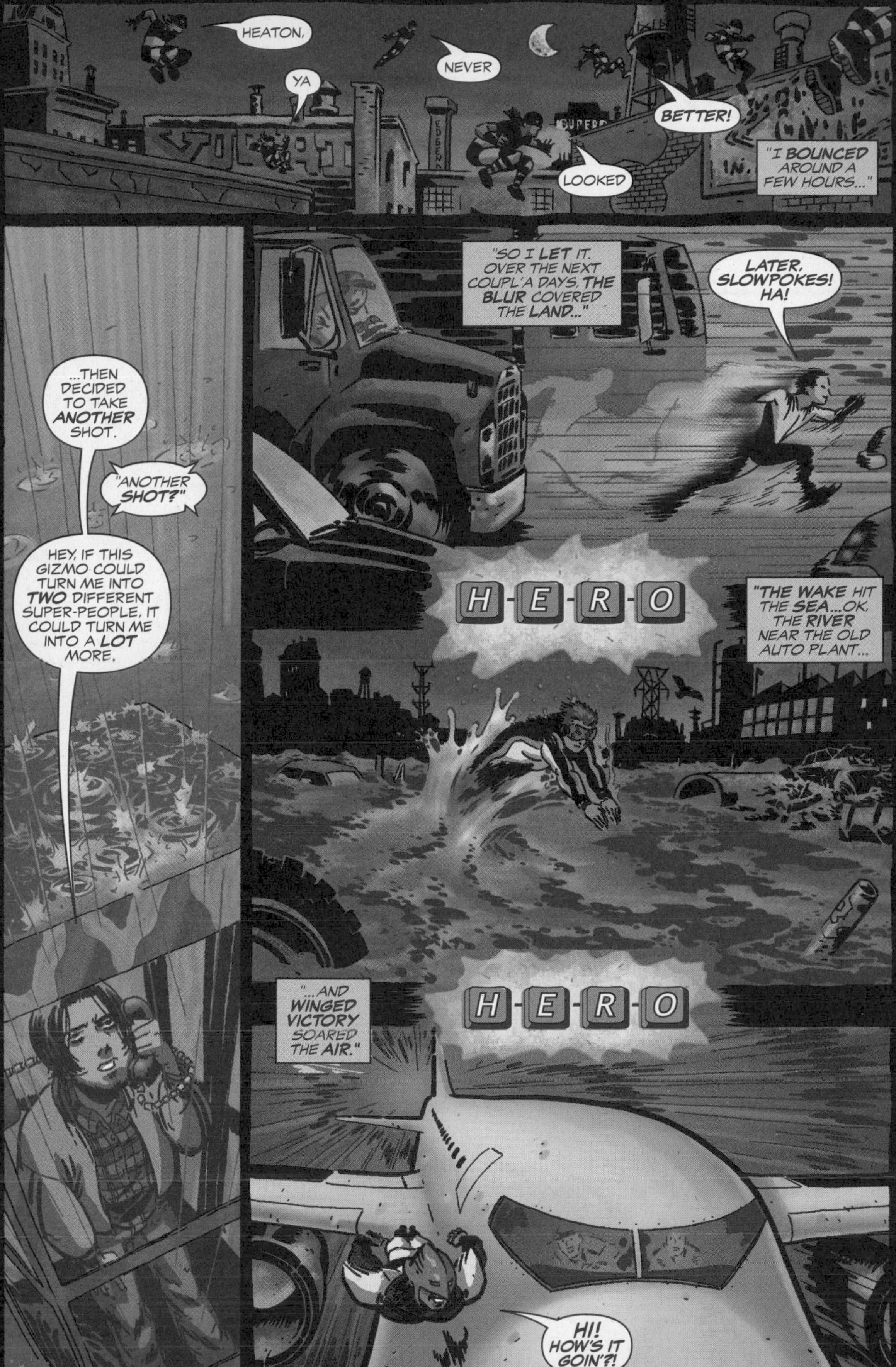
HEATON,
YA
NEVER
LOOKED
BETTER!
"I BOUNCED AROUND A FEW HOURS..."
"SO I LET IT. OVER THE NEXT COUPL'A DAYS, THE BLUR COVERED THE LAND..."
LATER, SLOWPOKES! HA!
...THEN DECIDED TO TAKE ANOTHER SHOT.
"ANOTHER SHOT?"
HEY, IF THIS GIZMO COULD TURN ME INTO TWO DIFFERENT SUPER-PEOPLE, IT COULD TURN ME INTO A LOT MORE.
H-E-R-O
"THE WAKE HIT THE SEA...OK, THE RIVER NEAR THE OLD AUTO PLANT...
H-E-R-O
"...AND WINGED VICTORY SOARED THE AIR."
HI! HOW'S IT GOIN'?!

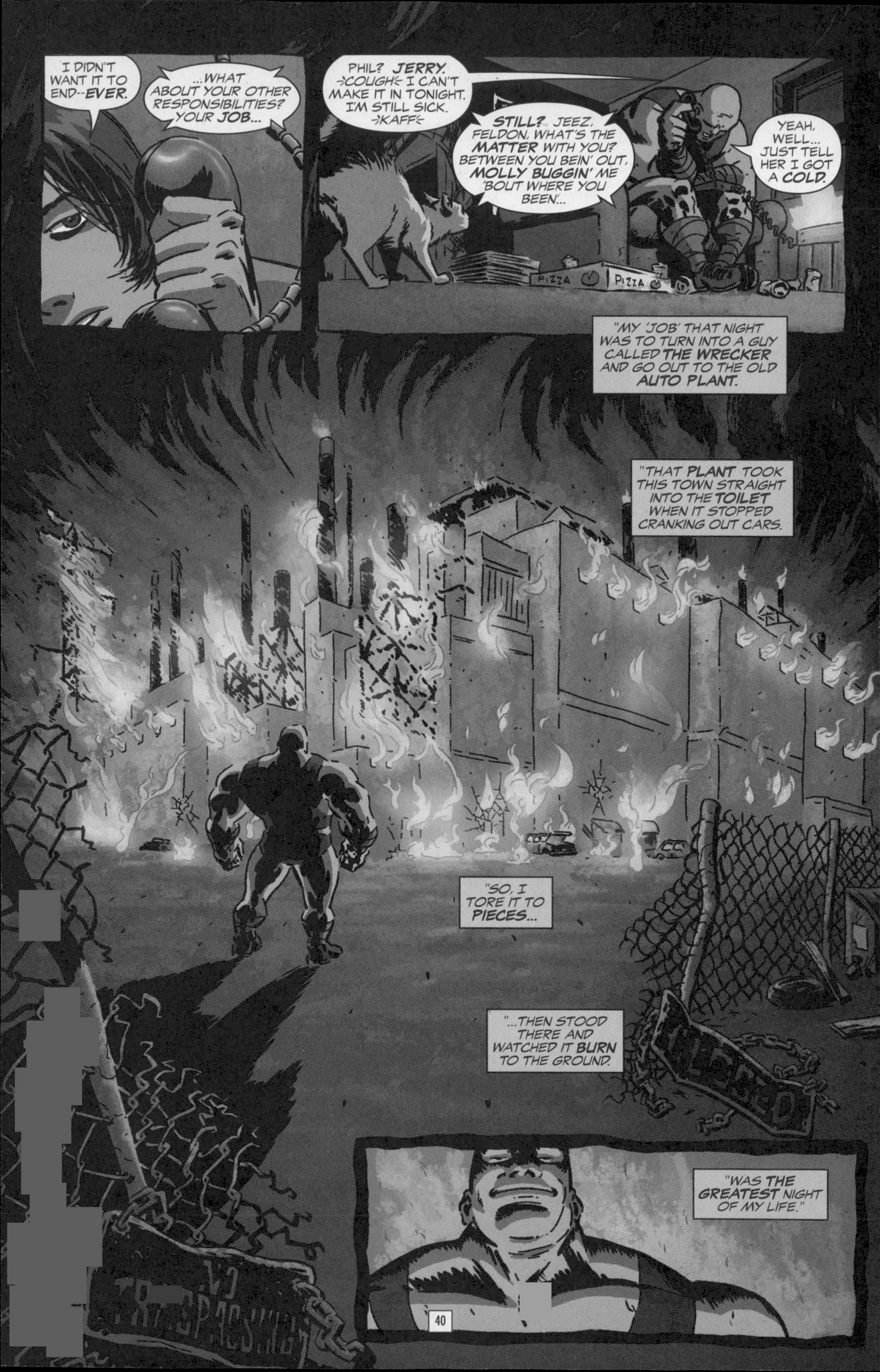
I DIDN'T WANT IT TO END--EVER.
...WHAT ABOUT YOUR OTHER RESPONSIBILITIES? YOUR JOB...
PHIL? JERRY. ⇢COUGH⇠ I CAN'T MAKE IT IN TONIGHT. I'M STILL SICK. ⇢KAFF⇠
STILL? JEEZ, FELDON, WHAT'S THE MATTER WITH YOU? BETWEEN YOU BEIN' OUT, MOLLY BUGGIN' ME 'BOUT WHERE YOU BEEN'...
YEAH, WELL... JUST TELL HER I GOT A COLD.
PIZZA
PIZZA
"MY 'JOB' THAT NIGHT WAS TO TURN INTO A GUY CALLED THE WRECKER AND GO OUT TO THE OLD AUTO PLANT.
"THAT PLANT TOOK THIS TOWN STRAIGHT INTO THE TOILET WHEN IT STOPPED CRANKING OUT CARS.
"SO, I TORE IT TO PIECES...
"...THEN STOOD THERE AND WATCHED IT BURN TO THE GROUND.
"WAS THE GREATEST NIGHT OF MY LIFE."

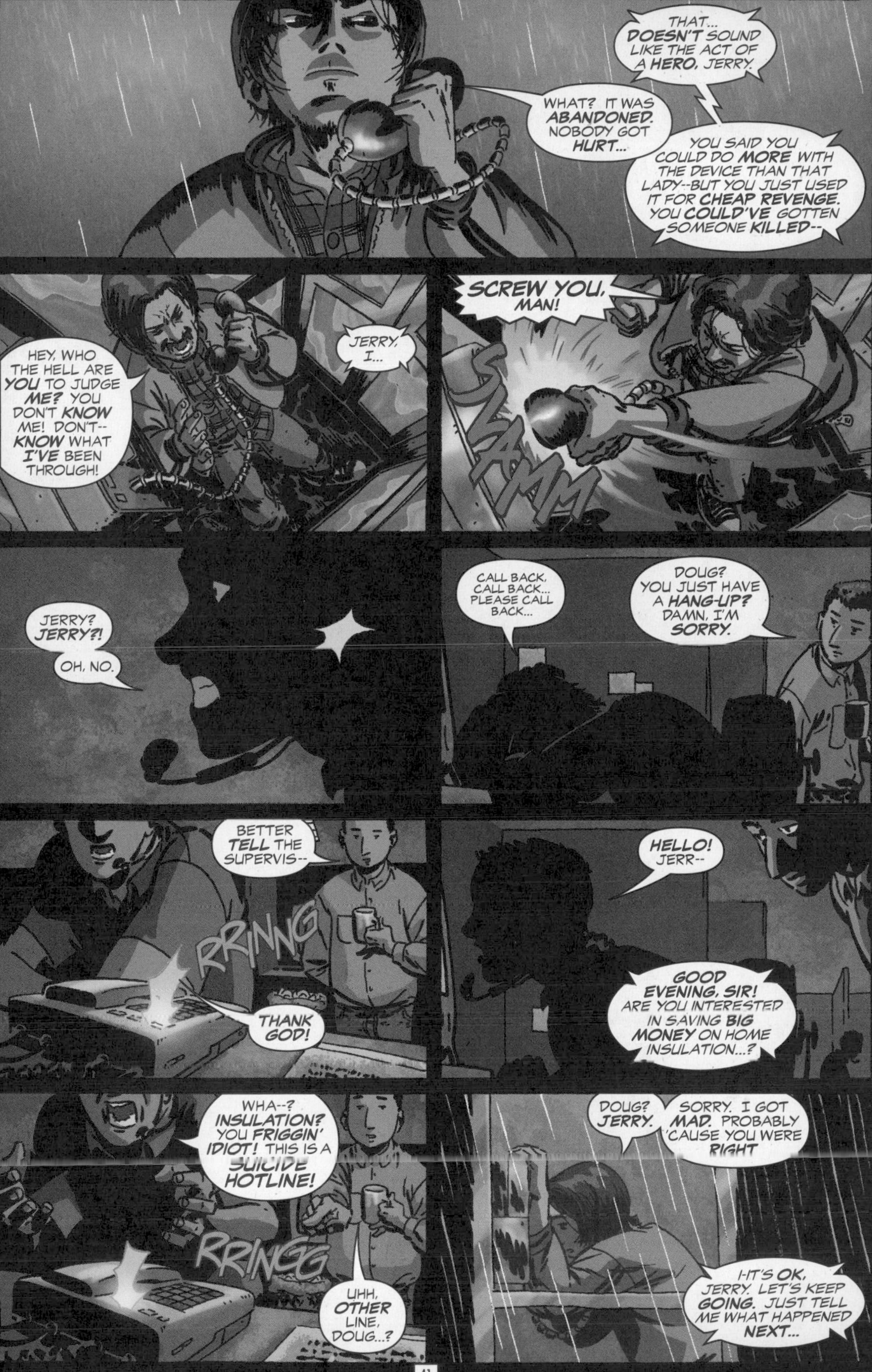

THAT... DOESN'T SOUND LIKE THE ACT OF A HERO, JERRY.
WHAT? IT WAS ABANDONED. NOBODY GOT HURT...
YOU SAID YOU COULD DO MORE WITH THE DEVICE THAN THAT LADY--BUT YOU JUST USED IT FOR CHEAP REVENGE. YOU COULD'VE GOTTEN SOMEONE KILLED--
HEY, WHO THE HELL ARE YOU TO JUDGE ME? YOU DON'T KNOW ME! DON'T-- KNOW WHAT I'VE BEEN THROUGH!
JERRY, I...
SCREW YOU, MAN!
SVAMM
JERRY? JERRY?!
OH, NO.
CALL BACK, CALL BACK... PLEASE CALL BACK...
DOUG? YOU JUST HAVE A HANG-UP? DAMN, I'M SORRY.
BETTER TELL THE SUPERVIS--
RRINNG
THANK GOD!
HELLO! JERR--
GOOD EVENING, SIR! ARE YOU INTERESTED IN SAVING BIG MONEY ON HOME INSULATION...?
WHA--? INSULATION? YOU FRIGGIN' IDIOT! THIS IS A SUICIDE HOTLINE!
RRINGG
UHH, OTHER LINE, DOUG...?
DOUG? JERRY.
SORRY. I GOT MAD. PROBABLY 'CAUSE YOU WERE RIGHT
I-IT'S OK, JERRY. LET'S KEEP GOING. JUST TELL ME WHAT HAPPENED NEXT...

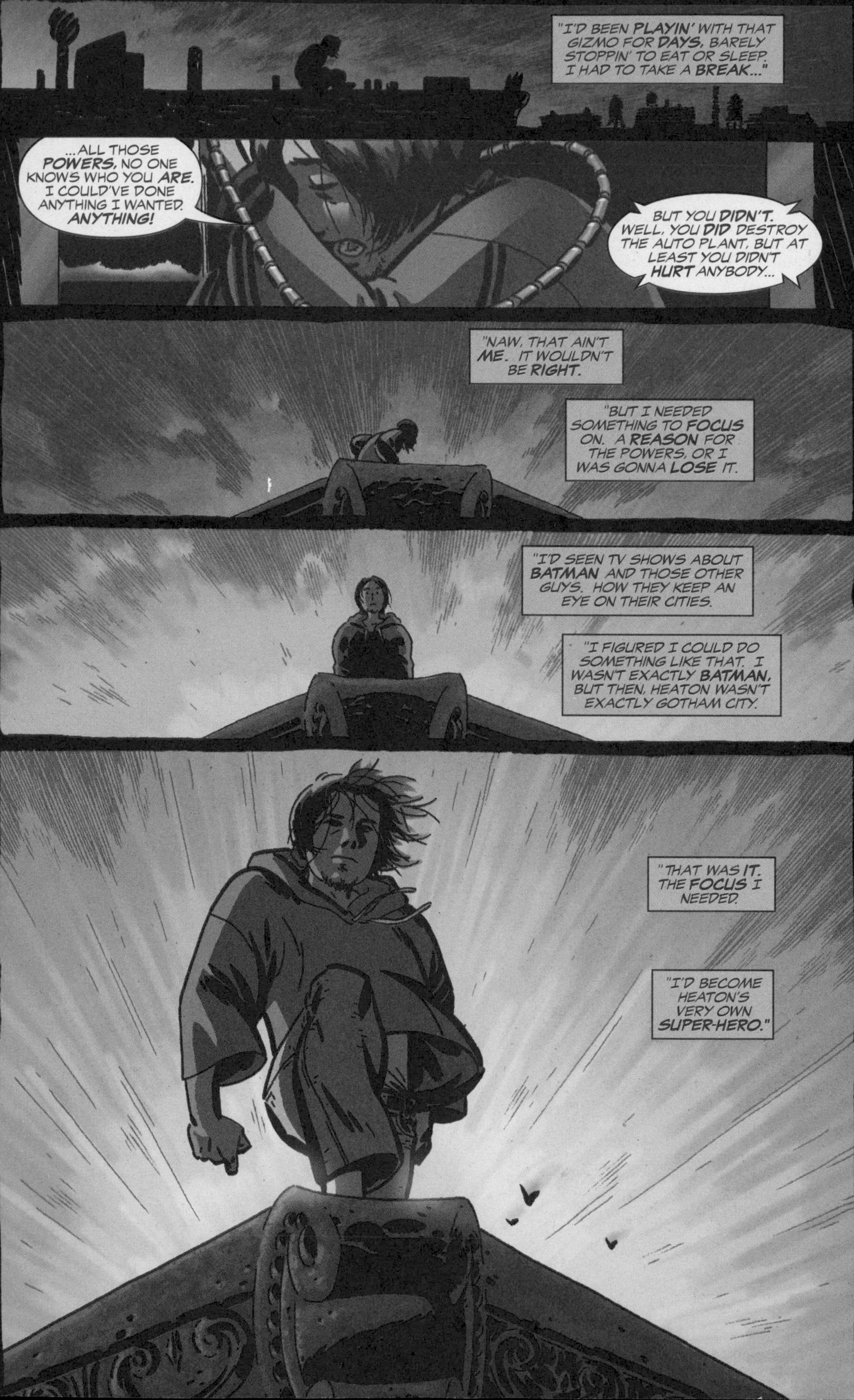
"I'D BEEN PLAYIN' WITH THAT GIZMO FOR DAYS, BARELY STOPPIN' TO EAT OR SLEEP. I HAD TO TAKE A BREAK..."
...ALL THOSE POWERS, NO ONE KNOWS WHO YOU ARE. I COULD'VE DONE ANYTHING I WANTED. ANYTHING!
BUT YOU DIDN'T. WELL, YOU DID DESTROY THE AUTO PLANT, BUT AT LEAST YOU DIDN'T HURT ANYBODY...
"NAW, THAT AIN'T ME. IT WOULDN'T BE RIGHT.
"BUT I NEEDED SOMETHING TO FOCUS ON. A REASON FOR THE POWERS, OR I WAS GONNA LOSE IT.
"I'D SEEN TV SHOWS ABOUT BATMAN AND THOSE OTHER GUYS. HOW THEY KEEP AN EYE ON THEIR CITIES.
"I FIGURED I COULD DO SOMETHING LIKE THAT. I WASN'T EXACTLY BATMAN, BUT THEN, HEATON WASN'T EXACTLY GOTHAM CITY.
"THAT WAS IT. THE FOCUS I NEEDED.
"I'D BECOME HEATON'S VERY OWN SUPER-HERO."

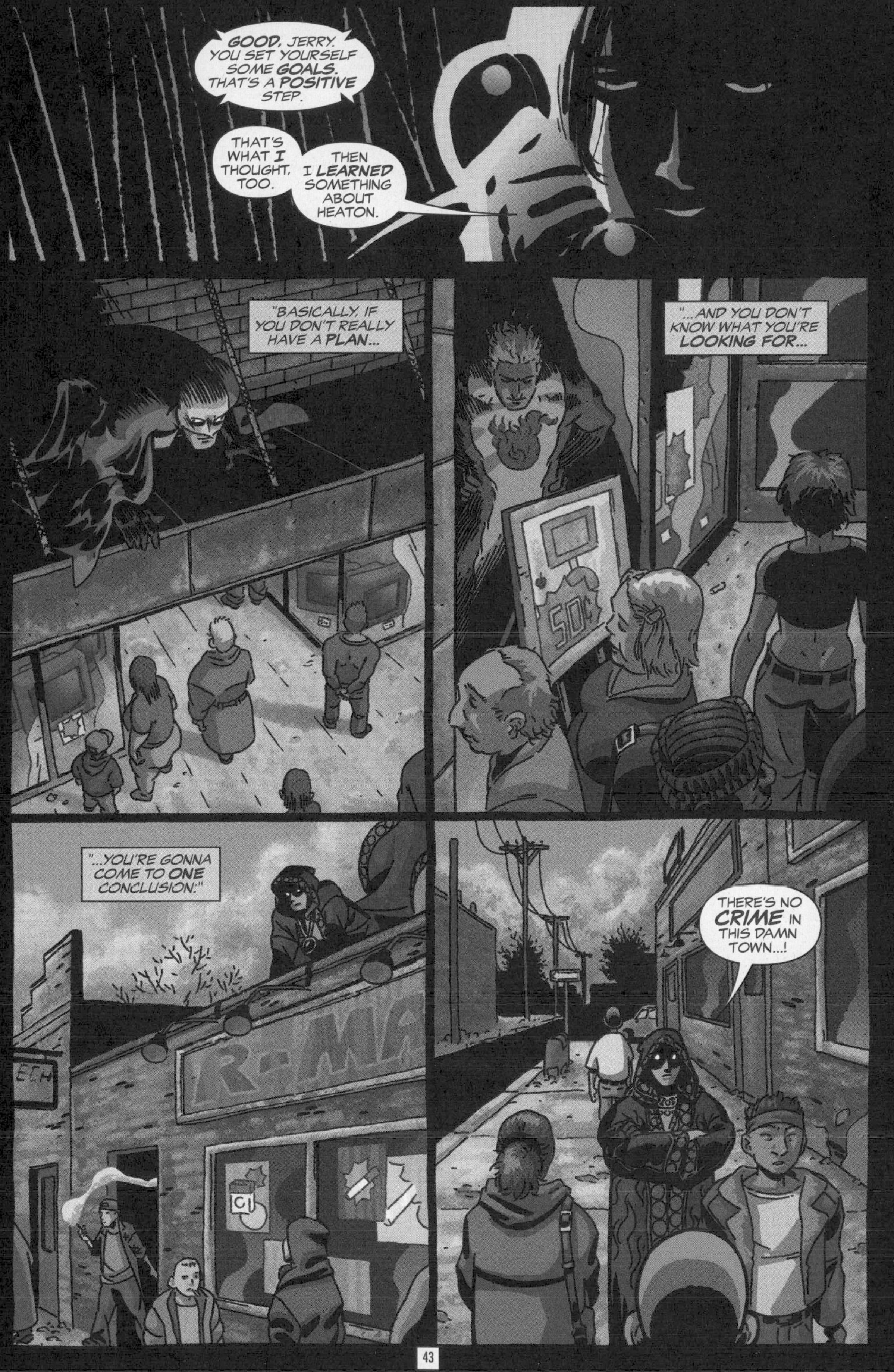
GOOD, JERRY. YOU SET YOURSELF SOME GOALS. THAT'S A POSITIVE STEP.
THAT'S WHAT I THOUGHT, TOO.
THEN I LEARNED SOMETHING ABOUT HEATON.
"BASICALLY, IF YOU DON'T REALLY HAVE A PLAN...
"...AND YOU DON'T KNOW WHAT YOU'RE LOOKING FOR...
50¢
"...YOU'RE GONNA COME TO ONE CONCLUSION:"
THERE'S NO CRIME IN THIS DAMN TOWN...!

'COURSE, I **KNEW** BETTER. HEATON'S **FULL** OF CRIME. I JUST WASN'T LOOKING IN THE **RIGHT** PLACES.

WOMAN, 78 STABBED IN KITCHEN

sdsj eíeíu v
fskl djlkjiasjjdkjyujekia sj

"ONLY IN OUR CASE, THE GOOD SIDE AIN'T THAT GREAT ..."

"YOU NEVER **BEEN** TO HEATON, RIGHT, DOUG? WELL, IT'S GOT ITS **GOOD** SIDE AND ITS **BAD** SIDE.

...POLICE OFFICIALS SAY THIS HOUSE HAS BEEN A CENTER FOR **DRUG ACTIVITY** ON SOUTH SIDE...

"...AND THE **BAD** SIDE IS AWFUL.

HEATON:

"AND IT'S JUST A **BUS RIDE** AWAY."

DAMN...!

44

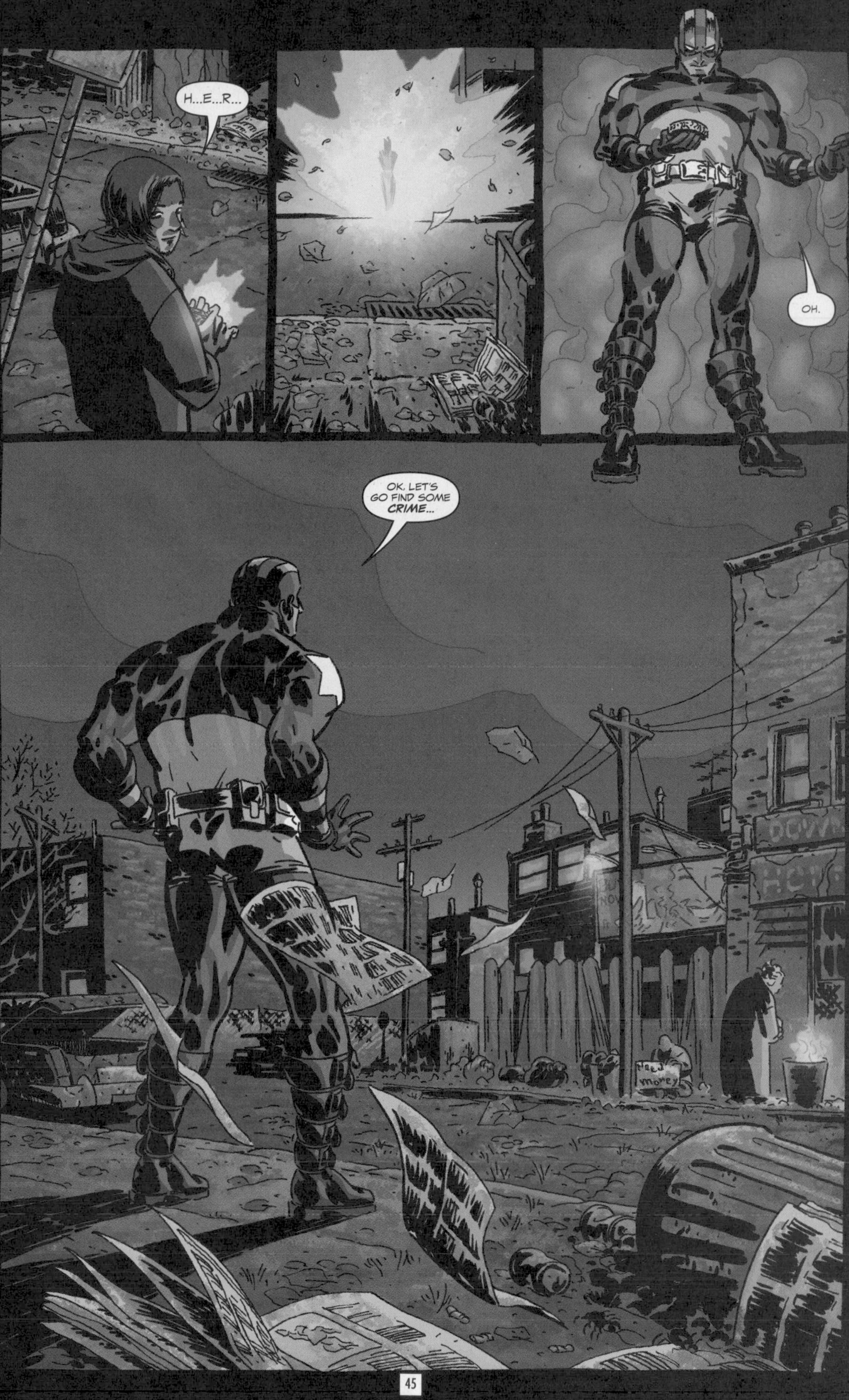

H...E...R...
OH.
OK, LET'S GO FIND SOME CRIME...
NEED money

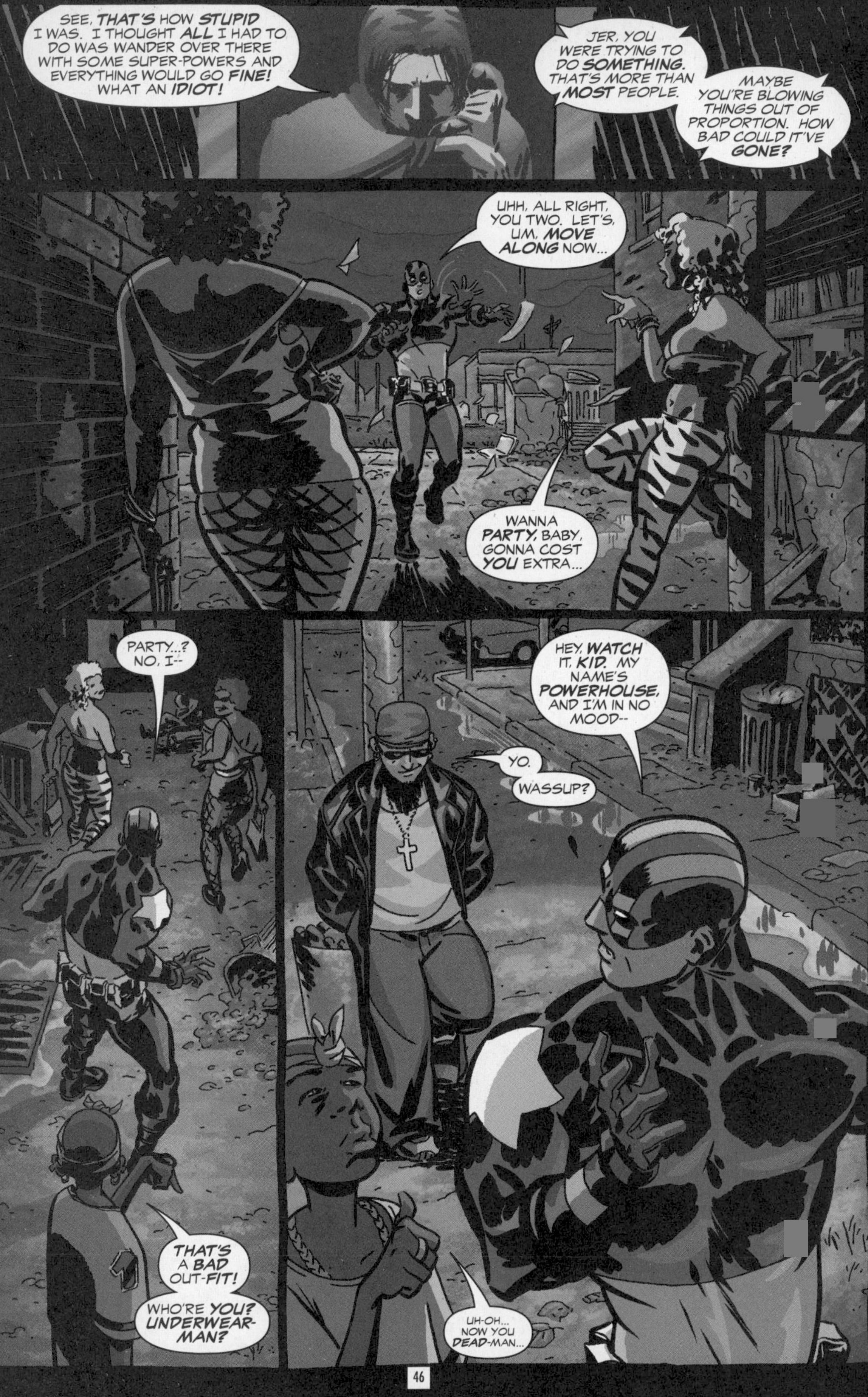
SEE, THAT'S HOW STUPID I WAS. I THOUGHT ALL I HAD TO DO WAS WANDER OVER THERE WITH SOME SUPER-POWERS AND EVERYTHING WOULD GO FINE! WHAT AN IDIOT!
JER, YOU WERE TRYING TO DO SOMETHING. THAT'S MORE THAN MOST PEOPLE.
MAYBE YOU'RE BLOWING THINGS OUT OF PROPORTION. HOW BAD COULD IT'VE GONE?
UHH, ALL RIGHT, YOU TWO. LET'S, UM, MOVE ALONG NOW...
WANNA PARTY, BABY, GONNA COST YOU EXTRA...
PARTY...? NO, I--
THAT'S A BAD OUT-FIT!
WHO'RE YOU? UNDERWEAR-MAN?
HEY, WATCH IT, KID. MY NAME'S POWERHOUSE, AND I'M IN NO MOOD--
YO. WASSUP?
UH-OH... NOW YOU DEAD-MAN...

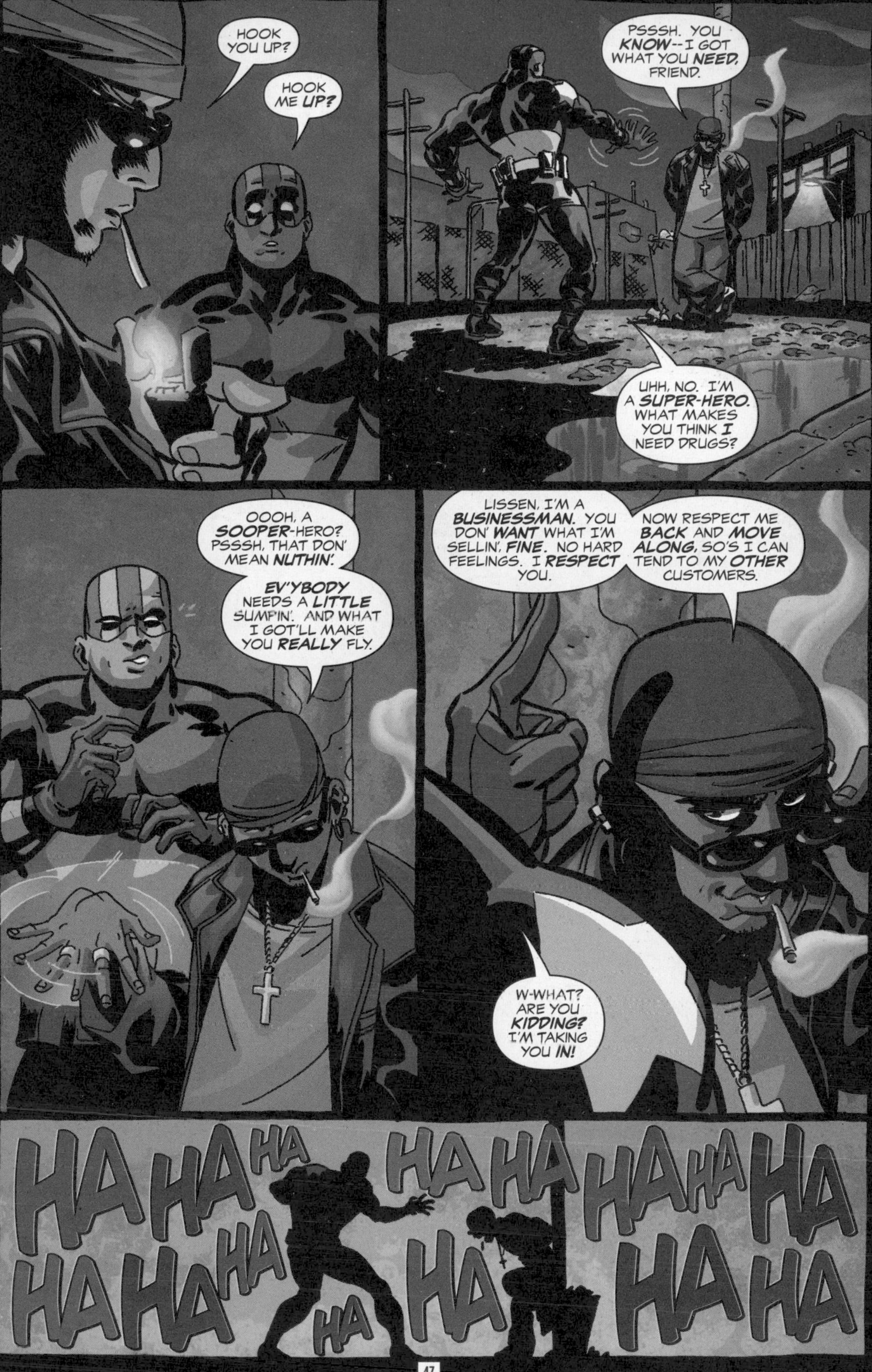
HOOK YOU UP?
HOOK ME UP?
PSSSH. YOU KNOW--I GOT WHAT YOU NEED, FRIEND.
UHH, NO. I'M A SUPER-HERO. WHAT MAKES YOU THINK I NEED DRUGS?
OOOH, A SOOPER-HERO? PSSSH, THAT DON' MEAN NUTHIN'.
EV'YBODY NEEDS A LITTLE SUMP'IN'. AND WHAT I GOT'LL MAKE YOU REALLY FLY.
LISSEN, I'M A BUSINESSMAN. YOU DON' WANT WHAT I'M SELLIN', FINE. NO HARD FEELINGS. I RESPECT YOU.
NOW RESPECT ME BACK AND MOVE ALONG, SO'S I CAN TEND TO MY OTHER CUSTOMERS.
W-WHAT? ARE YOU KIDDING? I'M TAKING YOU IN!
HA HA HA HA HA HA HA HA HA HA HA HA
HA HA HA HA HA HA HA HA HA

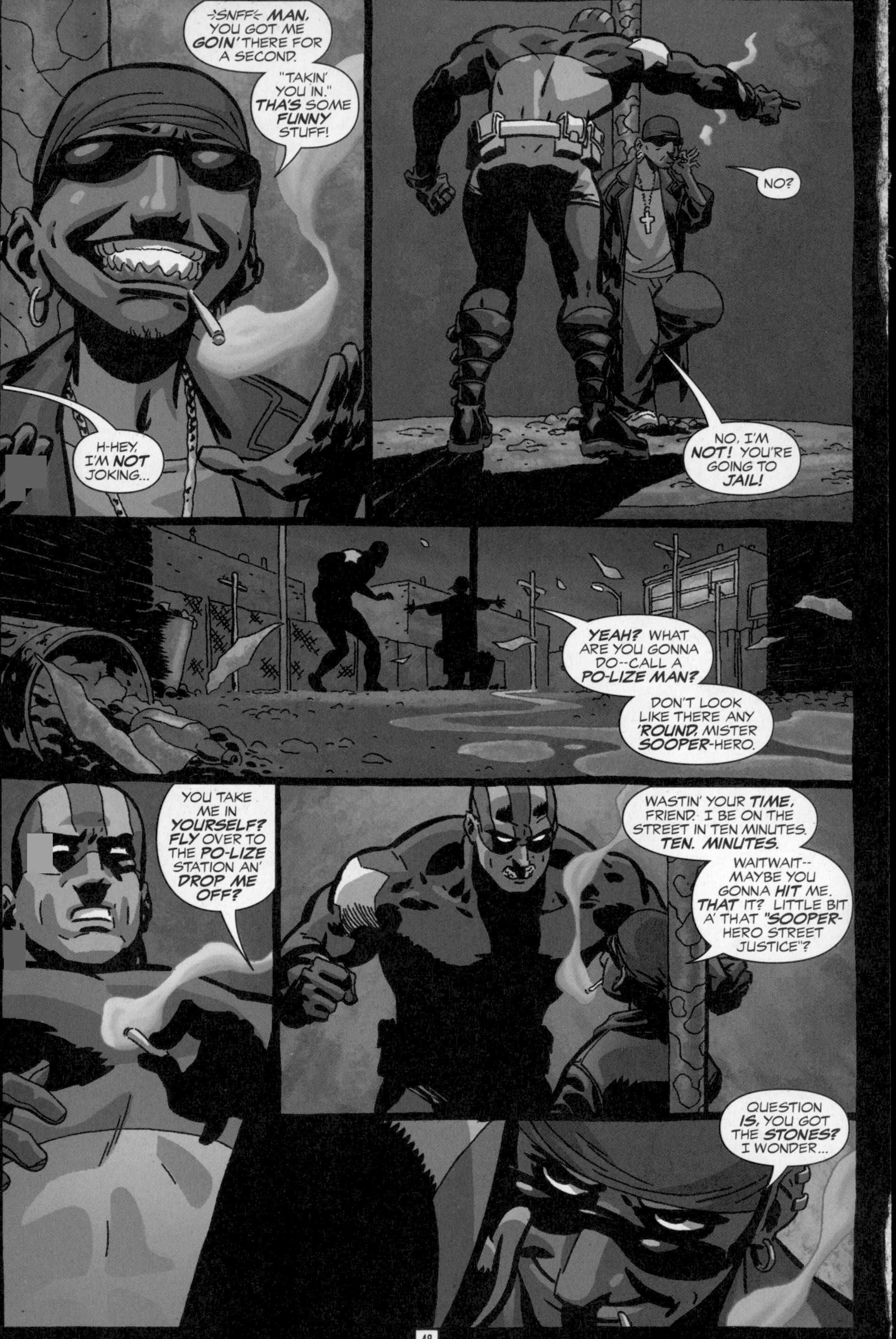

>SNFF< MAN, YOU GOT ME GOIN' THERE FOR A SECOND.
"TAKIN' YOU IN." THA'S SOME FUNNY STUFF!
H-HEY, I'M NOT JOKING...
NO?
NO, I'M NOT! YOU'RE GOING TO JAIL!
YEAH? WHAT ARE YOU GONNA DO--CALL A PO-LIZE MAN?
DON'T LOOK LIKE THERE ANY 'ROUND, MISTER SOOPER-HERO.
YOU TAKE ME IN YOURSELF? FLY OVER TO THE PO-LIZE STATION AN' DROP ME OFF?
WASTIN' YOUR TIME, FRIEND. I BE ON THE STREET IN TEN MINUTES. TEN. MINUTES.
WAITWAIT-- MAYBE YOU GONNA HIT ME. THAT IT? LITTLE BIT A' THAT "SOOPER-HERO STREET JUSTICE"?
QUESTION IS, YOU GOT THE STONES? I WONDER...

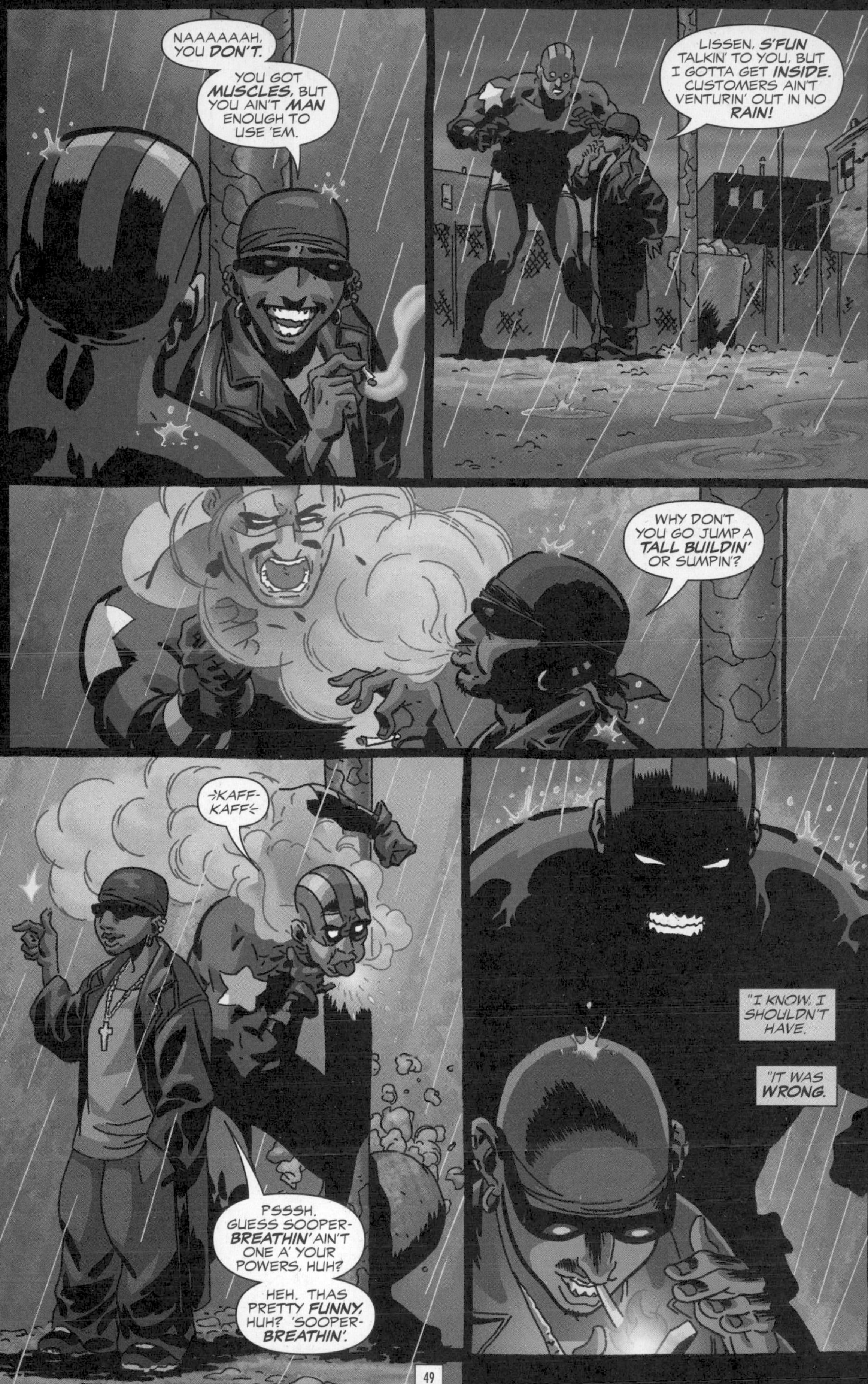
NAAAAAAH, YOU DON'T.
YOU GOT MUSCLES, BUT YOU AIN'T MAN ENOUGH TO USE 'EM.
LISSEN, S'FUN TALKIN' TO YOU, BUT I GOTTA GET INSIDE. CUSTOMERS AIN'T VENTURIN' OUT IN NO RAIN!
WHY DON'T YOU GO JUMP A TALL BUILDIN' OR SUMPIN'?
KAFF-KAFF
PSSSH. GUESS SOOPER-BREATHIN' AIN'T ONE A' YOUR POWERS, HUH?
HEH. THAS PRETTY FUNNY, HUH? 'SOOPER-BREATHIN'.
"I KNOW, I SHOULDN'T HAVE.
"IT WAS WRONG.

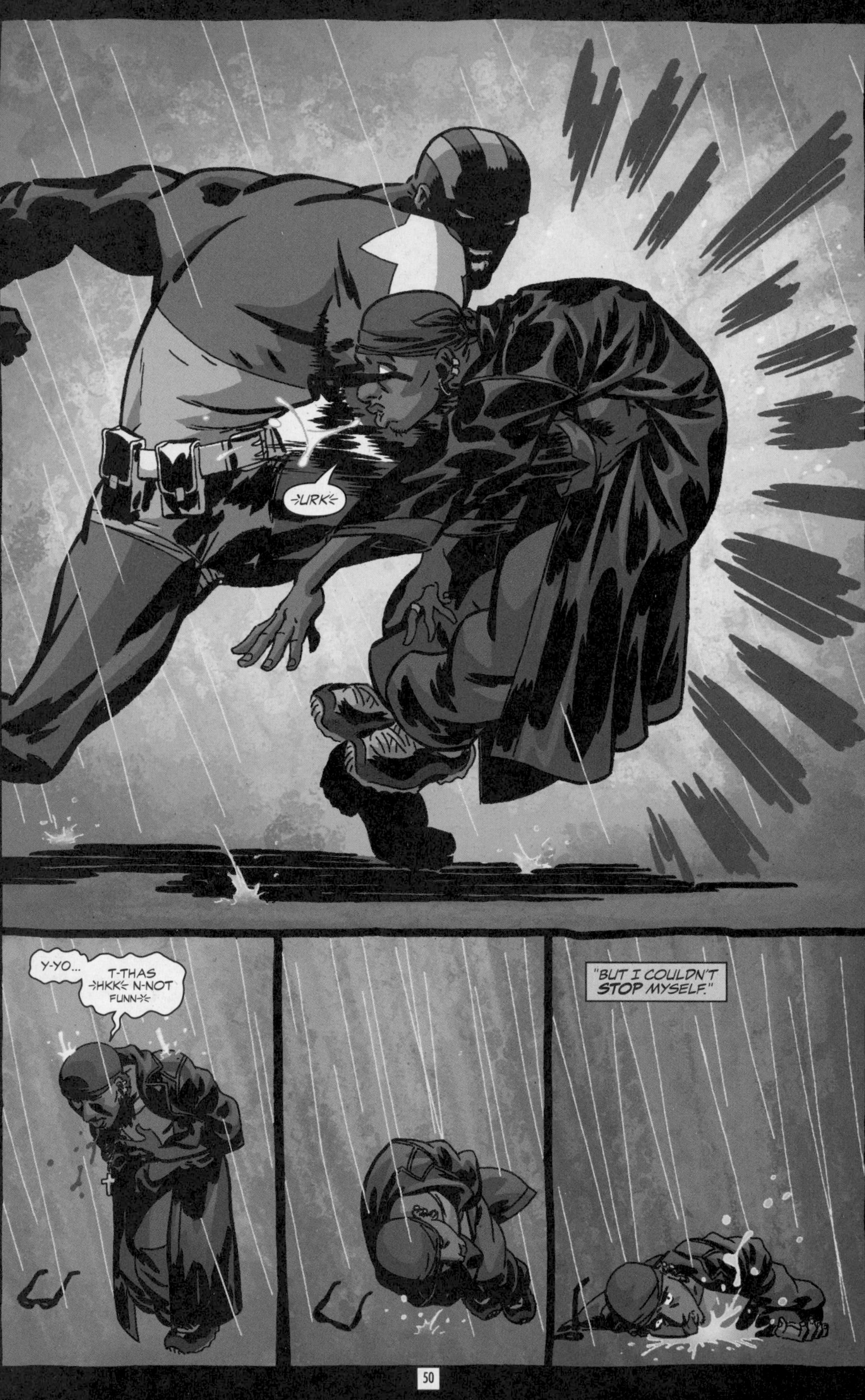
URK
Y-YO...
T-THAS HKK N-NOT FUNN
"BUT I COULDN'T STOP MYSELF."

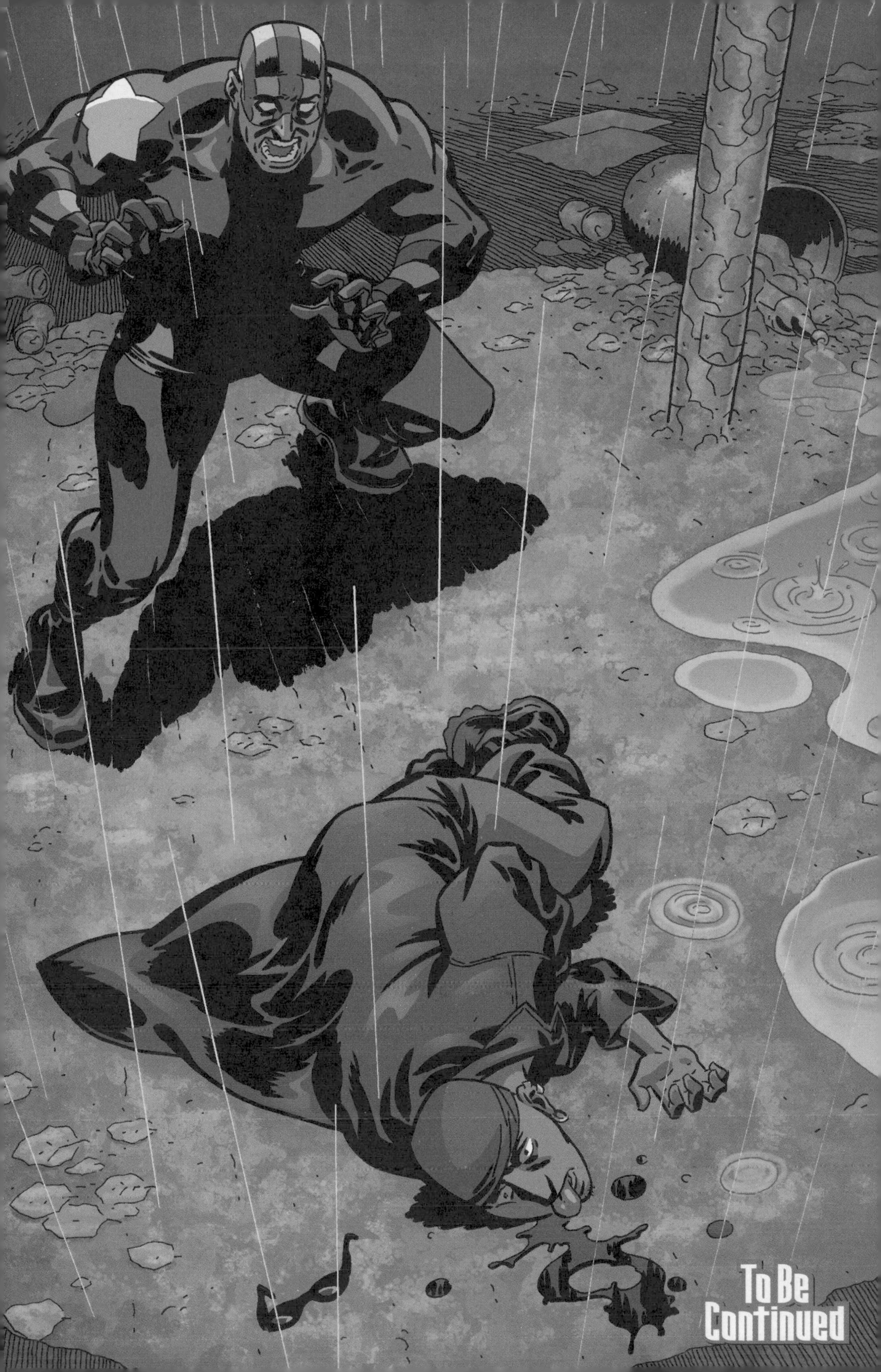
To Be
Continued

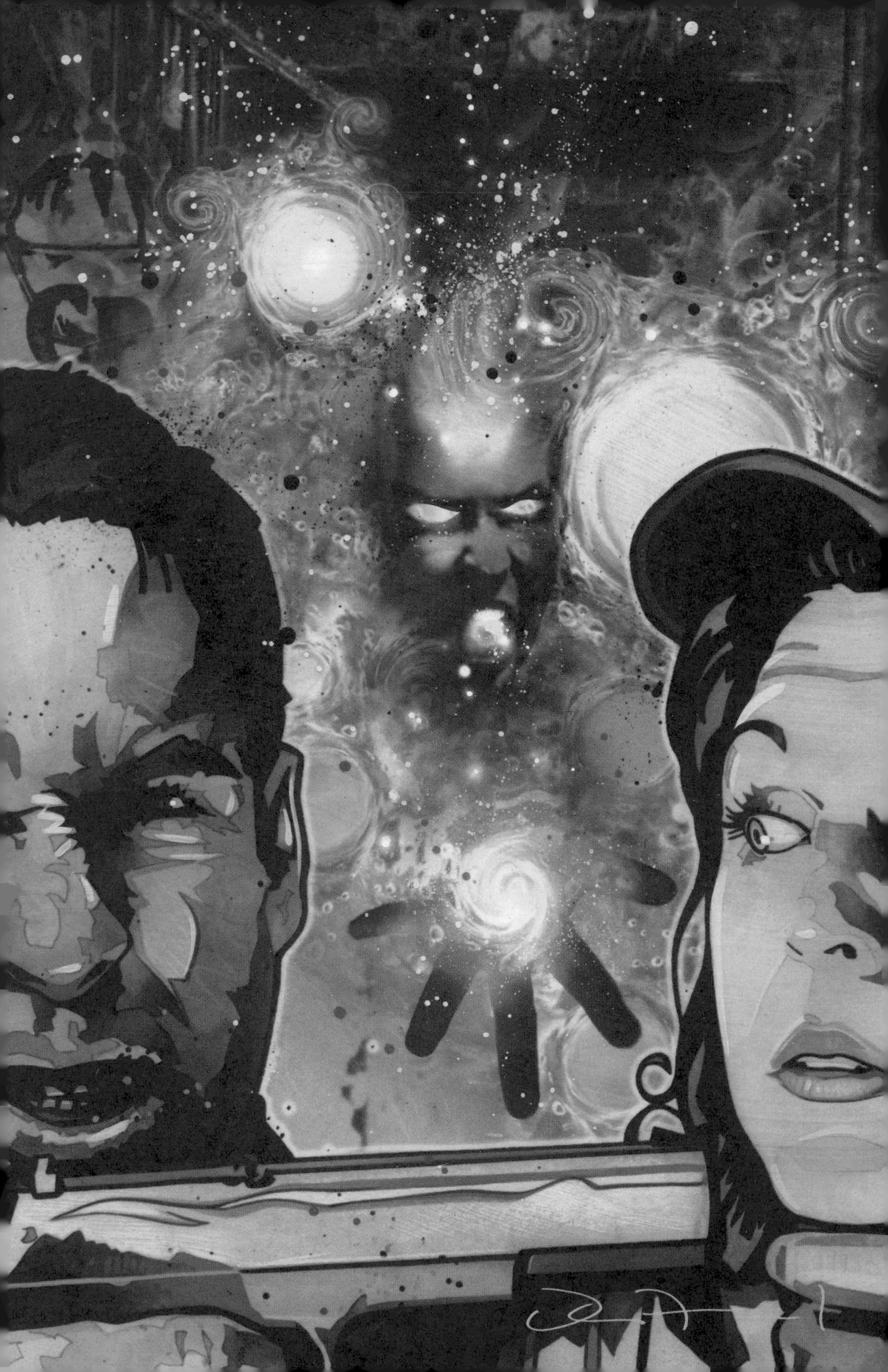

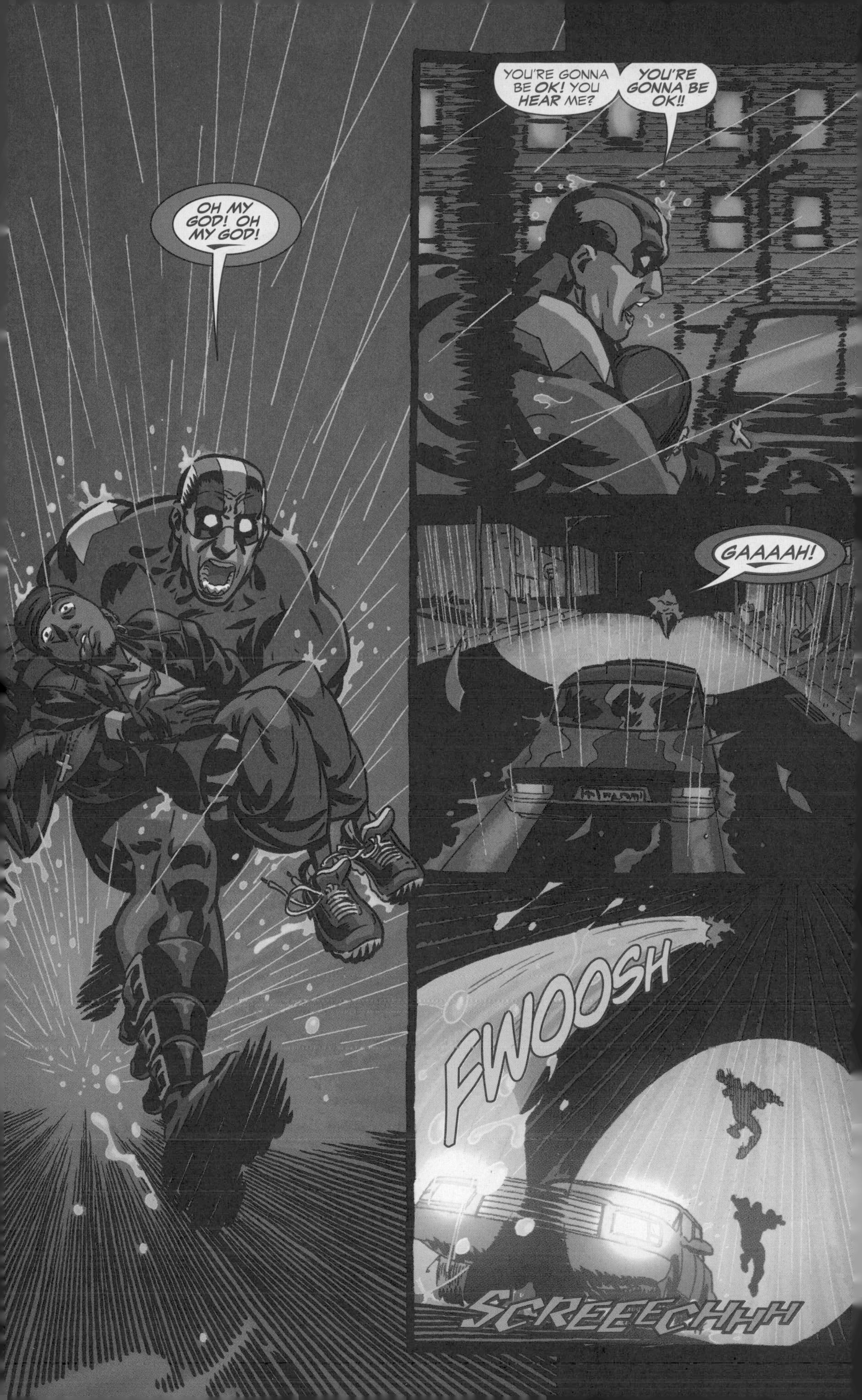
OH MY GOD! OH MY GOD!
YOU'RE GONNA BE OK! YOU HEAR ME?
YOU'RE GONNA BE OK!!
GAAAAH!
FWOOSH
SCREEECHHH

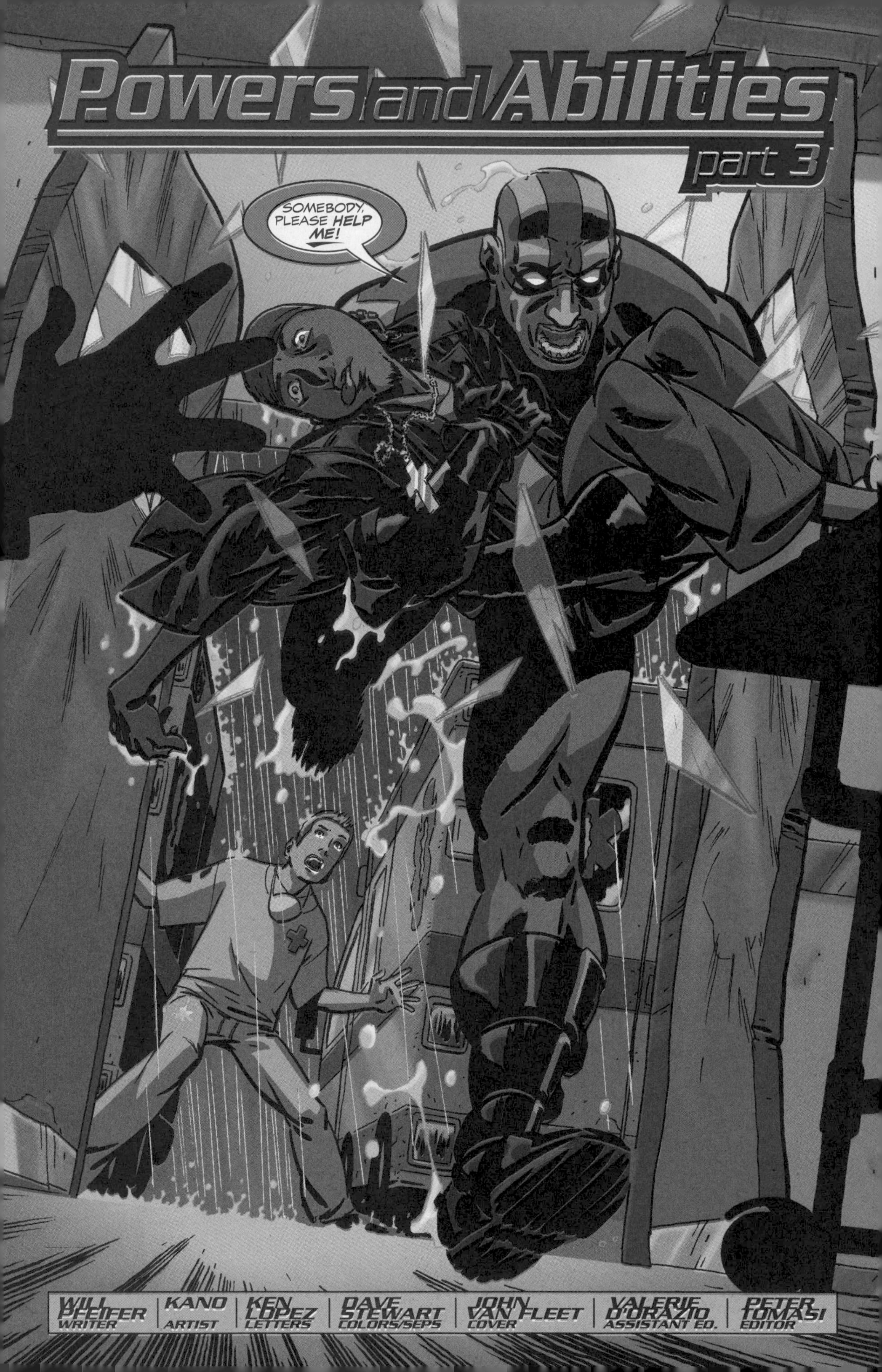
Powers and Abilities
part 3
SOMEBODY, PLEASE HELP ME!
WILL PFEIFER WRITER
KANO ARTIST
KEN LOPEZ LETTERS
DAVE STEWART COLORS/SEPS
JOHN VAN FLEET COVER
VALERIE D'ORAZIO ASSISTANT ED.
PETER TOMASI EDITOR

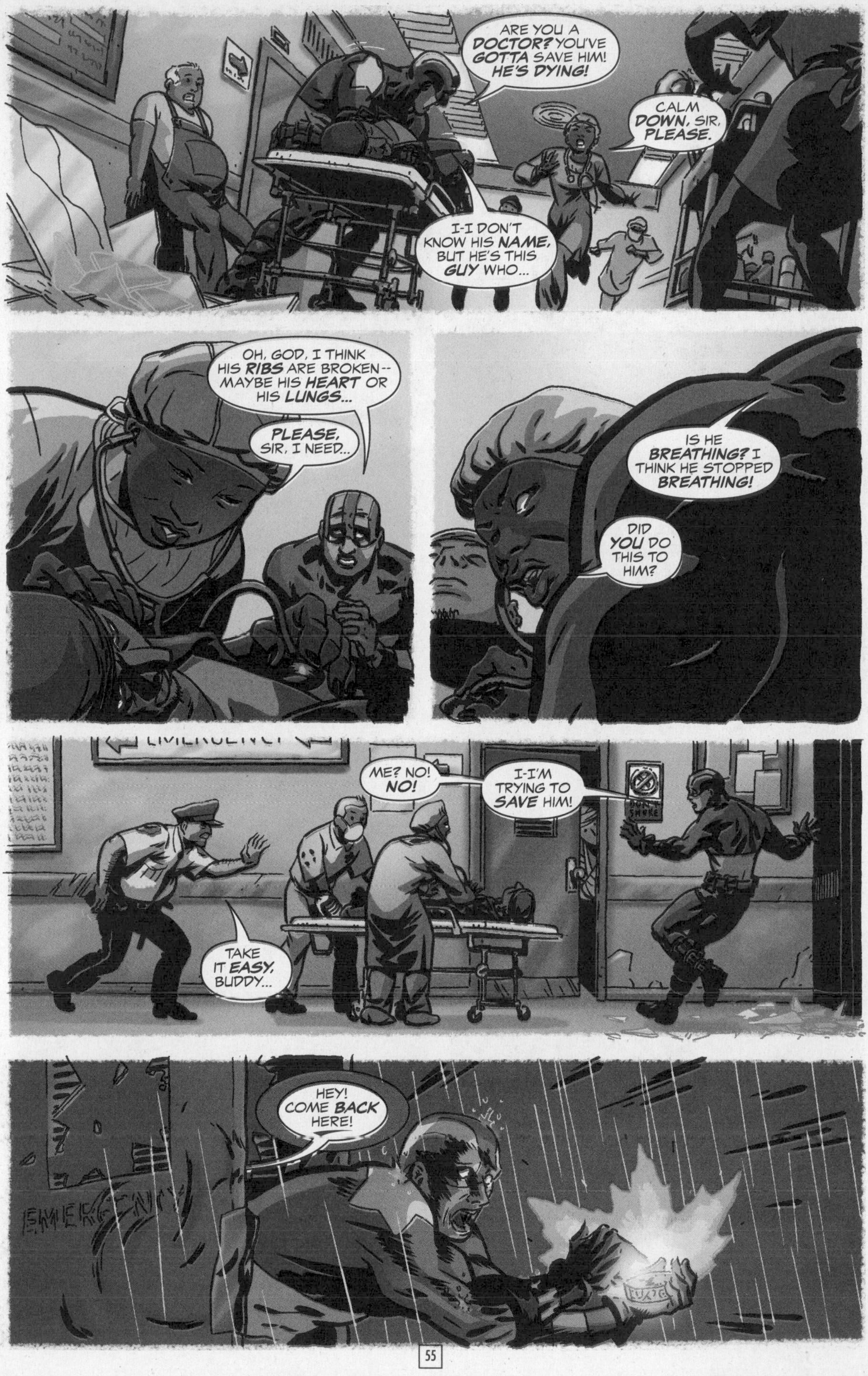
ARE YOU A DOCTOR? YOU'VE GOTTA SAVE HIM! HE'S DYING!
CALM DOWN, SIR, PLEASE.
I-I DON'T KNOW HIS NAME, BUT HE'S THIS GUY WHO...
OH, GOD, I THINK HIS RIBS ARE BROKEN-- MAYBE HIS HEART OR HIS LUNGS...
PLEASE, SIR, I NEED...
IS HE BREATHING? I THINK HE STOPPED BREATHING!
DID YOU DO THIS TO HIM?
ME? NO! NO!
I-I'M TRYING TO SAVE HIM!
TAKE IT EASY, BUDDY...
HEY! COME BACK HERE!

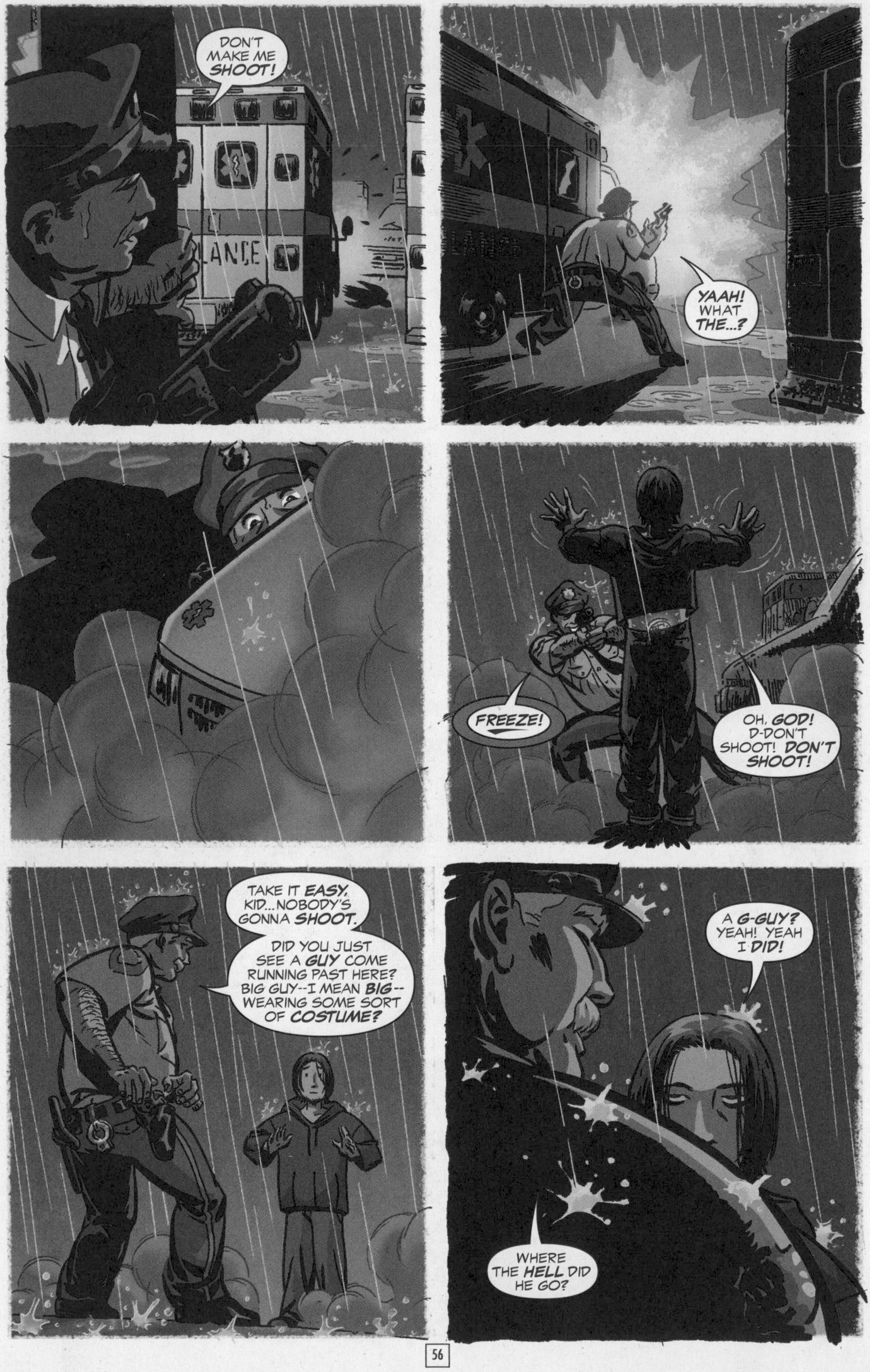
DON'T MAKE ME SHOOT!
YAAH! WHAT THE...?
FREEZE!
OH, GOD! D-DON'T SHOOT! DON'T SHOOT!
TAKE IT EASY, KID...NOBODY'S GONNA SHOOT.
DID YOU JUST SEE A GUY COME RUNNING PAST HERE? BIG GUY--I MEAN BIG--WEARING SOME SORT OF COSTUME?
A G-GUY? YEAH! YEAH I DID!
WHERE THE HELL DID HE GO?

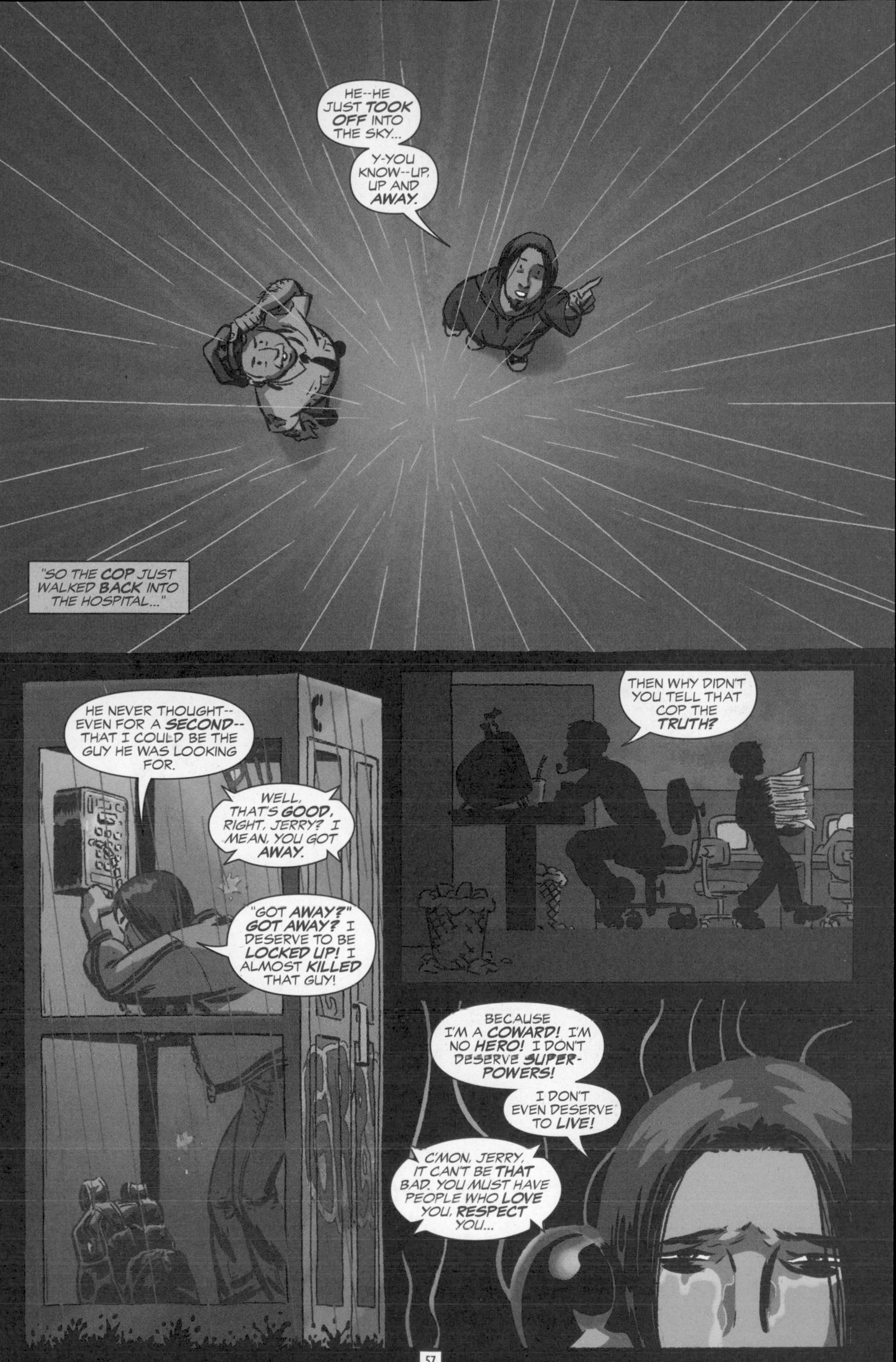

HE--HE JUST TOOK OFF INTO THE SKY...
Y-YOU KNOW--UP, UP AND AWAY.
"SO THE COP JUST WALKED BACK INTO THE HOSPITAL..."
HE NEVER THOUGHT--EVEN FOR A SECOND--THAT I COULD BE THE GUY HE WAS LOOKING FOR.
WELL, THAT'S GOOD, RIGHT, JERRY? I MEAN, YOU GOT AWAY.
"GOT AWAY?" GOT AWAY? I DESERVE TO BE LOCKED UP! I ALMOST KILLED THAT GUY!
THEN WHY DIDN'T YOU TELL THAT COP THE TRUTH?
BECAUSE I'M A COWARD! I'M NO HERO! I DON'T DESERVE SUPER-POWERS!
I DON'T EVEN DESERVE TO LIVE!
C'MON, JERRY, IT CAN'T BE THAT BAD. YOU MUST HAVE PEOPLE WHO LOVE YOU, RESPECT YOU...

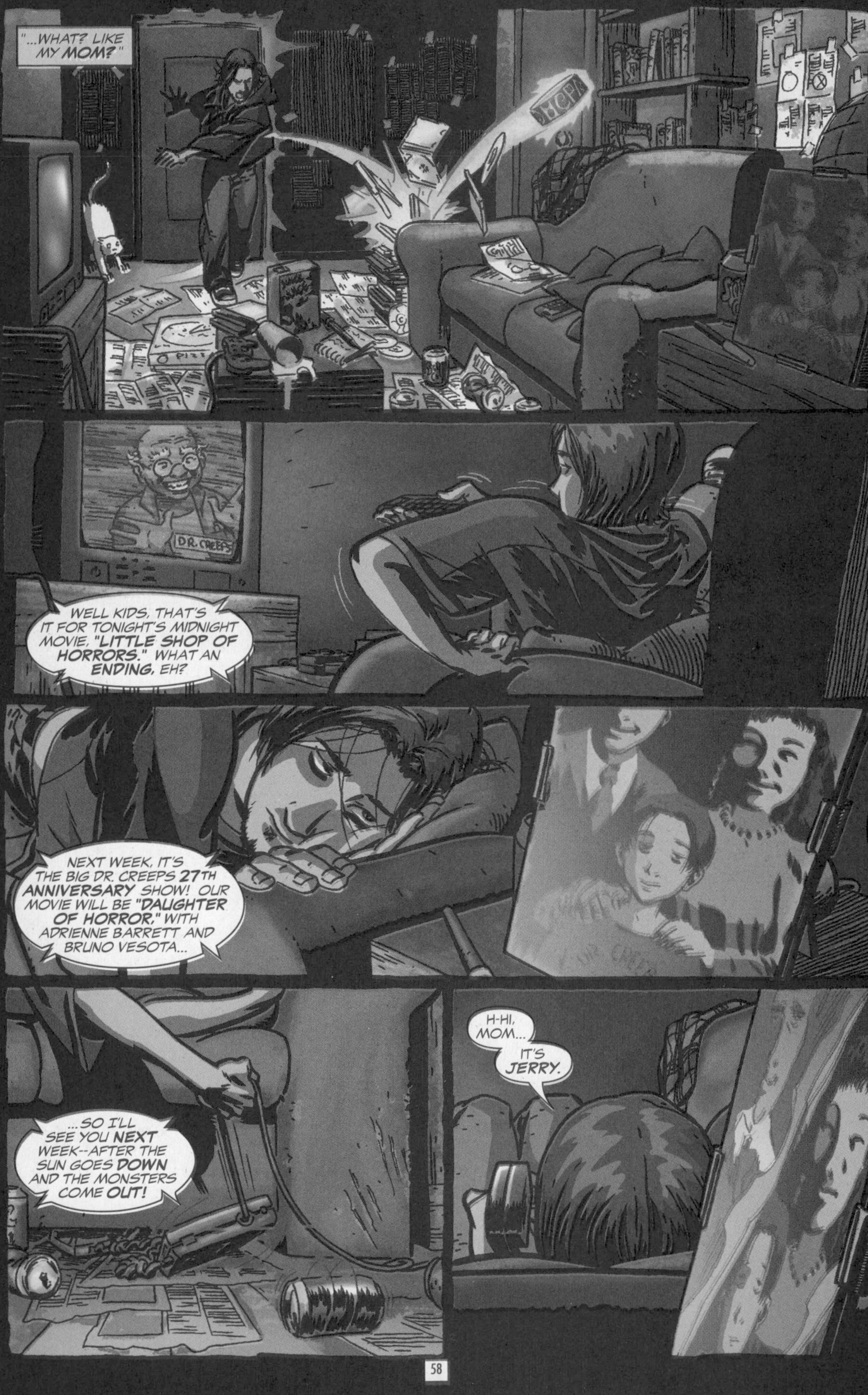
"...WHAT? LIKE MY MOM?"
WELL KIDS, THAT'S IT FOR TONIGHT'S MIDNIGHT MOVIE, "LITTLE SHOP OF HORRORS." WHAT AN ENDING, EH?
NEXT WEEK, IT'S THE BIG DR. CREEPS 27TH ANNIVERSARY SHOW! OUR MOVIE WILL BE "DAUGHTER OF HORROR," WITH ADRIENNE BARRETT AND BRUNO VESOTA...
...SO I'LL SEE YOU NEXT WEEK--AFTER THE SUN GOES DOWN AND THE MONSTERS COME OUT!
H-HI, MOM...
IT'S JERRY.

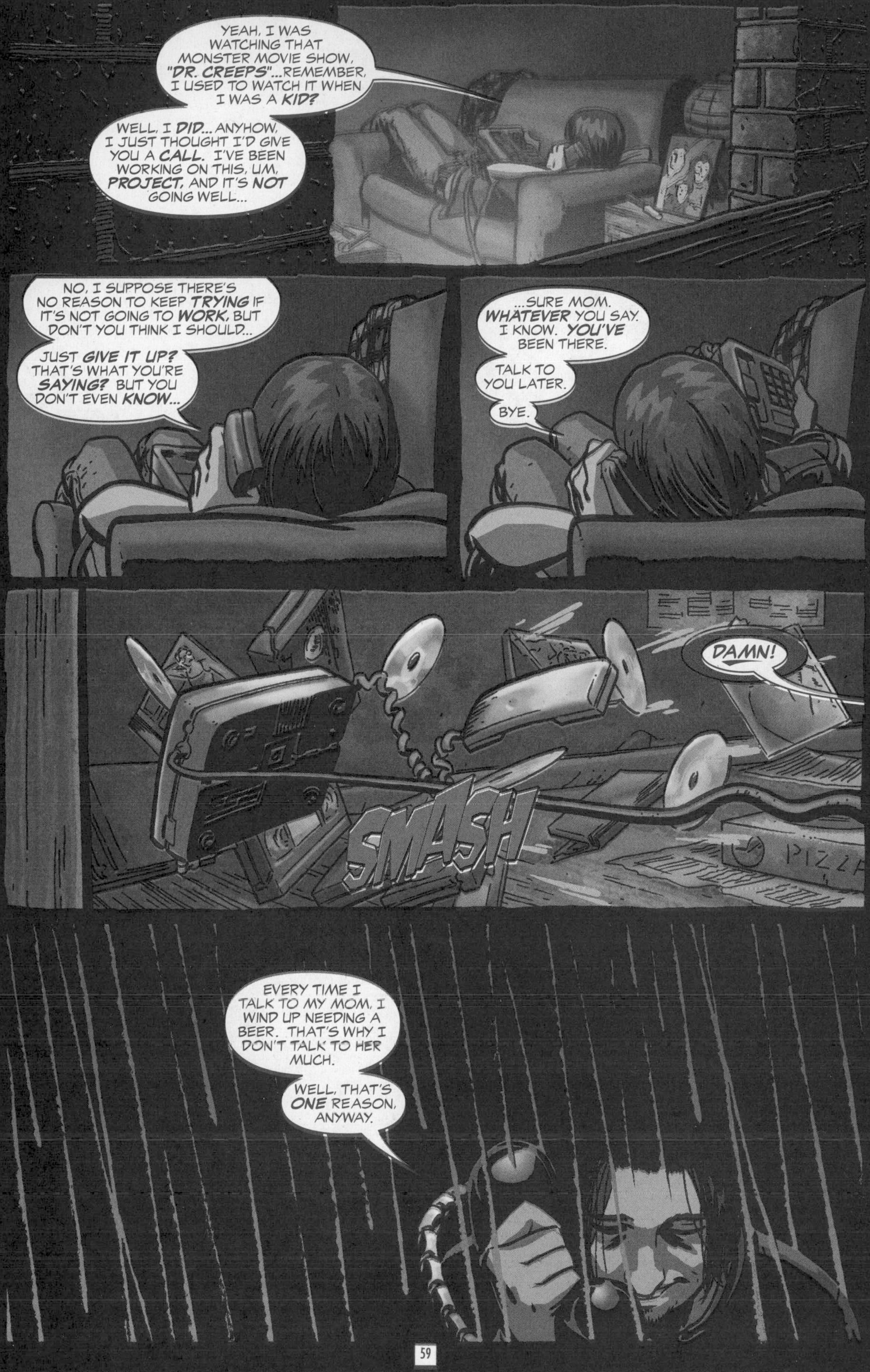
YEAH, I WAS WATCHING THAT MONSTER MOVIE SHOW, "DR. CREEPS"...REMEMBER, I USED TO WATCH IT WHEN I WAS A KID?
WELL, I DID... ANYHOW, I JUST THOUGHT I'D GIVE YOU A CALL. I'VE BEEN WORKING ON THIS, UM, PROJECT, AND IT'S NOT GOING WELL...
NO, I SUPPOSE THERE'S NO REASON TO KEEP TRYING IF IT'S NOT GOING TO WORK, BUT DON'T YOU THINK I SHOULD...
JUST GIVE IT UP? THAT'S WHAT YOU'RE SAYING? BUT YOU DON'T EVEN KNOW...
...SURE MOM. WHATEVER YOU SAY. I KNOW. YOU'VE BEEN THERE.
TALK TO YOU LATER.
BYE.
DAMN!
SMASH
PIZZA
EVERY TIME I TALK TO MY MOM, I WIND UP NEEDING A BEER. THAT'S WHY I DON'T TALK TO HER MUCH.
WELL, THAT'S ONE REASON, ANYWAY.

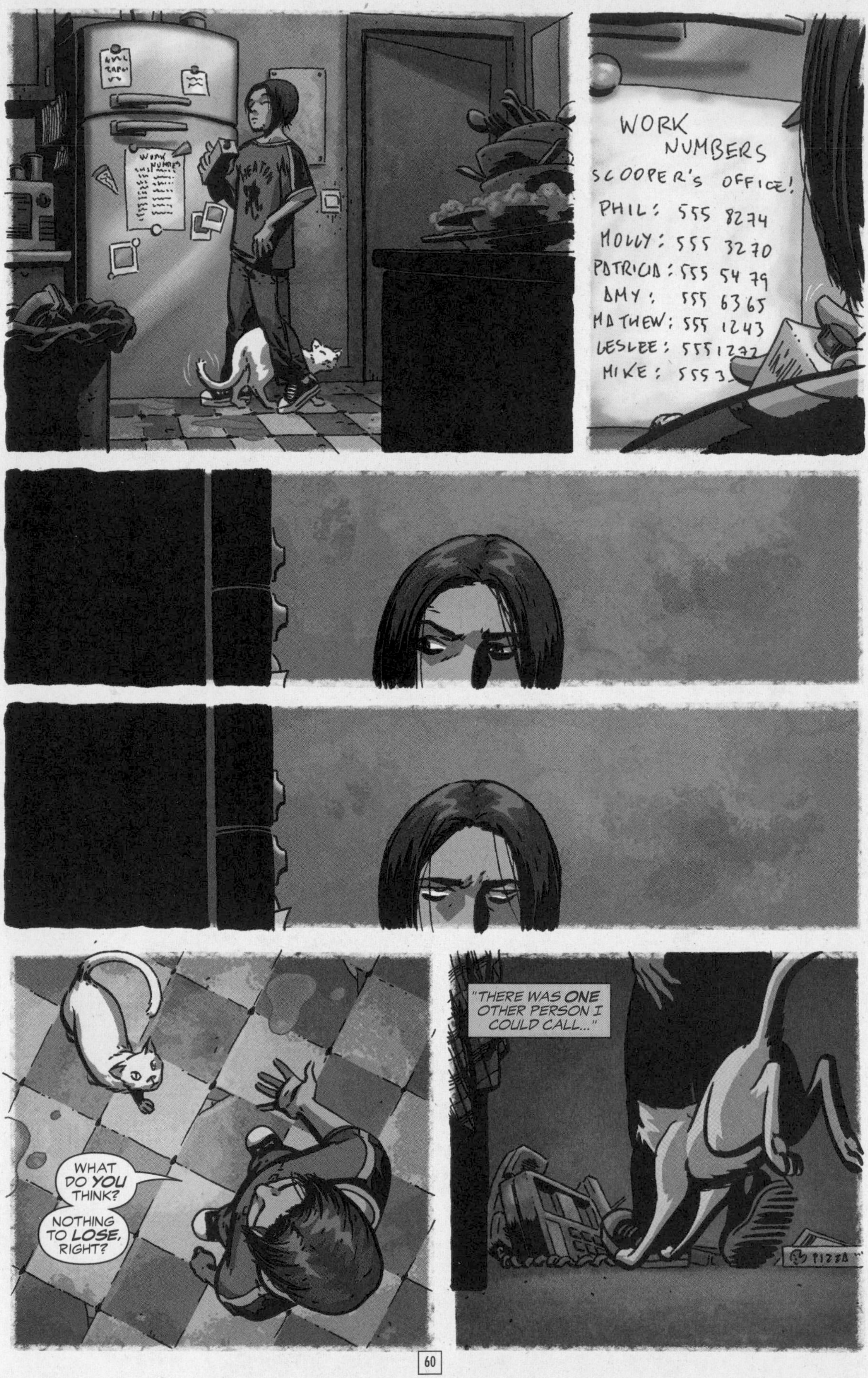

WORK NUMBERS
SCOOPER'S OFFICE!
PHIL: 555 8274
MOLLY: 555 3270
PATRICIA: 555 5479
AMY: 555 6365
MATHEW: 555 1243
LESLEE: 5551
MIKE: 5553
WHAT DO YOU THINK?
NOTHING TO LOSE, RIGHT?
"THERE WAS ONE OTHER PERSON I COULD CALL..."
PIZZA

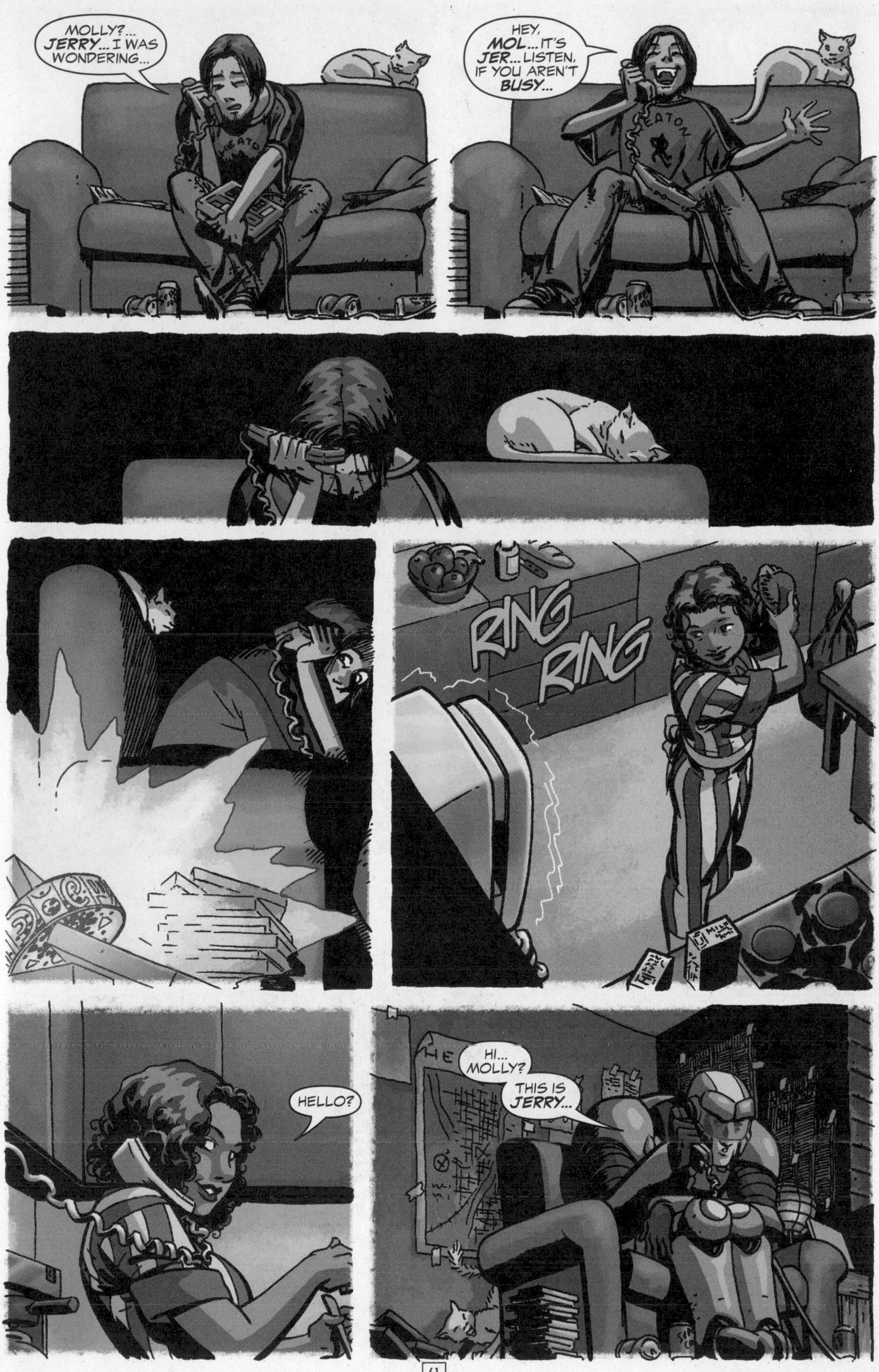
MOLLY?... JERRY... I WAS WONDERING...
HEY, MOL... IT'S JER... LISTEN, IF YOU AREN'T BUSY...
RING RING
HELLO?
HI... MOLLY?
THIS IS JERRY...

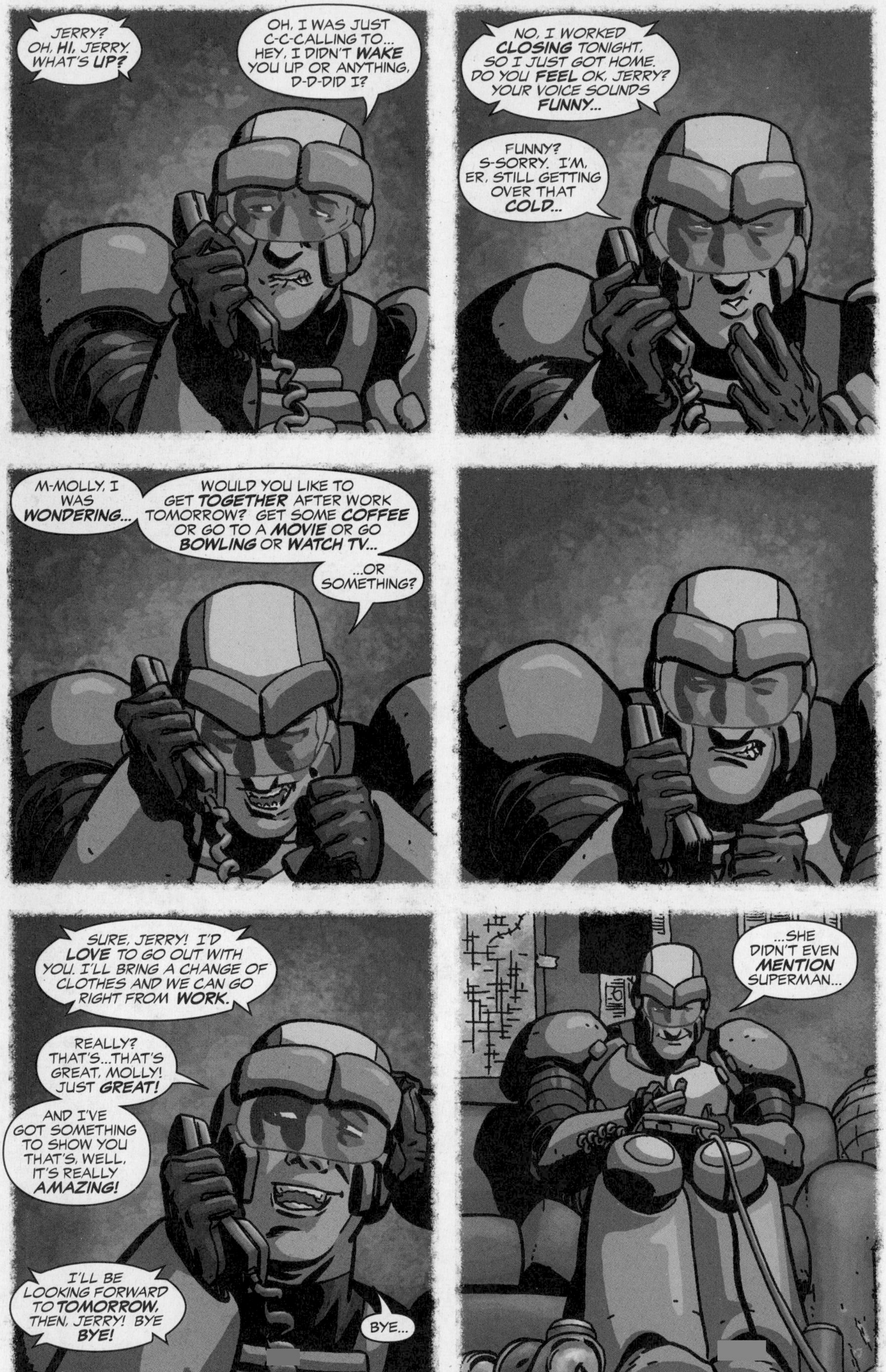
JERRY? OH, HI, JERRY. WHAT'S UP?
OH, I WAS JUST C-C-CALLING TO... HEY, I DIDN'T WAKE YOU UP OR ANYTHING, D-D-DID I?
NO, I WORKED CLOSING TONIGHT, SO I JUST GOT HOME. DO YOU FEEL OK, JERRY? YOUR VOICE SOUNDS FUNNY...
FUNNY? S-SORRY. I'M, ER, STILL GETTING OVER THAT COLD...
M-MOLLY, I WAS WONDERING...
WOULD YOU LIKE TO GET TOGETHER AFTER WORK TOMORROW? GET SOME COFFEE OR GO TO A MOVIE OR GO BOWLING OR WATCH TV...
...OR SOMETHING?
SURE, JERRY! I'D LOVE TO GO OUT WITH YOU. I'LL BRING A CHANGE OF CLOTHES AND WE CAN GO RIGHT FROM WORK.
REALLY? THAT'S...THAT'S GREAT, MOLLY! JUST GREAT!
AND I'VE GOT SOMETHING TO SHOW YOU THAT'S, WELL, IT'S REALLY AMAZING!
I'LL BE LOOKING FORWARD TO TOMORROW, THEN, JERRY! BYE BYE!
BYE...
...SHE DIDN'T EVEN MENTION SUPERMAN...

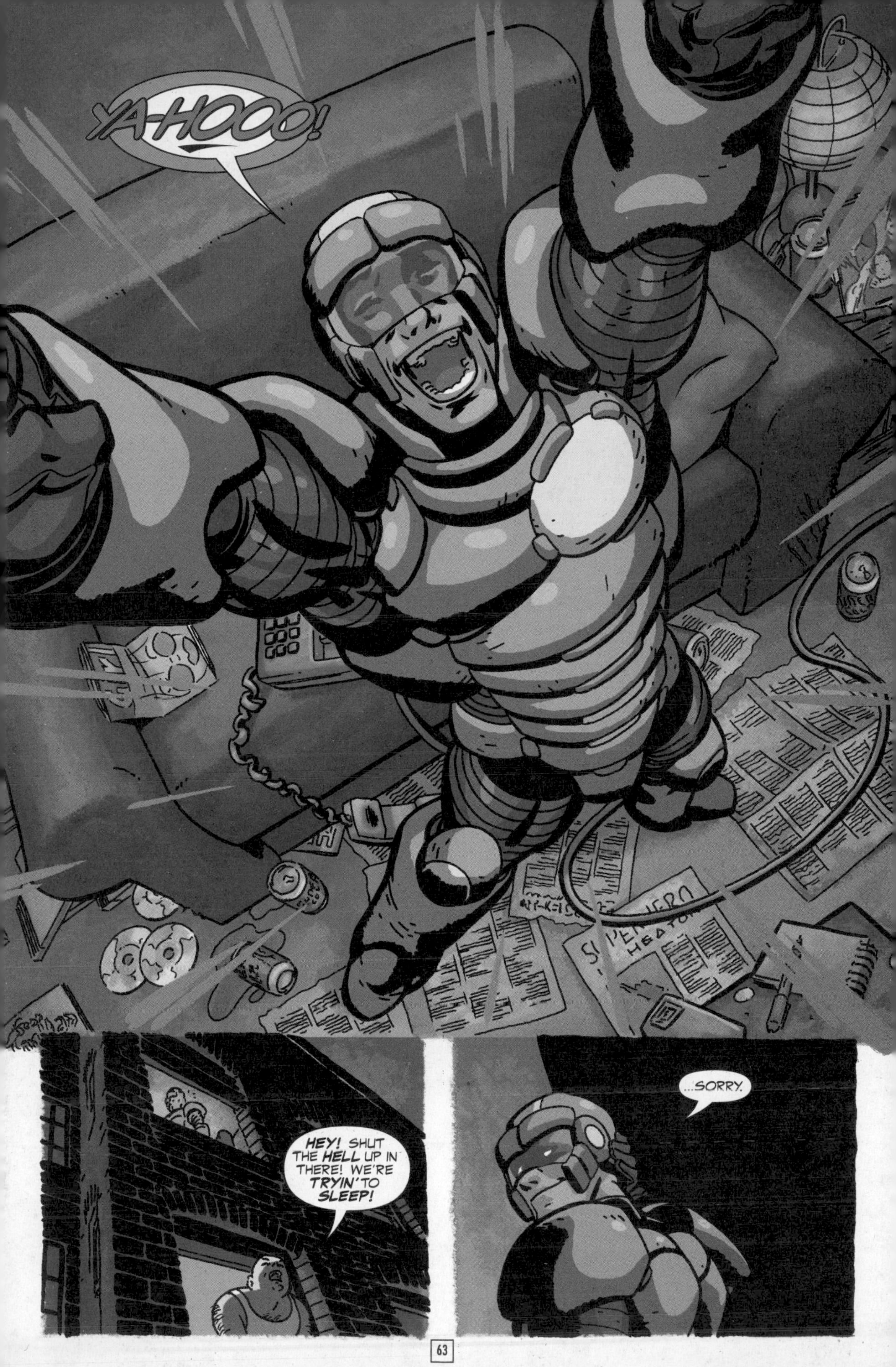
YA-HOOO!
HEY! SHUT THE HELL UP IN THERE! WE'RE TRYIN' TO SLEEP!
...SORRY.

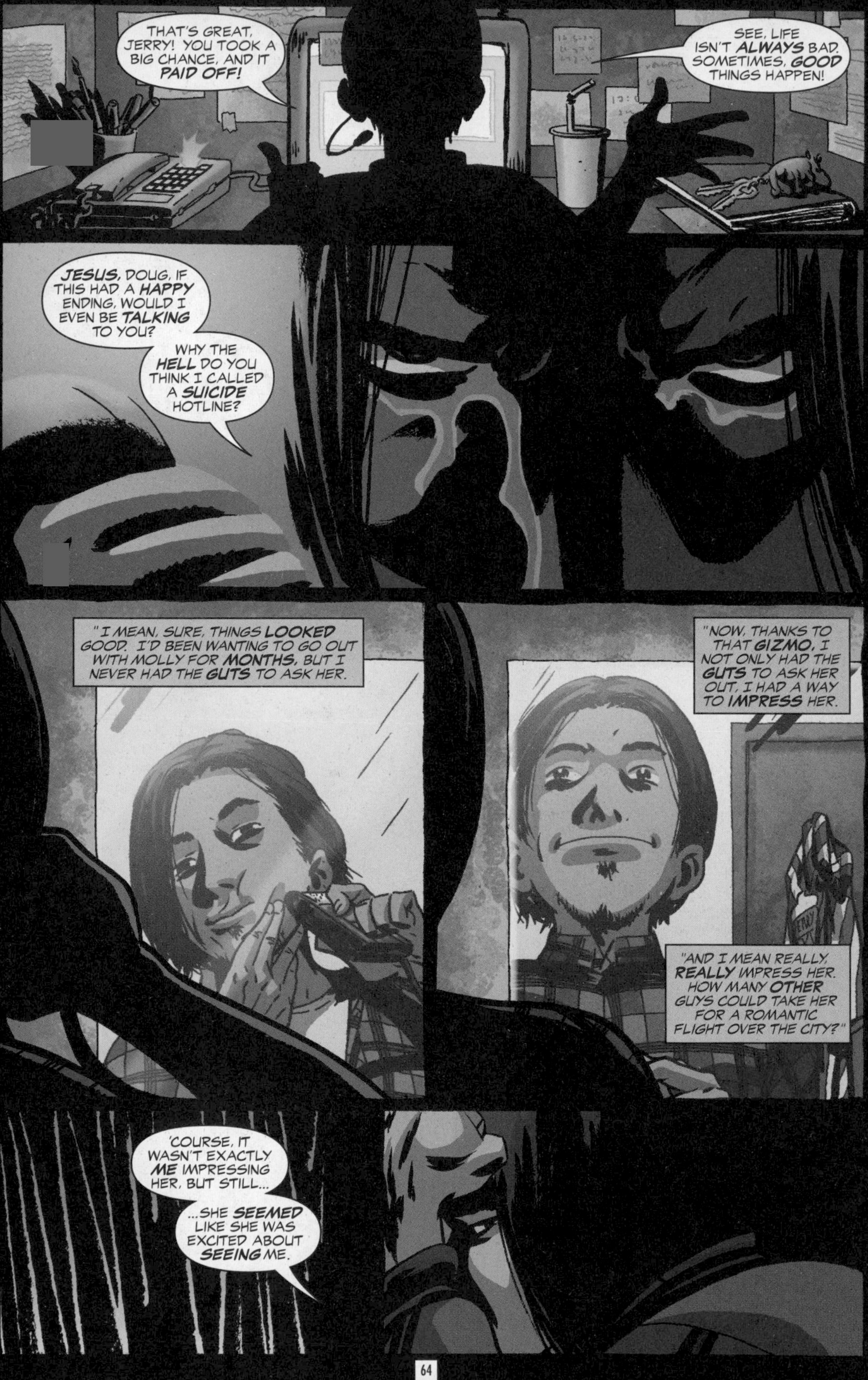

THAT'S GREAT, JERRY! YOU TOOK A BIG CHANCE, AND IT PAID OFF!
SEE, LIFE ISN'T ALWAYS BAD. SOMETIMES, GOOD THINGS HAPPEN!
JESUS, DOUG, IF THIS HAD A HAPPY ENDING, WOULD I EVEN BE TALKING TO YOU?
WHY THE HELL DO YOU THINK I CALLED A SUICIDE HOTLINE?
"I MEAN, SURE, THINGS LOOKED GOOD. I'D BEEN WANTING TO GO OUT WITH MOLLY FOR MONTHS, BUT I NEVER HAD THE GUTS TO ASK HER.
"NOW, THANKS TO THAT GIZMO, I NOT ONLY HAD THE GUTS TO ASK HER OUT, I HAD A WAY TO IMPRESS HER.
"AND I MEAN REALLY, REALLY IMPRESS HER. HOW MANY OTHER GUYS COULD TAKE HER FOR A ROMANTIC FLIGHT OVER THE CITY?"
'COURSE, IT WASN'T EXACTLY ME IMPRESSING HER, BUT STILL...
...SHE SEEMED LIKE SHE WAS EXCITED ABOUT SEEING ME.

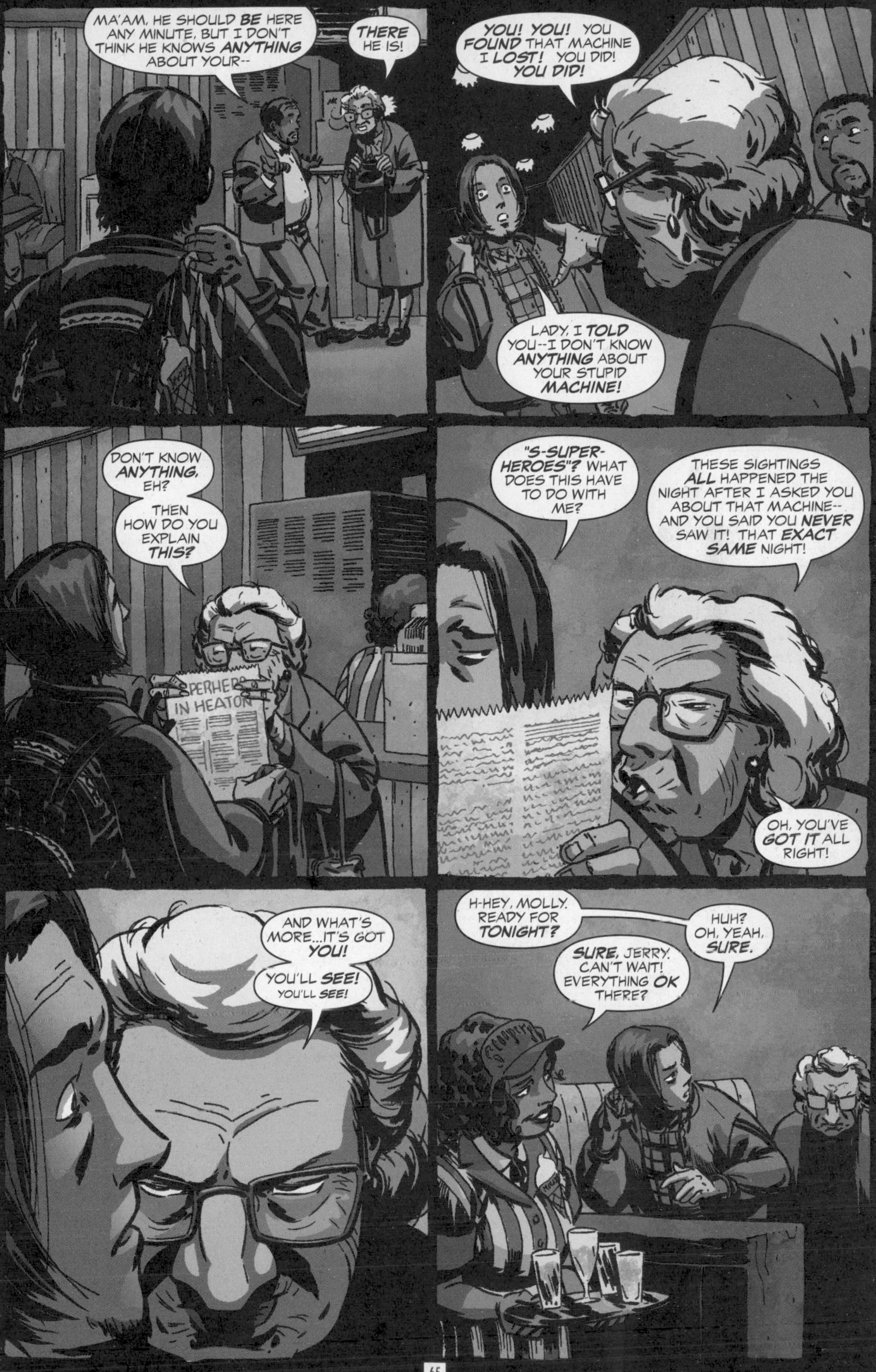
MA'AM, HE SHOULD BE HERE ANY MINUTE, BUT I DON'T THINK HE KNOWS ANYTHING ABOUT YOUR--
THERE HE IS!
YOU! YOU! YOU FOUND THAT MACHINE I LOST! YOU DID! YOU DID!
LADY, I TOLD YOU--I DON'T KNOW ANYTHING ABOUT YOUR STUPID MACHINE!
DON'T KNOW ANYTHING, EH?
THEN HOW DO YOU EXPLAIN THIS?
SUPERHEROS IN HEATON
"S-SUPER-HEROES"? WHAT DOES THIS HAVE TO DO WITH ME?
THESE SIGHTINGS ALL HAPPENED THE NIGHT AFTER I ASKED YOU ABOUT THAT MACHINE-- AND YOU SAID YOU NEVER SAW IT! THAT EXACT SAME NIGHT!
OH, YOU'VE GOT IT ALL RIGHT!
AND WHAT'S MORE...IT'S GOT YOU!
YOU'LL SEE! YOU'LL SEE!
H-HEY, MOLLY. READY FOR TONIGHT?
HUH? OH, YEAH, SURE.
SURE, JERRY. CAN'T WAIT! EVERYTHING OK THERE?

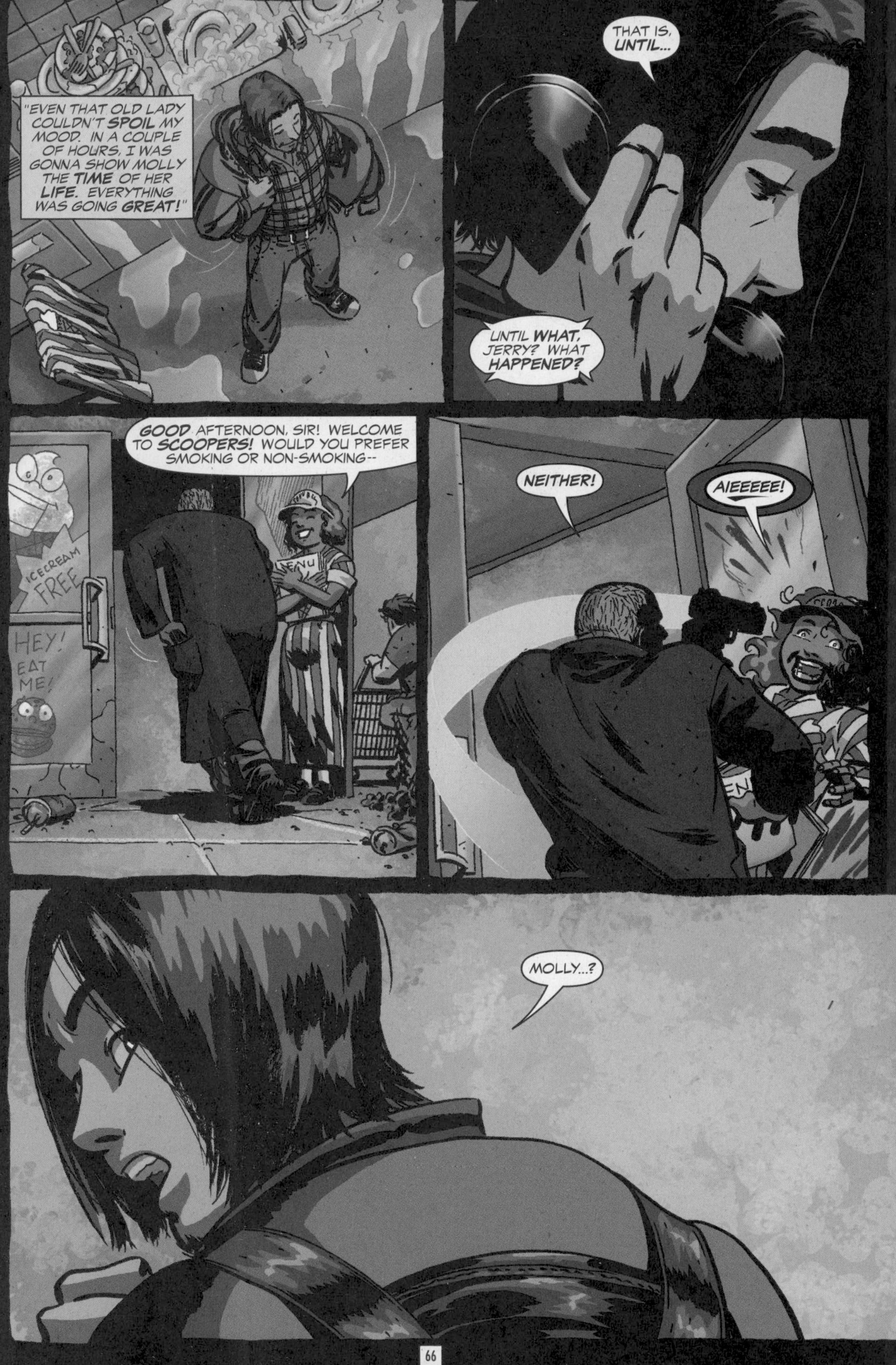
"EVEN THAT OLD LADY COULDN'T SPOIL MY MOOD. IN A COUPLE OF HOURS, I WAS GONNA SHOW MOLLY THE TIME OF HER LIFE. EVERYTHING WAS GOING GREAT!"
THAT IS, UNTIL...
UNTIL WHAT, JERRY? WHAT HAPPENED?
GOOD AFTERNOON, SIR! WELCOME TO SCOOPERS! WOULD YOU PREFER SMOKING OR NON-SMOKING--
ICECREAM FREE
HEY! EAT ME!
NEITHER!
AIEEEEE!
MOLLY...?

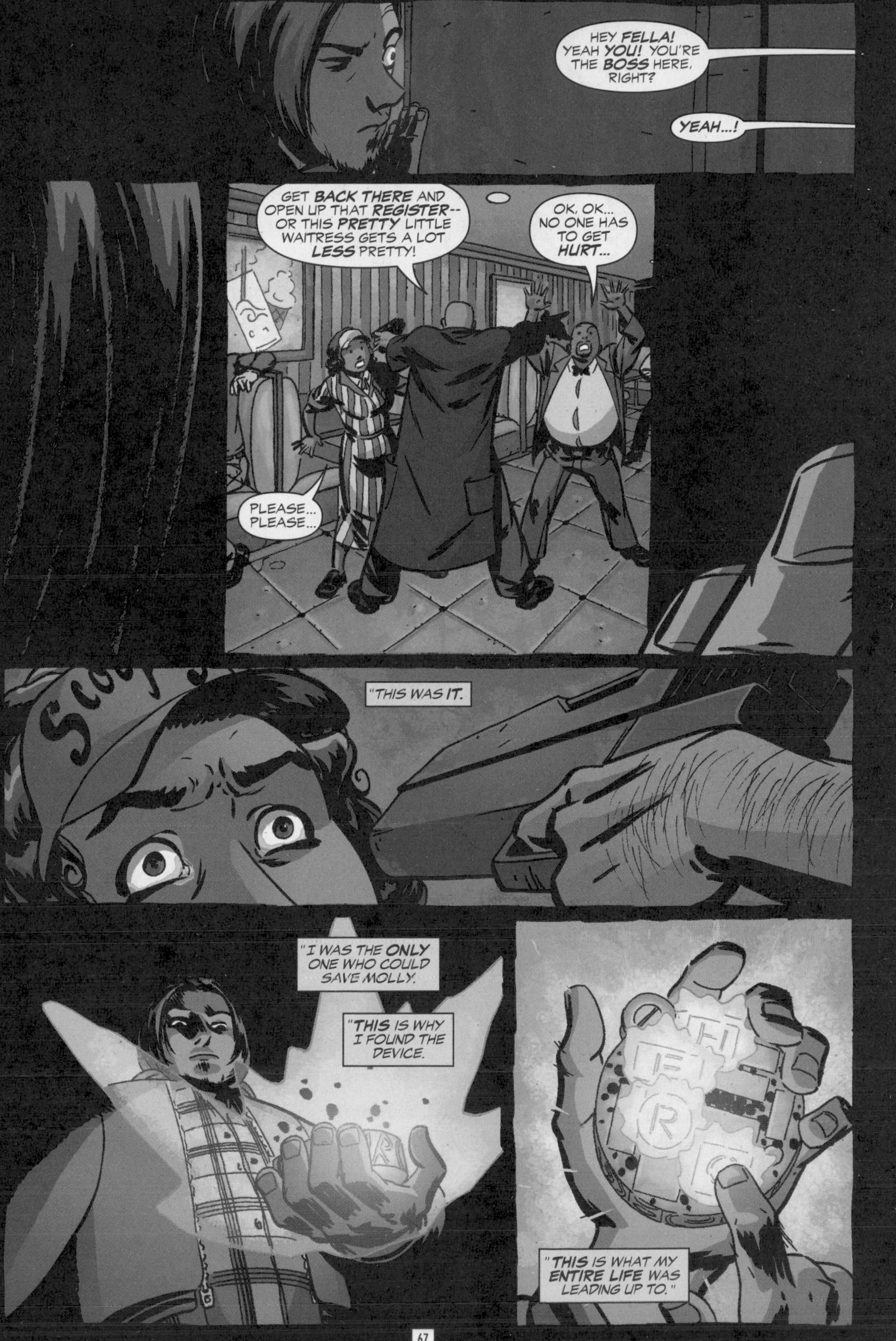
HEY FELLA! YEAH YOU! YOU'RE THE BOSS HERE, RIGHT?
YEAH...!
GET BACK THERE AND OPEN UP THAT REGISTER-- OR THIS PRETTY LITTLE WAITRESS GETS A LOT LESS PRETTY!
OK, OK... NO ONE HAS TO GET HURT...
PLEASE... PLEASE...
"THIS WAS IT.
"I WAS THE ONLY ONE WHO COULD SAVE MOLLY.
"THIS IS WHY I FOUND THE DEVICE.
"THIS IS WHAT MY ENTIRE LIFE WAS LEADING UP TO."

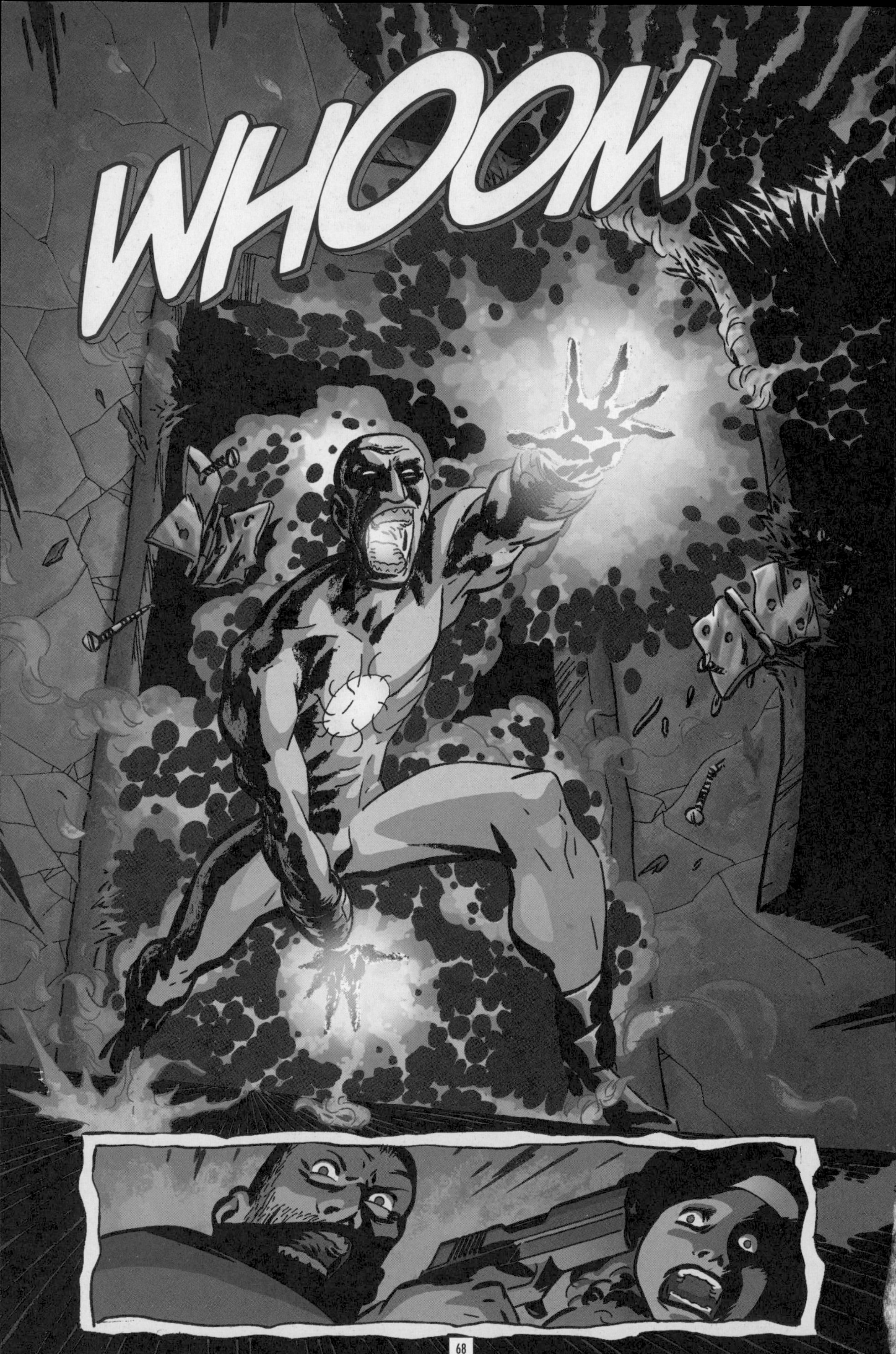
WHOOM

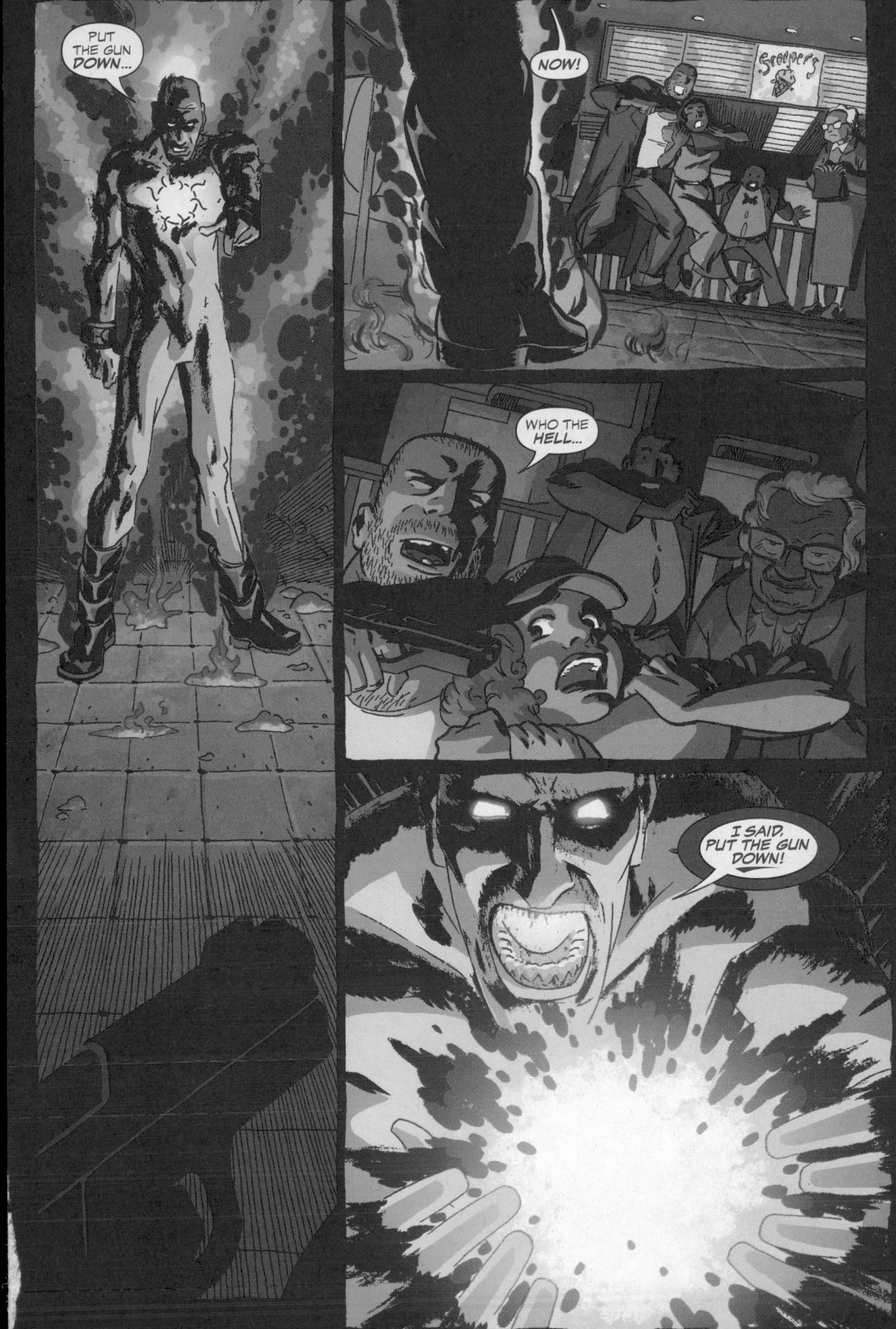
PUT THE GUN DOWN...
NOW!
Scoopers
WHO THE HELL...
I SAID, PUT THE GUN DOWN!

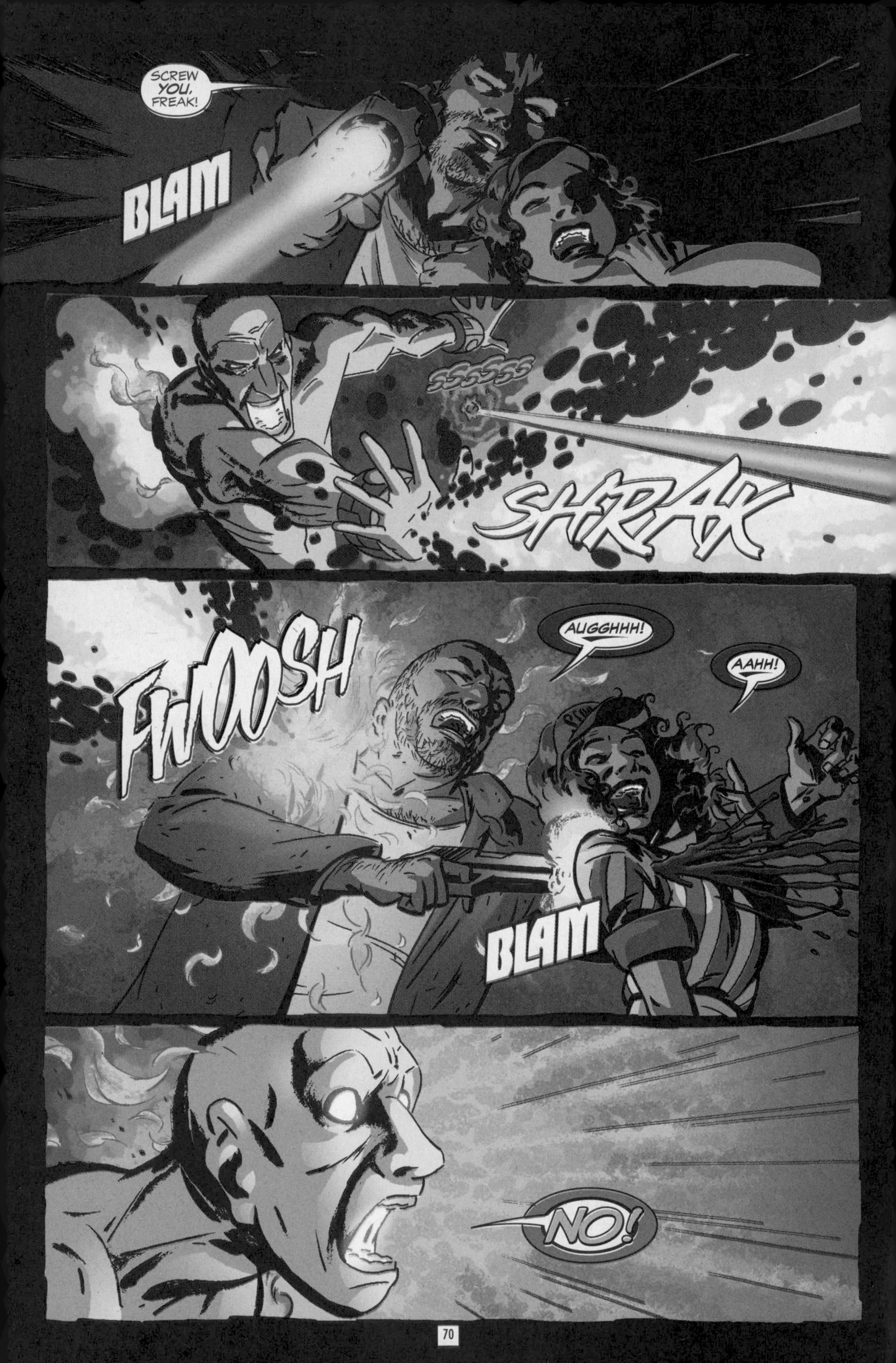
SCREW YOU, FREAK!
BLAM
SSSSSS
SHRAK
FWOOSH
AUGGHHH!
AAHH!
BLAM
NO!

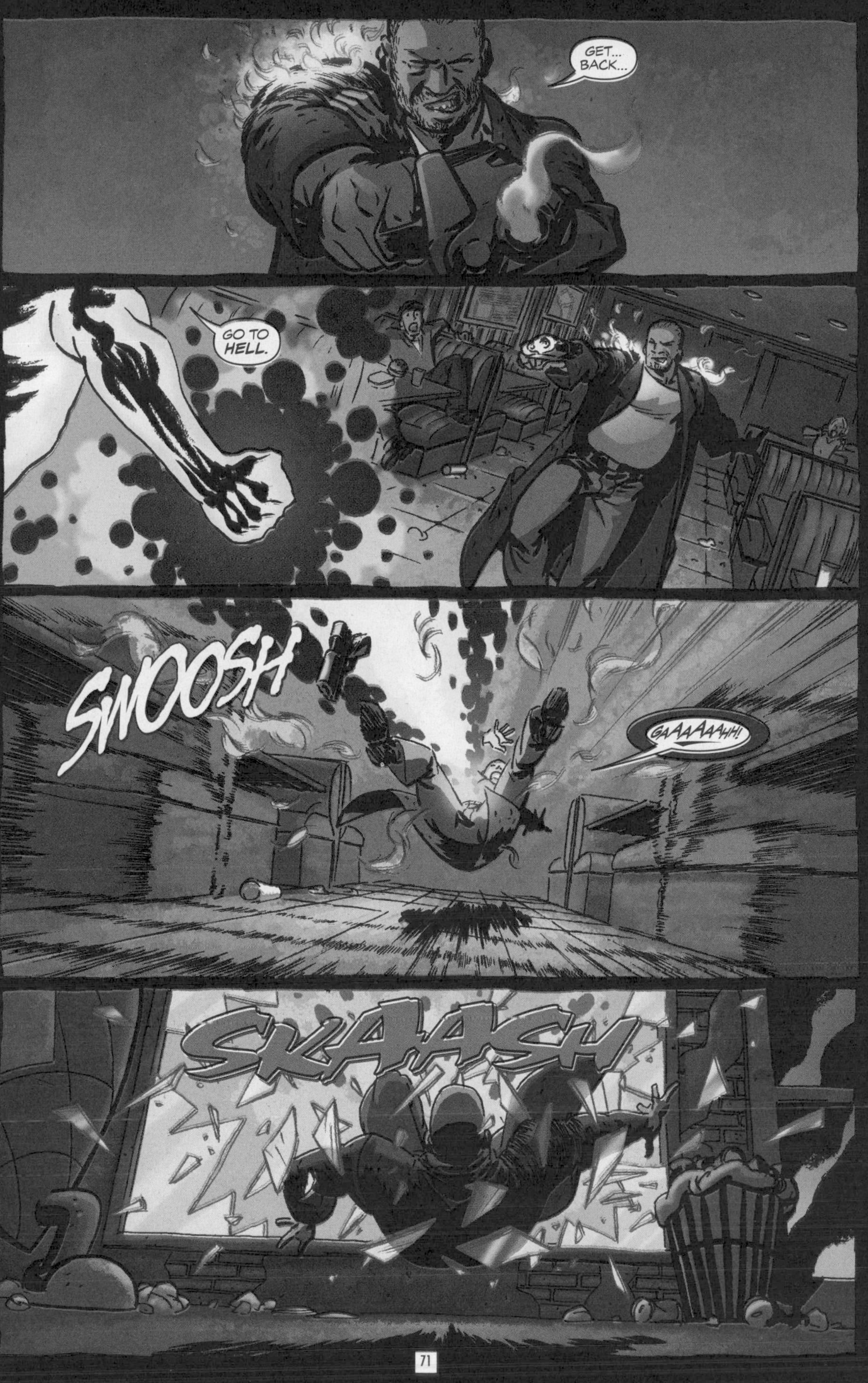
GET... BACK...
GO TO HELL.
SWOOSH
GAAAAAAHH!
SKAASH

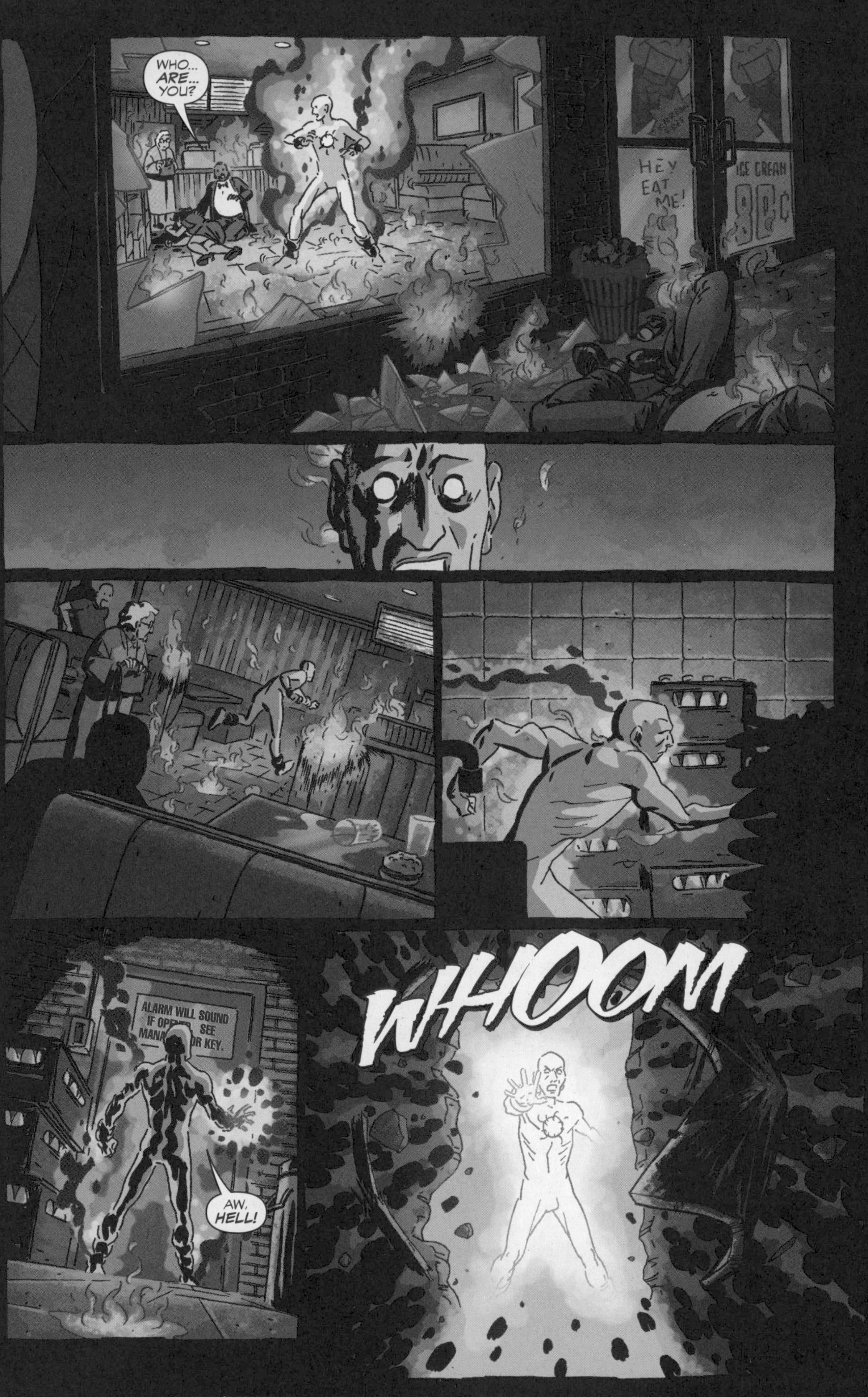
WHO... ARE... YOU?
HEY EAT ME!
ICE CREAM
ALARM WILL SOUND
AW, HELL!
WHOOM

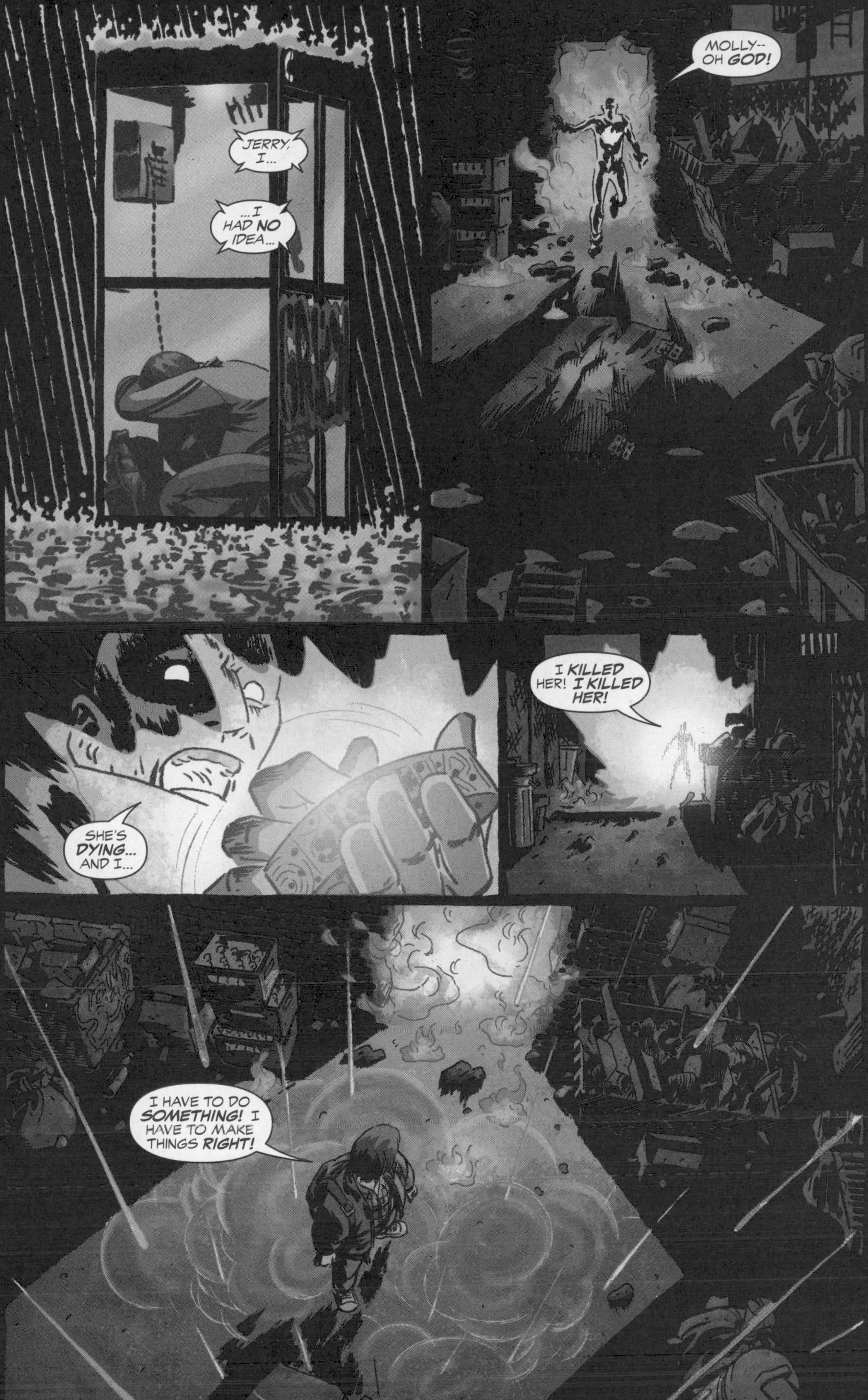
JERRY, I...
...I HAD NO IDEA...
MOLLY-- OH GOD!
SHE'S DYING... AND I...
I KILLED HER! I KILLED HER!
I HAVE TO DO SOMETHING! I HAVE TO MAKE THINGS RIGHT!

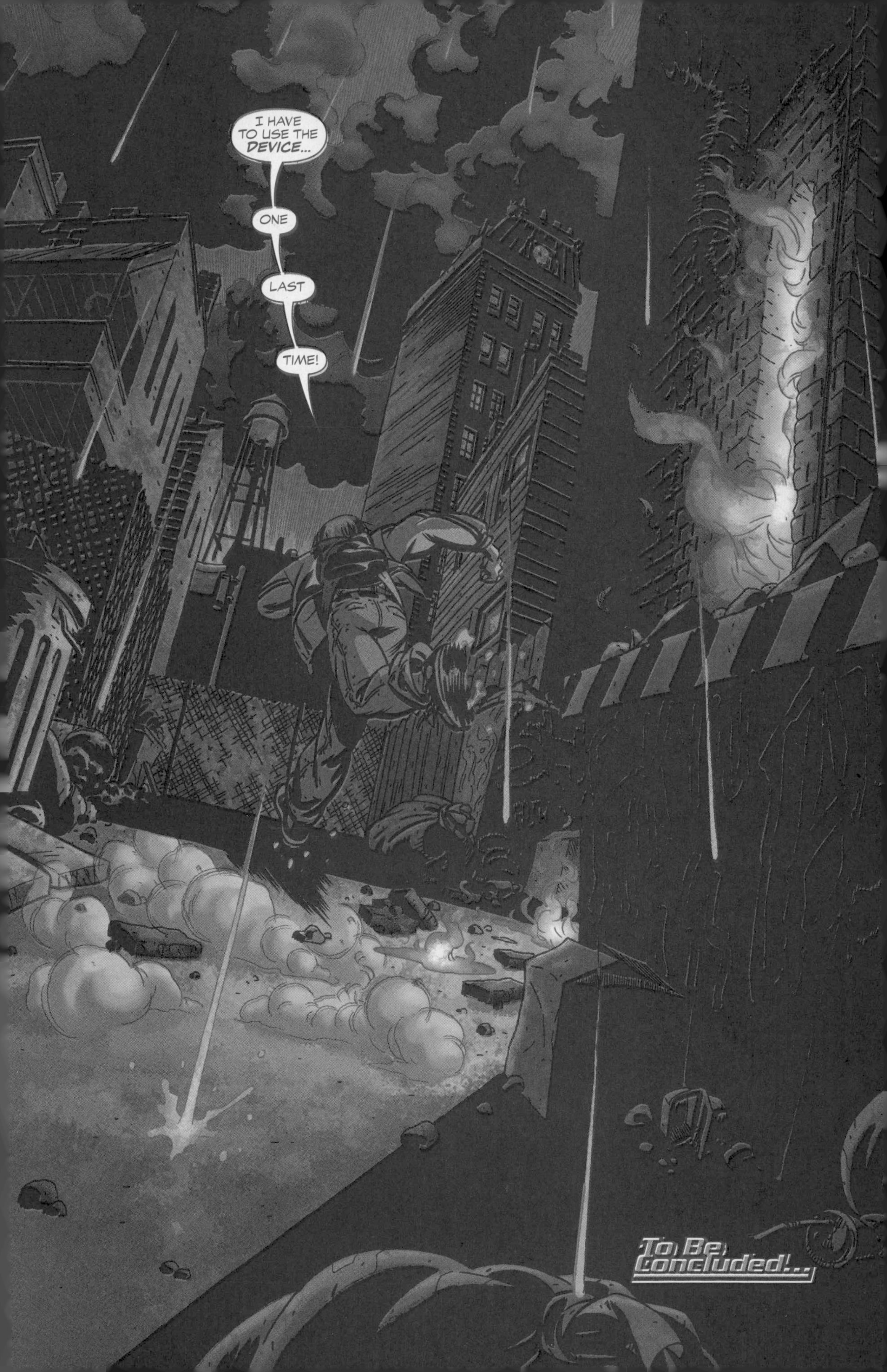
I HAVE TO USE THE DEVICE...
ONE
LAST
TIME!
To Be Concluded!...

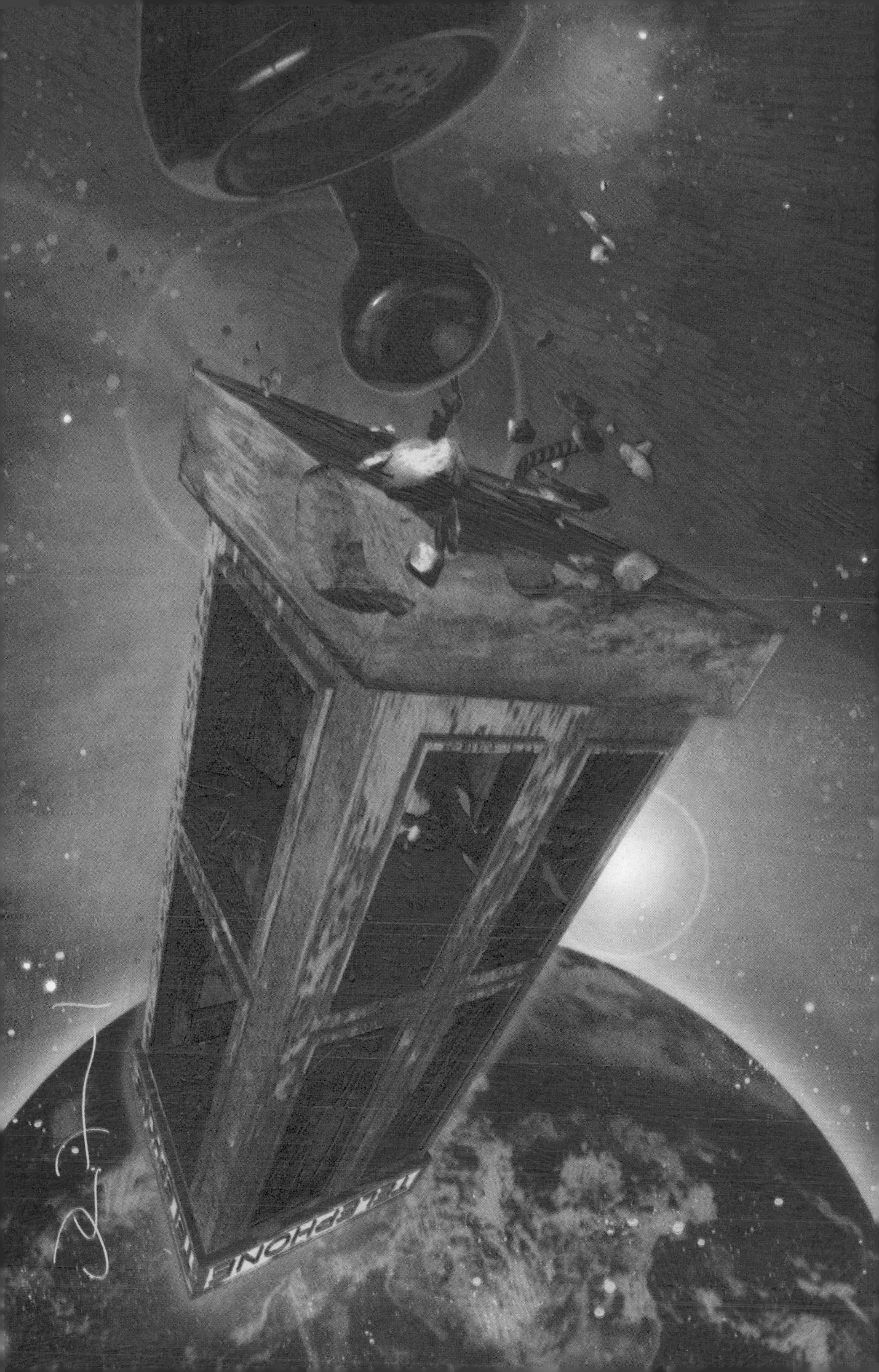

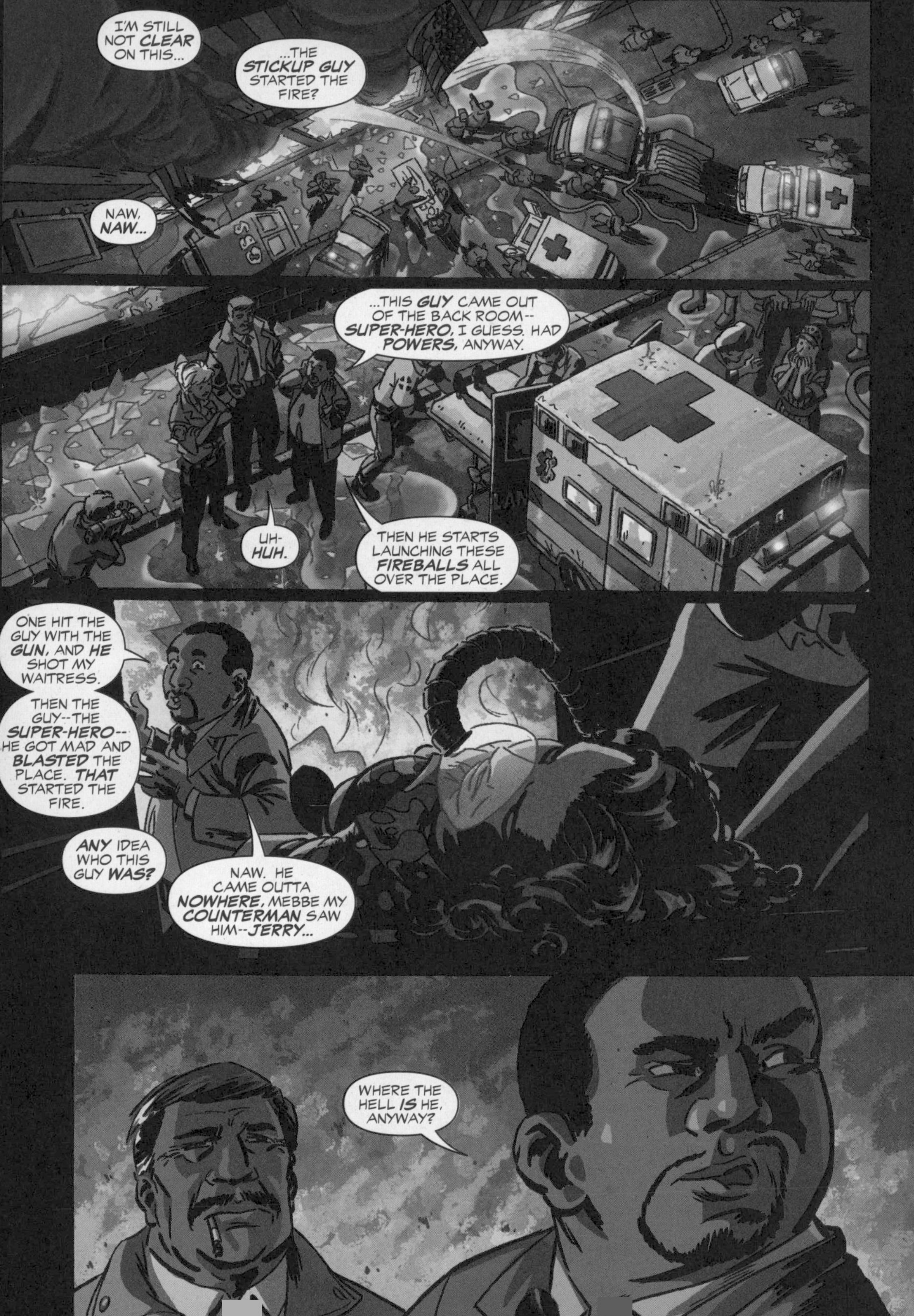
I'M STILL NOT CLEAR ON THIS...
...THE STICKUP GUY STARTED THE FIRE?
NAW, NAW...
...THIS GUY CAME OUT OF THE BACK ROOM-- SUPER-HERO, I GUESS. HAD POWERS, ANYWAY.
UH-HUH.
THEN HE STARTS LAUNCHING THESE FIREBALLS ALL OVER THE PLACE.
ONE HIT THE GUY WITH THE GUN, AND HE SHOT MY WAITRESS.
THEN THE GUY--THE SUPER-HERO-- HE GOT MAD AND BLASTED THE PLACE. THAT STARTED THE FIRE.
ANY IDEA WHO THIS GUY WAS?
NAW. HE CAME OUTTA NOWHERE. MEBBE MY COUNTERMAN SAW HIM--JERRY...
WHERE THE HELL IS HE, ANYWAY?

POWERS and ABILITIES:
CONCLUSION

| WILL PFEIFER | KANO | KEN LOPEZ | DAVE STEWART | JOHN VAN FLEET | VALERIE D'ORAZIO | PETER TOMASI |
| WRITER | ARTIST | LETTERS | COLORS/SEPS | COVER | ASSISTANT EDITOR | EDITOR |

DUNNO WHY I RAN...

I DIDN'T HAVE ANY PLACE TO GO.

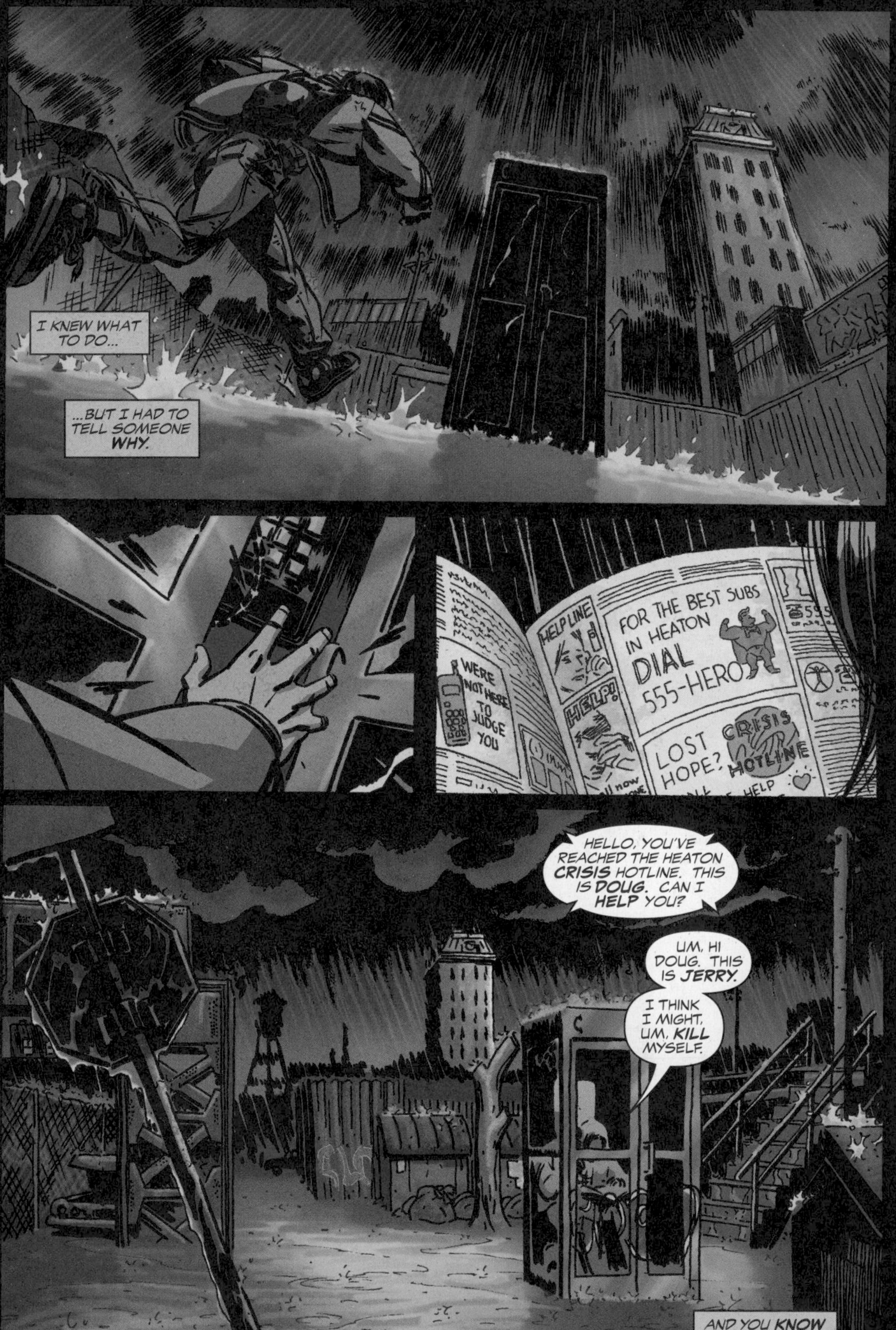

I KNEW WHAT TO DO...
...BUT I HAD TO TELL SOMEONE WHY.
HELP LINE
WERE NOT HERE TO JUDGE YOU
HELP!
FOR THE BEST SUBS IN HEATON DIAL 555-HERO
LOST HOPE?
CRISIS HOTLINE
HELLO. YOU'VE REACHED THE HEATON CRISIS HOTLINE. THIS IS DOUG. CAN I HELP YOU?
UM, HI DOUG. THIS IS JERRY.
I THINK I MIGHT, UM, KILL MYSELF.
AND YOU KNOW WHAT HAPPENED NEXT.

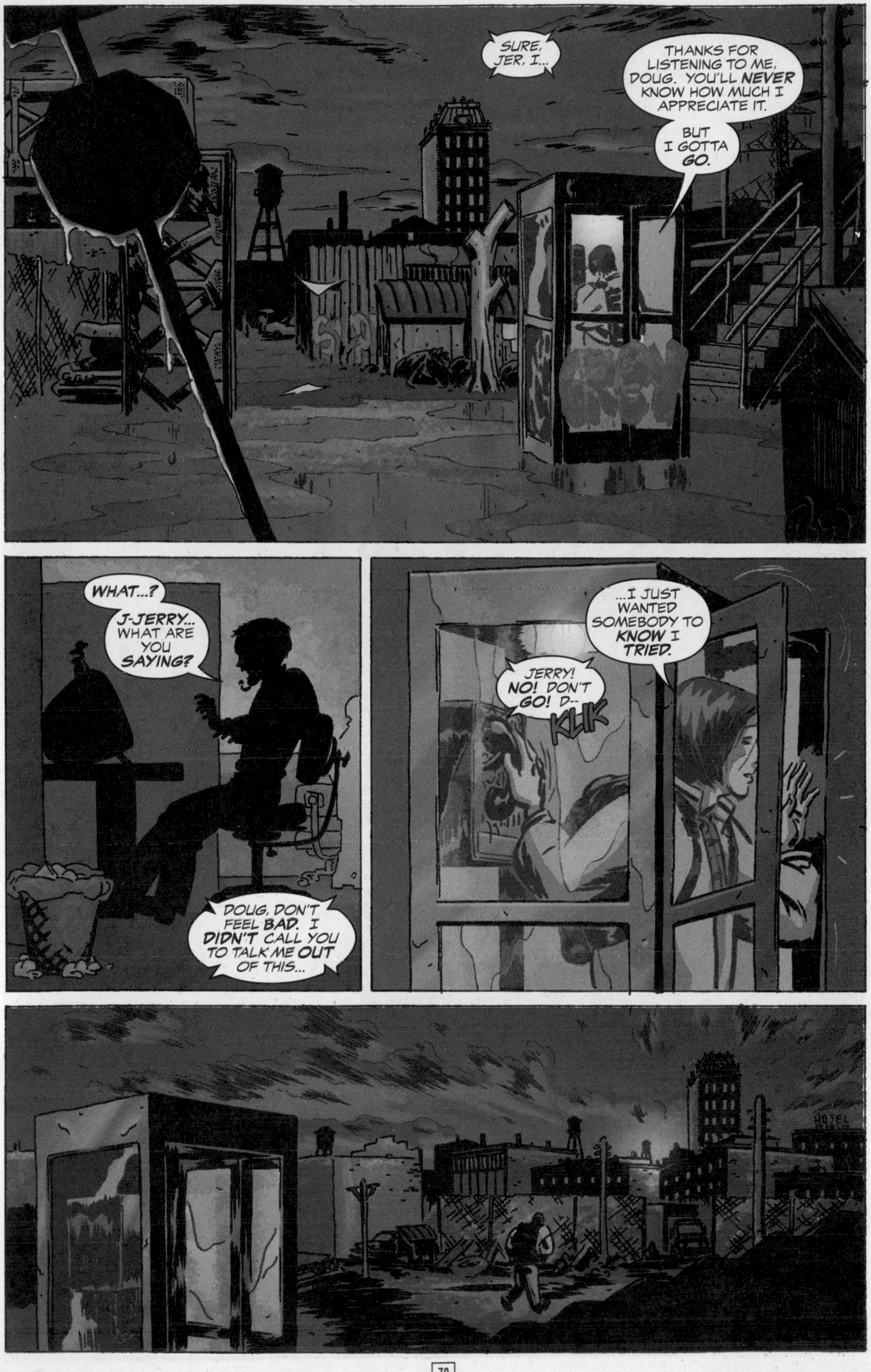
SURE, JER, I...
THANKS FOR LISTENING TO ME, DOUG. YOU'LL **NEVER** KNOW HOW MUCH I APPRECIATE IT.
BUT I GOTTA **GO.**
WHAT...?
J-JERRY... WHAT ARE YOU **SAYING?**
DOUG, DON'T FEEL **BAD.** I **DIDN'T** CALL YOU TO TALK ME **OUT** OF THIS...
...I JUST WANTED SOMEBODY TO **KNOW** I **TRIED.**
JERRY! **NO!** DON'T **GO!** D--
KLIK

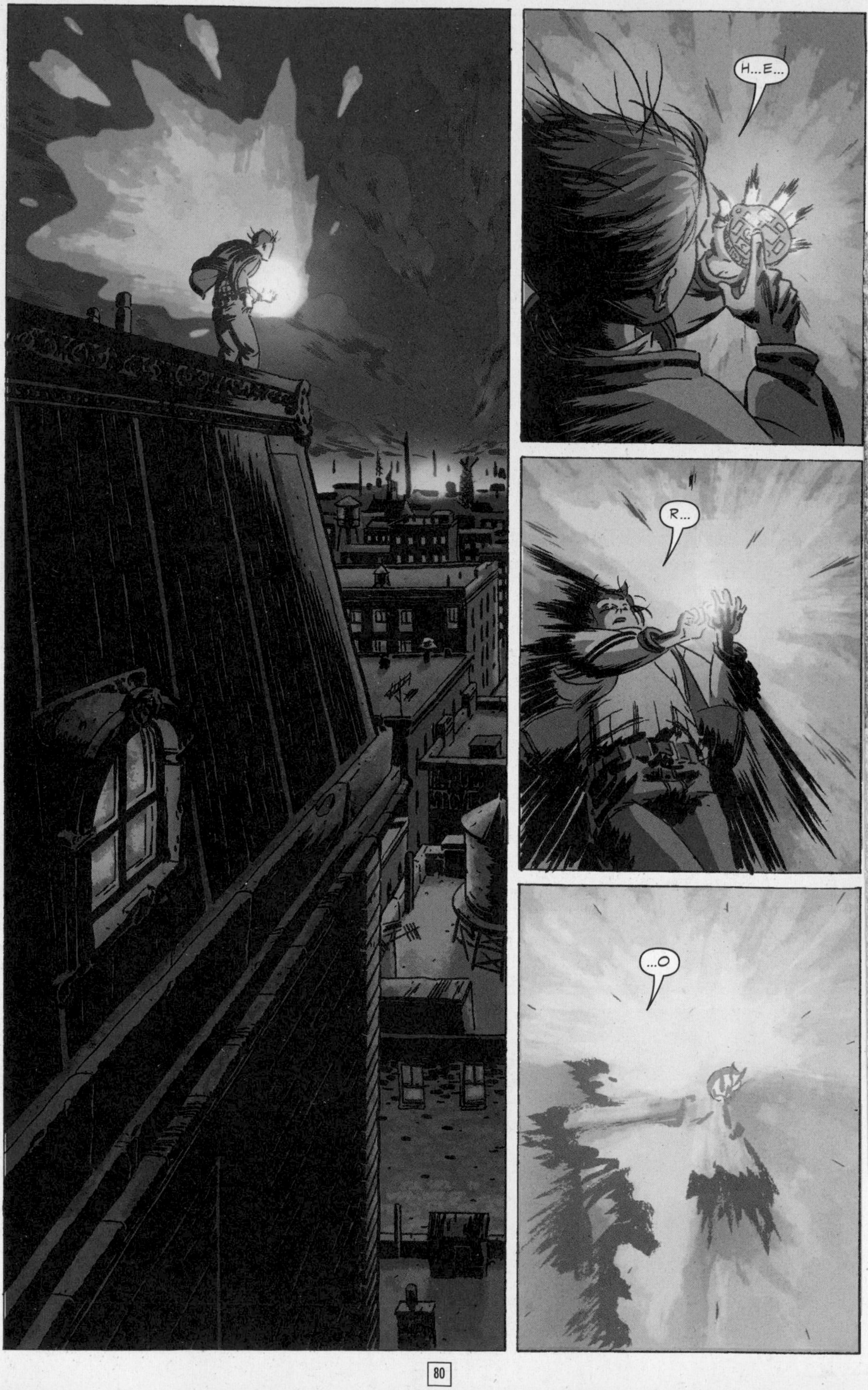
H...E...
R...
...O

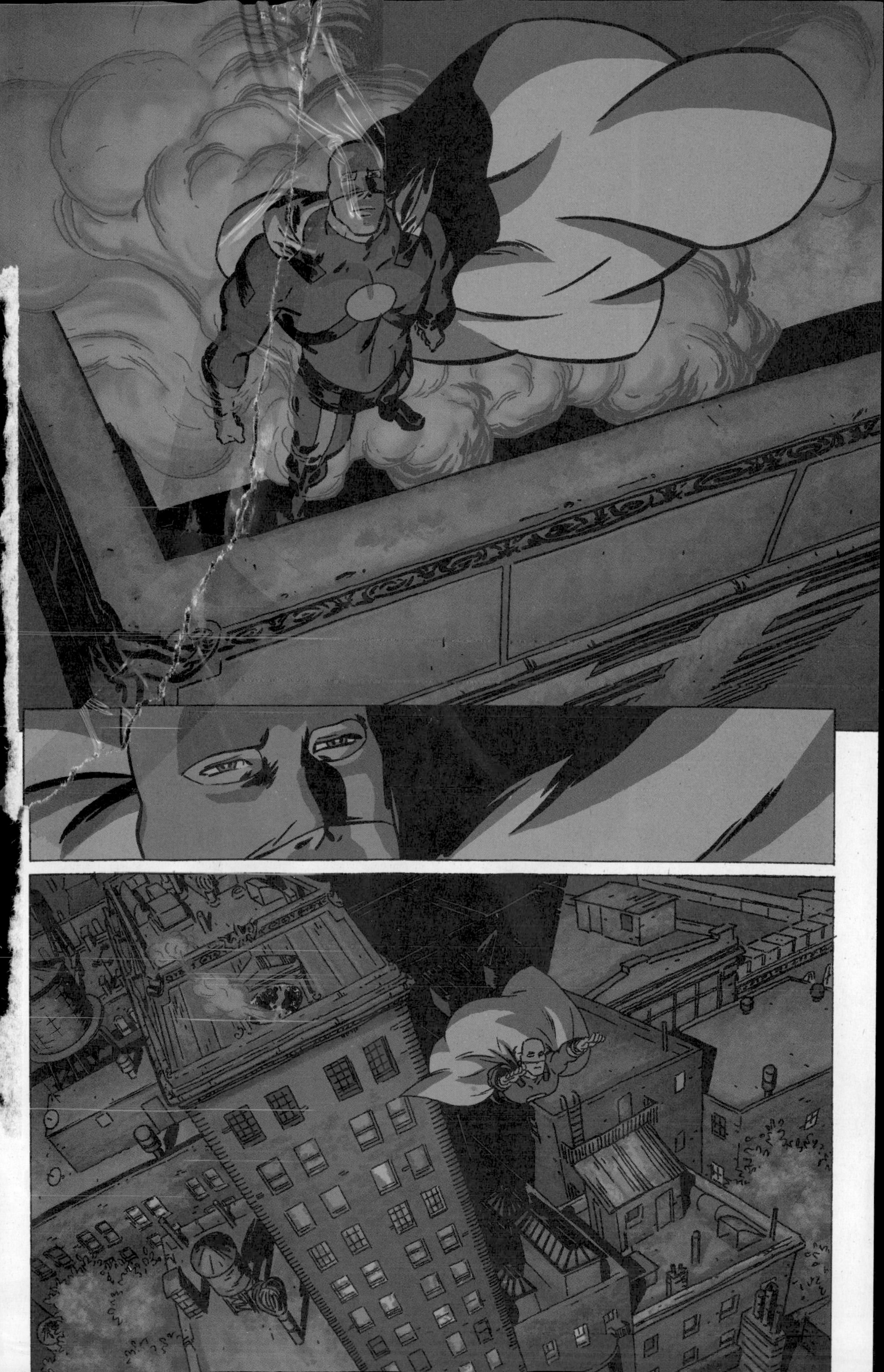

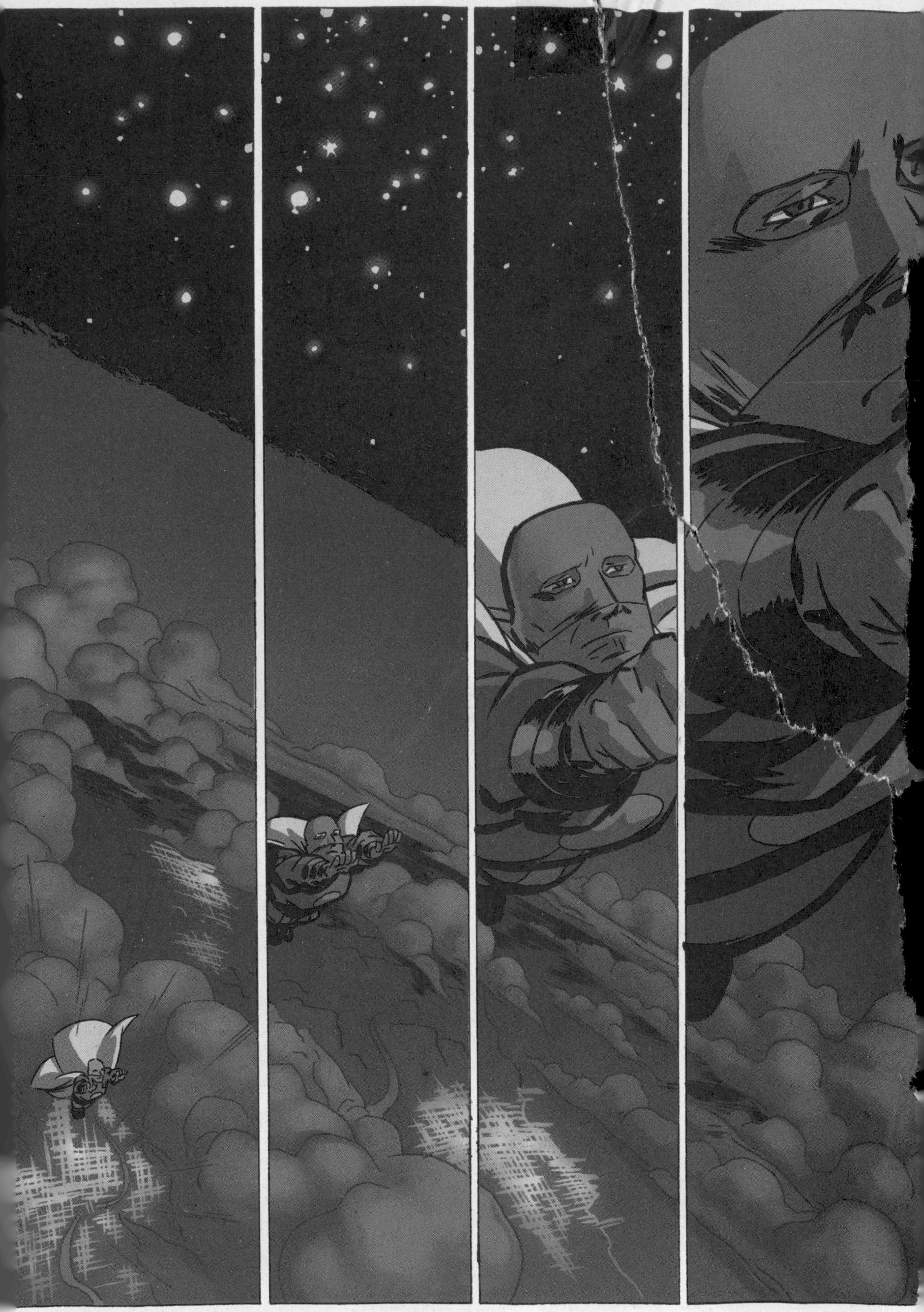

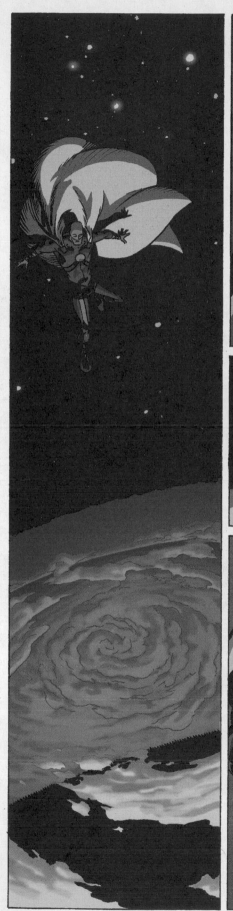

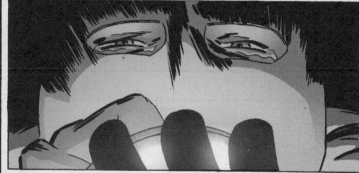

I'M
SORRY.

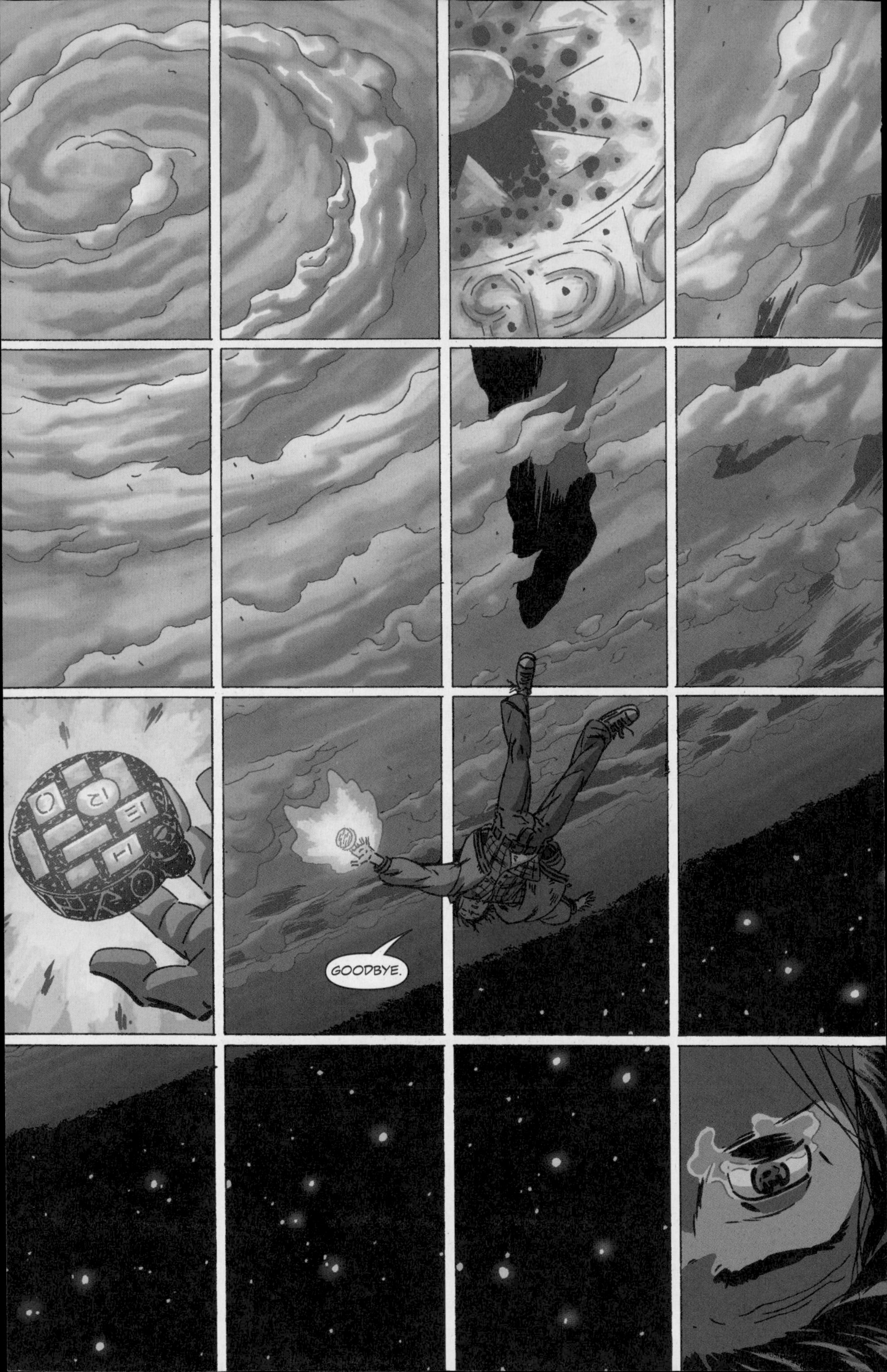
GOODBYE.

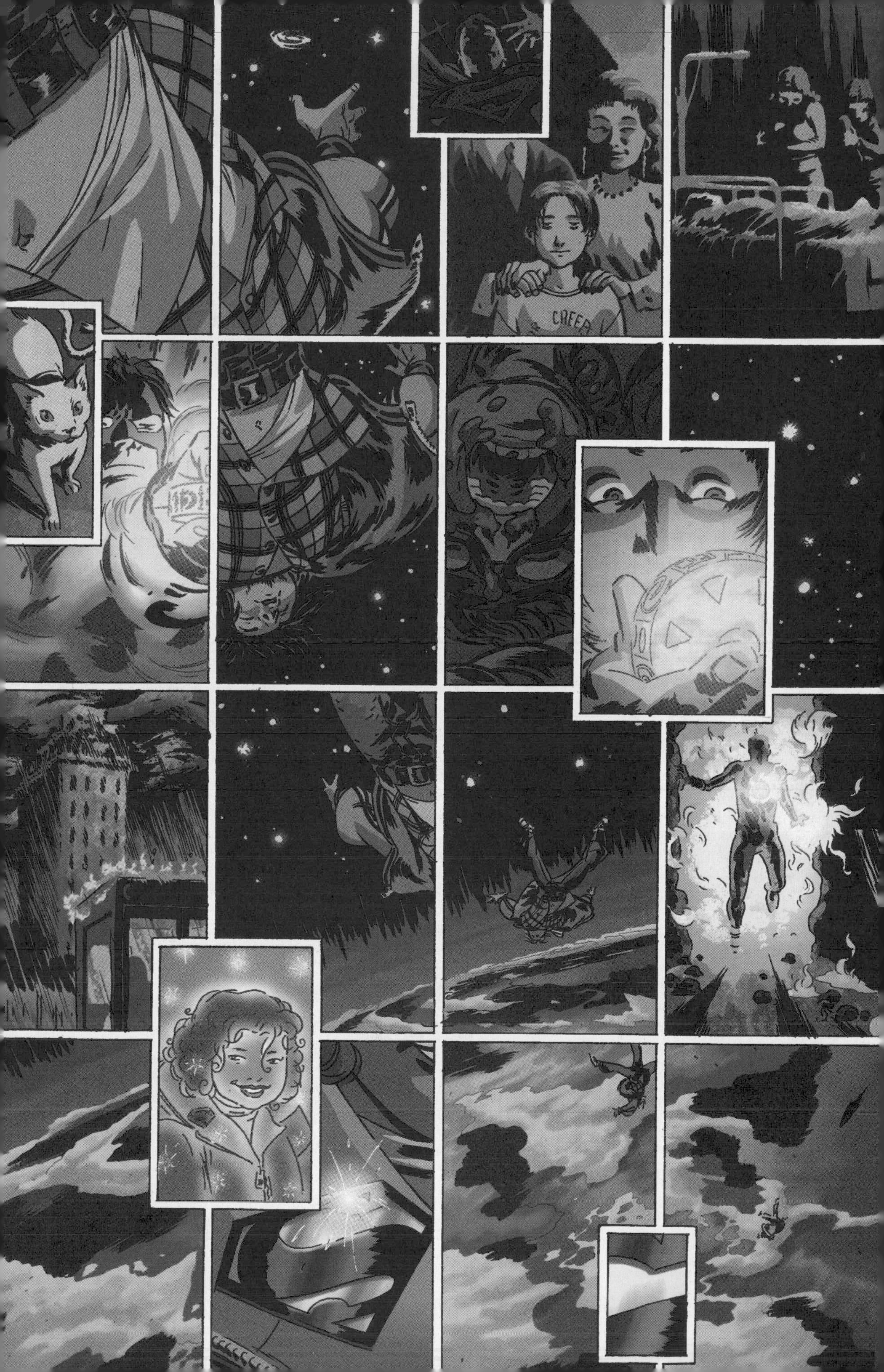

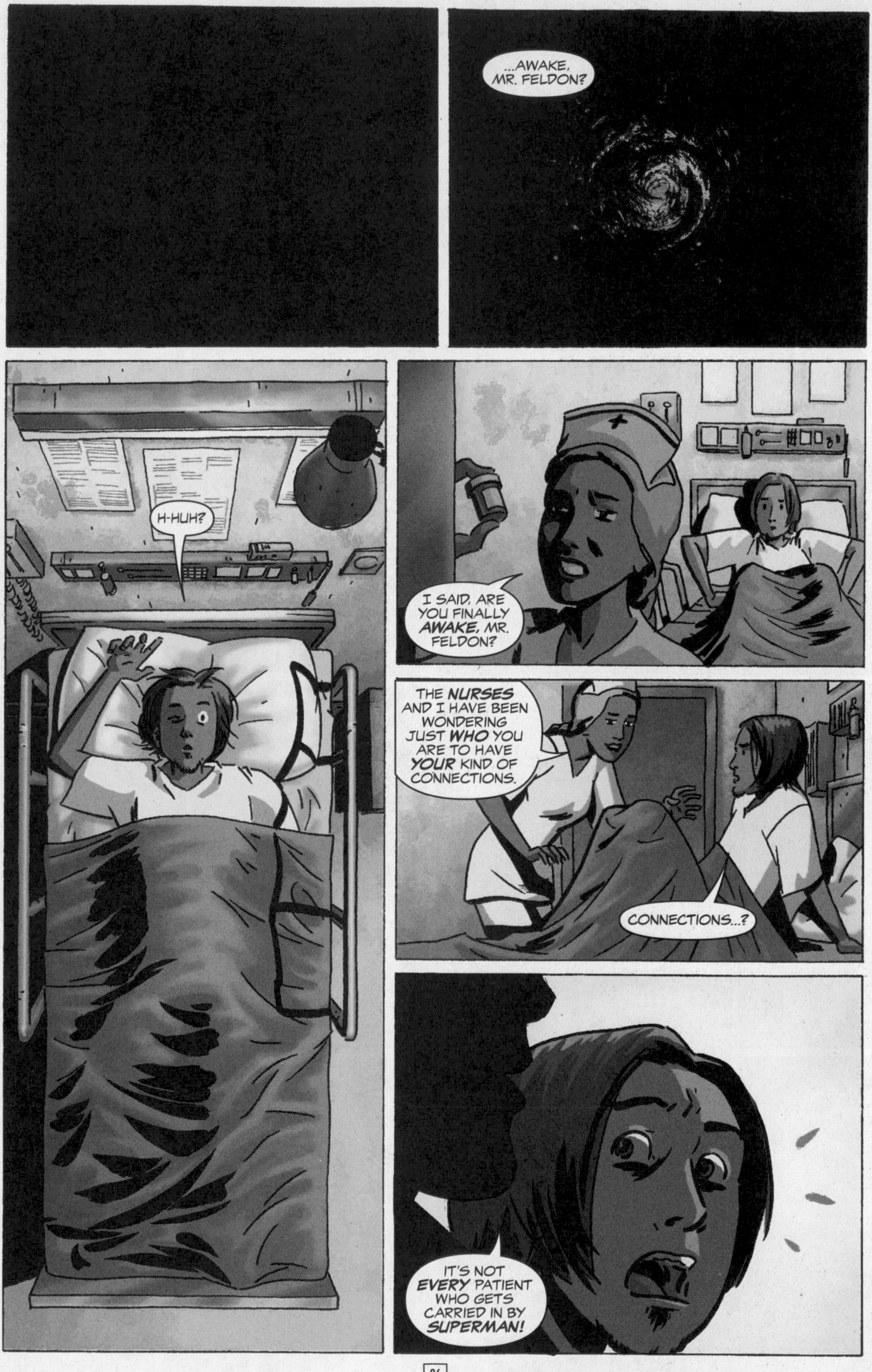
...AWAKE, MR. FELDON?
H-HUH?
I SAID, ARE YOU FINALLY AWAKE, MR. FELDON?
THE NURSES AND I HAVE BEEN WONDERING JUST WHO YOU ARE TO HAVE YOUR KIND OF CONNECTIONS.
CONNECTIONS...?
IT'S NOT EVERY PATIENT WHO GETS CARRIED IN BY SUPERMAN!

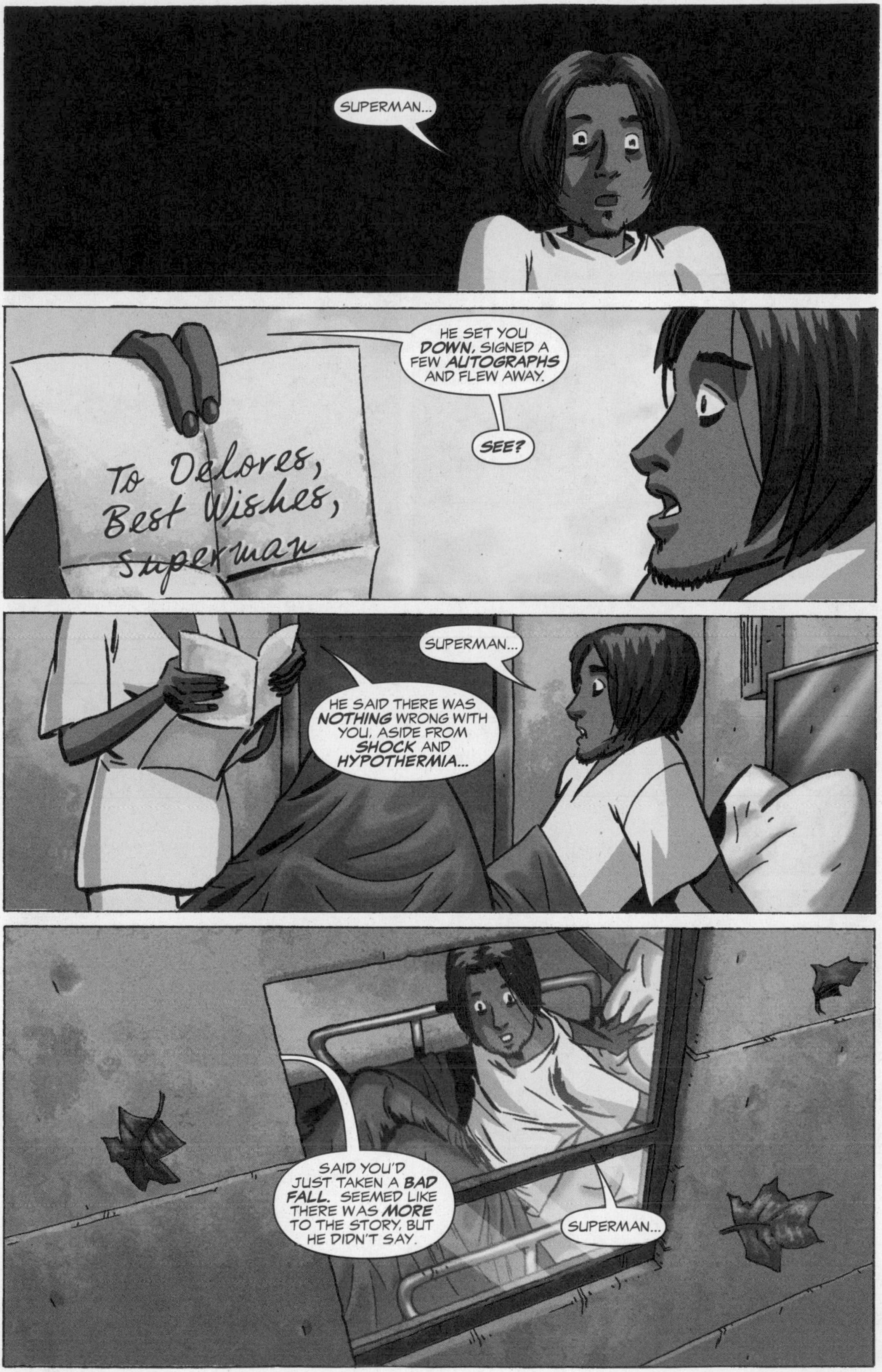
SUPERMAN...
HE SET YOU DOWN, SIGNED A FEW AUTOGRAPHS AND FLEW AWAY.
SEE?
To Delores, Best Wishes, Superman
SUPERMAN...
HE SAID THERE WAS NOTHING WRONG WITH YOU, ASIDE FROM SHOCK AND HYPOTHERMIA...
SAID YOU'D JUST TAKEN A BAD FALL. SEEMED LIKE THERE WAS MORE TO THE STORY, BUT HE DIDN'T SAY.
SUPERMAN...

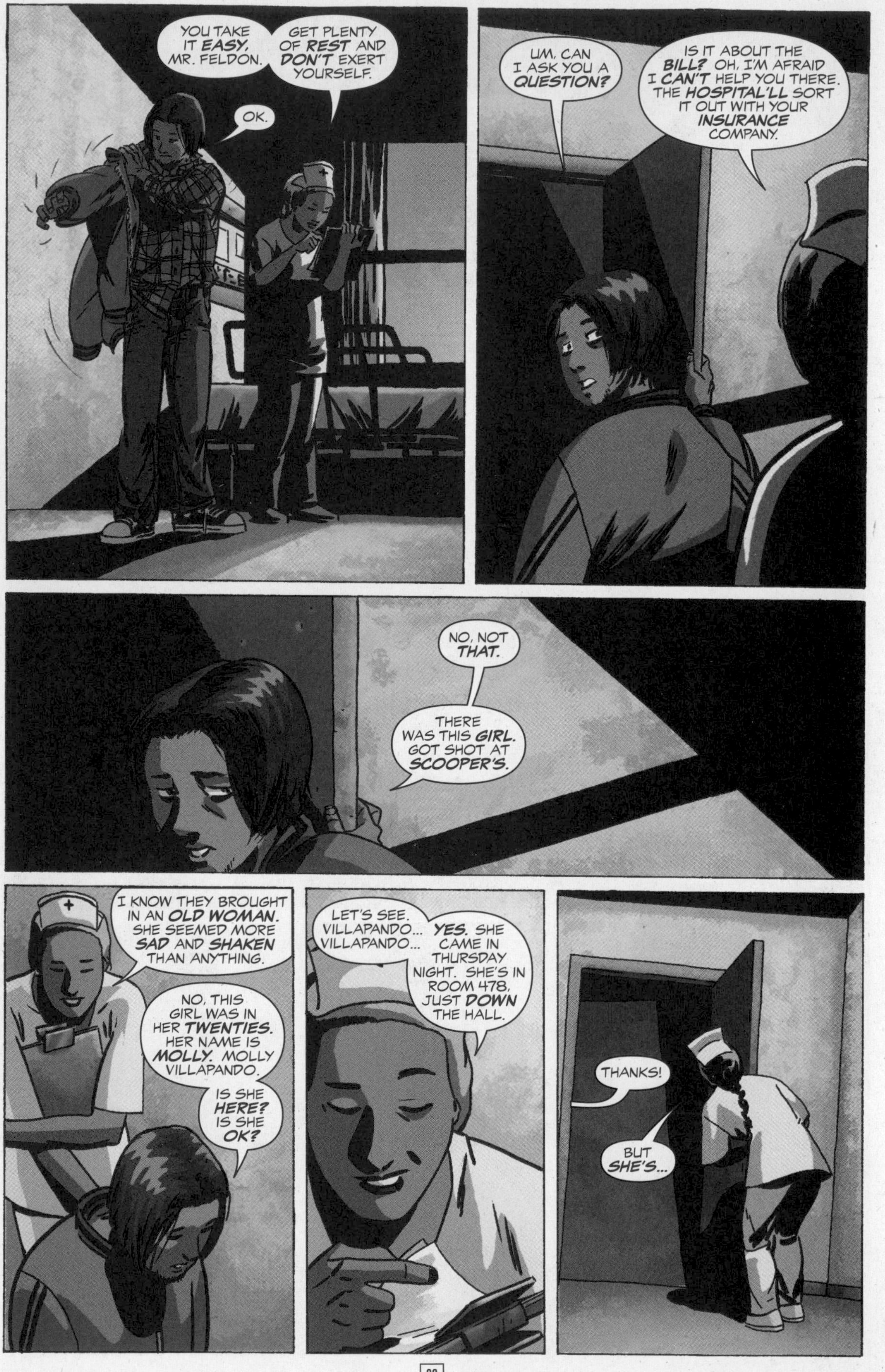
YOU TAKE IT EASY, MR. FELDON.
GET PLENTY OF REST AND DON'T EXERT YOURSELF.
OK.
UM, CAN I ASK YOU A QUESTION?
IS IT ABOUT THE BILL? OH, I'M AFRAID I CAN'T HELP YOU THERE. THE HOSPITAL'LL SORT IT OUT WITH YOUR INSURANCE COMPANY.
NO, NOT THAT.
THERE WAS THIS GIRL. GOT SHOT AT SCOOPER'S.
I KNOW THEY BROUGHT IN AN OLD WOMAN. SHE SEEMED MORE SAD AND SHAKEN THAN ANYTHING.
NO, THIS GIRL WAS IN HER TWENTIES. HER NAME IS MOLLY. MOLLY VILLAPANDO.
IS SHE HERE? IS SHE OK?
LET'S SEE. VILLAPANDO... VILLAPANDO...
YES. SHE CAME IN THURSDAY NIGHT. SHE'S IN ROOM 478, JUST DOWN THE HALL.
THANKS!
BUT SHE'S...

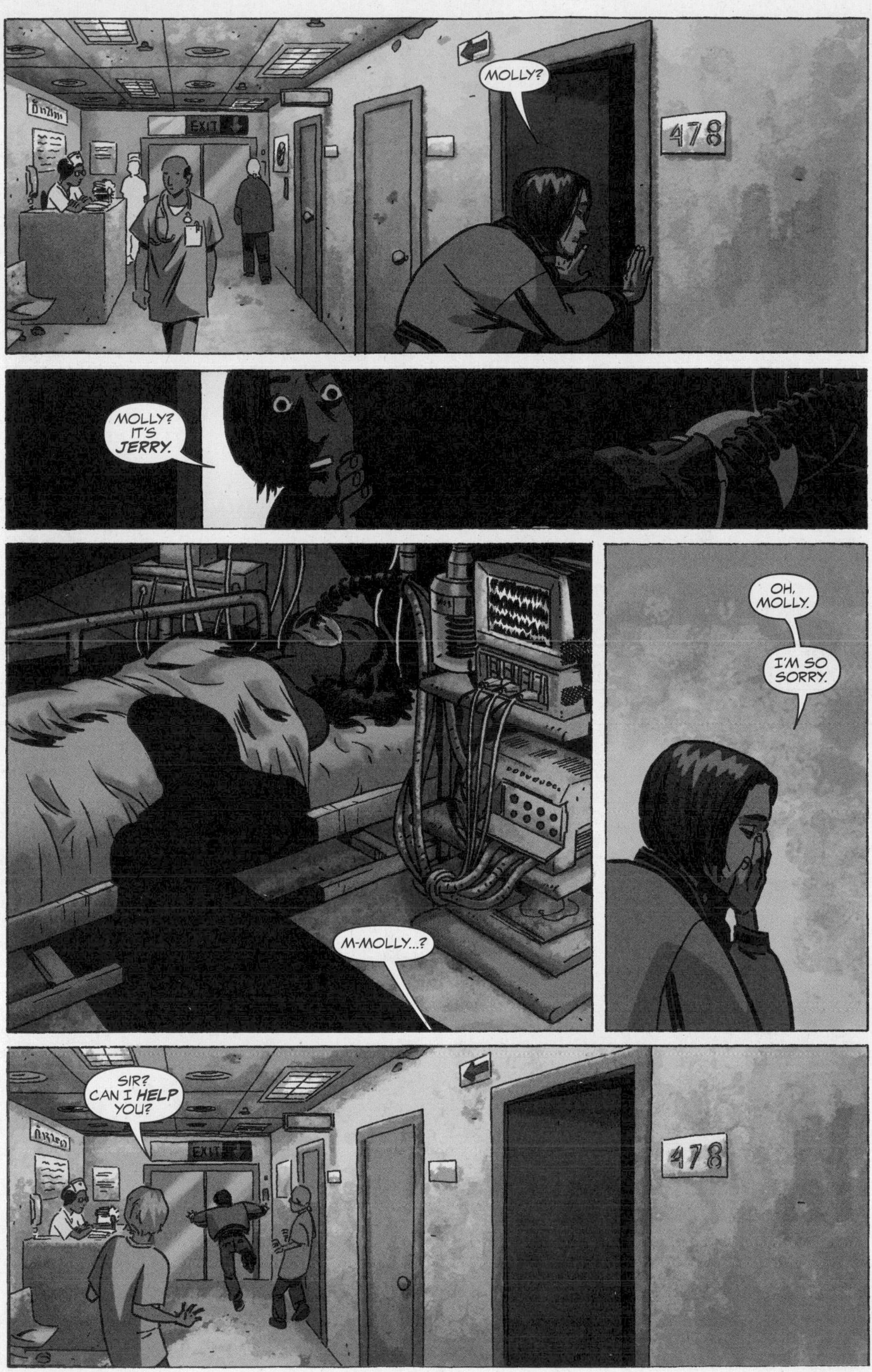

EXIT
MOLLY?
478
MOLLY? IT'S JERRY.
OH, MOLLY.
I'M SO SORRY.
M-MOLLY...?
SIR? CAN I HELP YOU?
EXIT
478

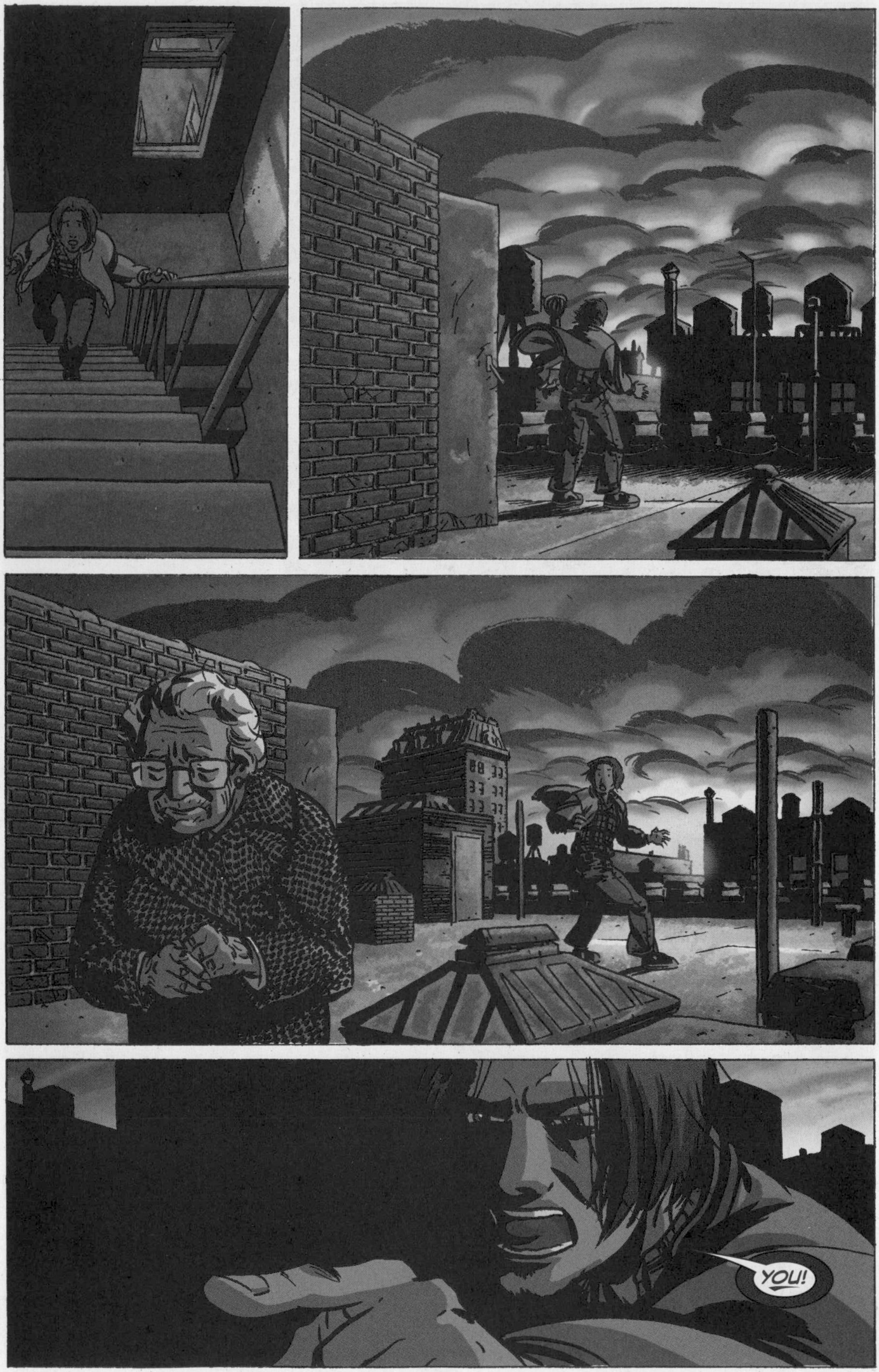
YOU!

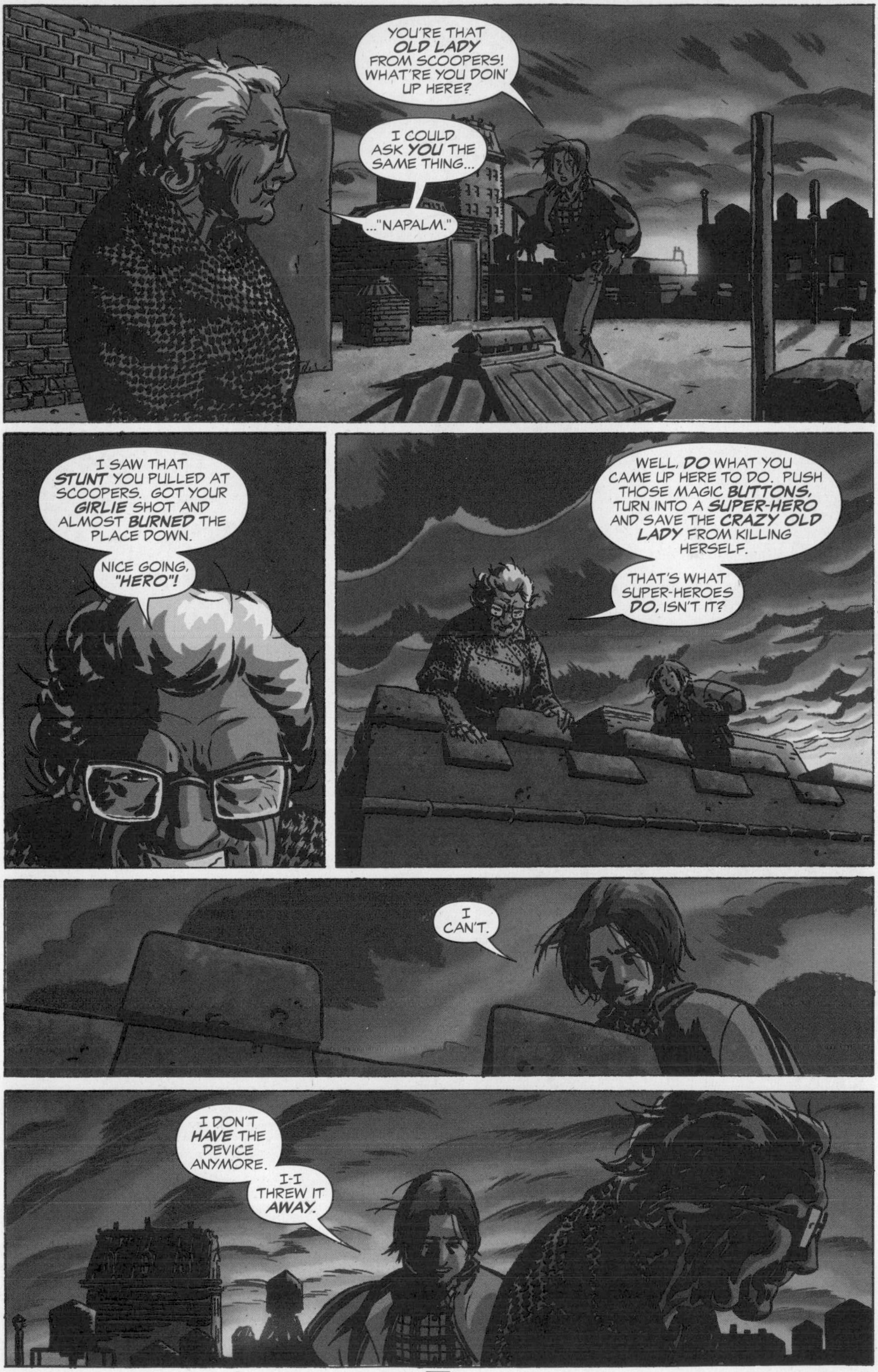
YOU'RE THAT OLD LADY FROM SCOOPERS! WHAT'RE YOU DOIN' UP HERE?
I COULD ASK YOU THE SAME THING...
..."NAPALM."
I SAW THAT STUNT YOU PULLED AT SCOOPERS. GOT YOUR GIRLIE SHOT AND ALMOST BURNED THE PLACE DOWN.
NICE GOING, "HERO"!
WELL, DO WHAT YOU CAME UP HERE TO DO. PUSH THOSE MAGIC BUTTONS, TURN INTO A SUPER-HERO AND SAVE THE CRAZY OLD LADY FROM KILLING HERSELF.
THAT'S WHAT SUPER-HEROES DO, ISN'T IT?
I CAN'T.
I DON'T HAVE THE DEVICE ANYMORE.
I-I THREW IT AWAY.

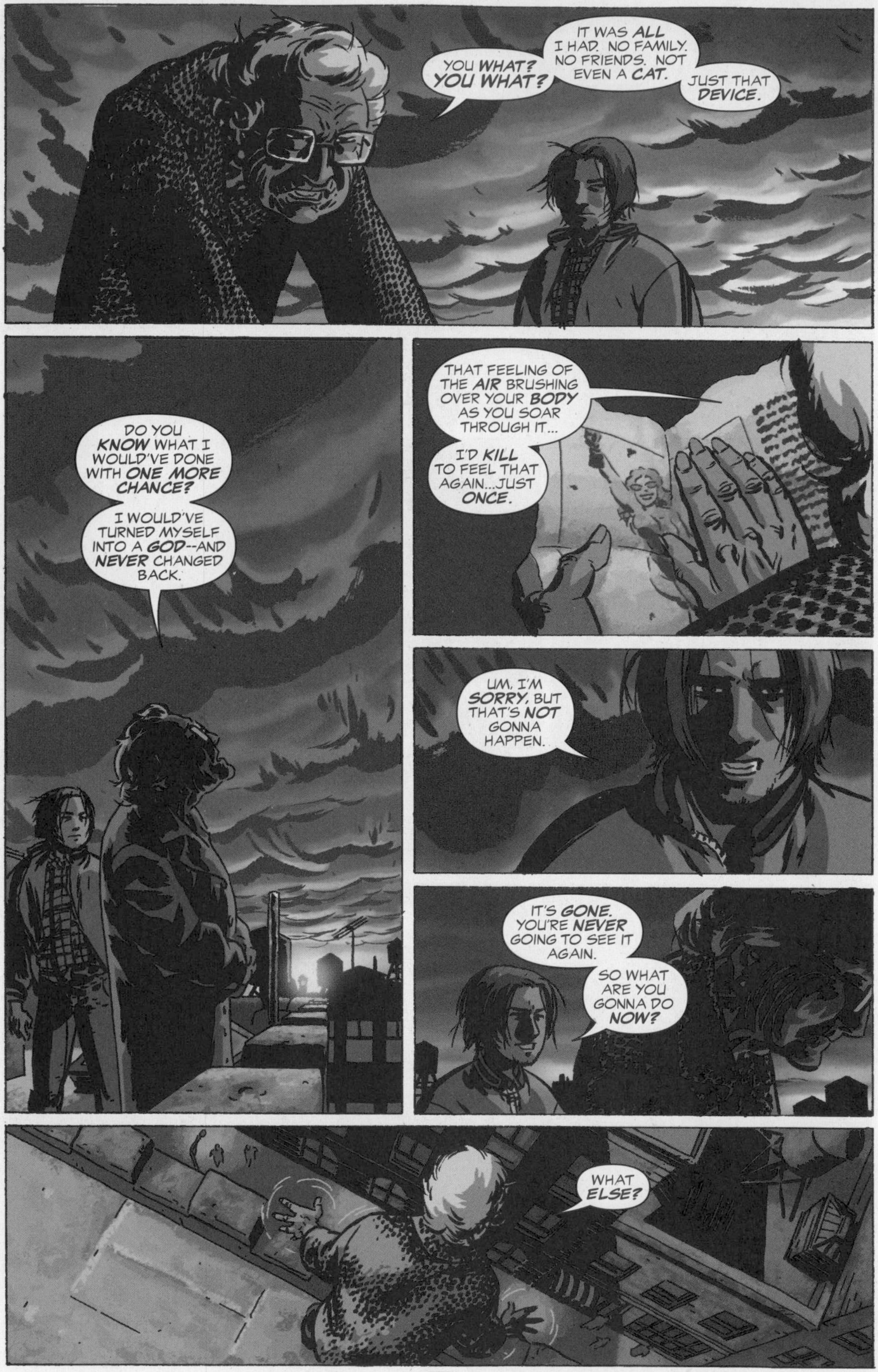
YOU WHAT? YOU WHAT?
IT WAS ALL I HAD. NO FAMILY. NO FRIENDS. NOT EVEN A CAT.
JUST THAT DEVICE.
DO YOU KNOW WHAT I WOULD'VE DONE WITH ONE MORE CHANCE?
I WOULD'VE TURNED MYSELF INTO A GOD--AND NEVER CHANGED BACK.
THAT FEELING OF THE AIR BRUSHING OVER YOUR BODY AS YOU SOAR THROUGH IT...
I'D KILL TO FEEL THAT AGAIN...JUST ONCE.
UM, I'M SORRY, BUT THAT'S NOT GONNA HAPPEN.
IT'S GONE. YOU'RE NEVER GOING TO SEE IT AGAIN.
SO WHAT ARE YOU GONNA DO NOW?
WHAT ELSE?

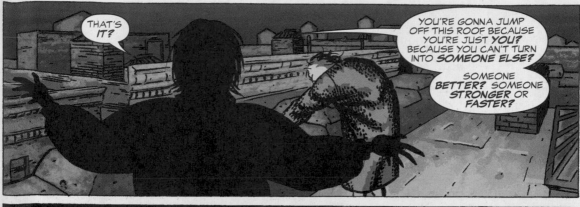

THAT'S *IT?*

YOU'RE GONNA JUMP OFF THIS ROOF BECAUSE YOU'RE JUST *YOU?* BECAUSE YOU CAN'T TURN INTO *SOMEONE ELSE?*

SOMEONE *BETTER?* SOMEONE *STRONGER* OR *FASTER?*

THAT'S WHAT *I WAS* GONNA DO, TOO.

BUT THINGS DIDN'T TURN OUT LIKE I *PLANNED,* AND NOW I GOTTA *DEAL* WITH IT.

LOOK, I'M JUST SOME *JERK* WHO TOOK THE GREATEST THING EITHER OF US EVER SAW AND *THREW* IT AWAY.

YOU GOT *NO* REASON TO LISTEN TO ME. I'M *NO* HERO.

IN FACT, I'LL PROBABLY BE BACK HERE *TOMORROW,* TRYING TO *KILL* MYSELF.

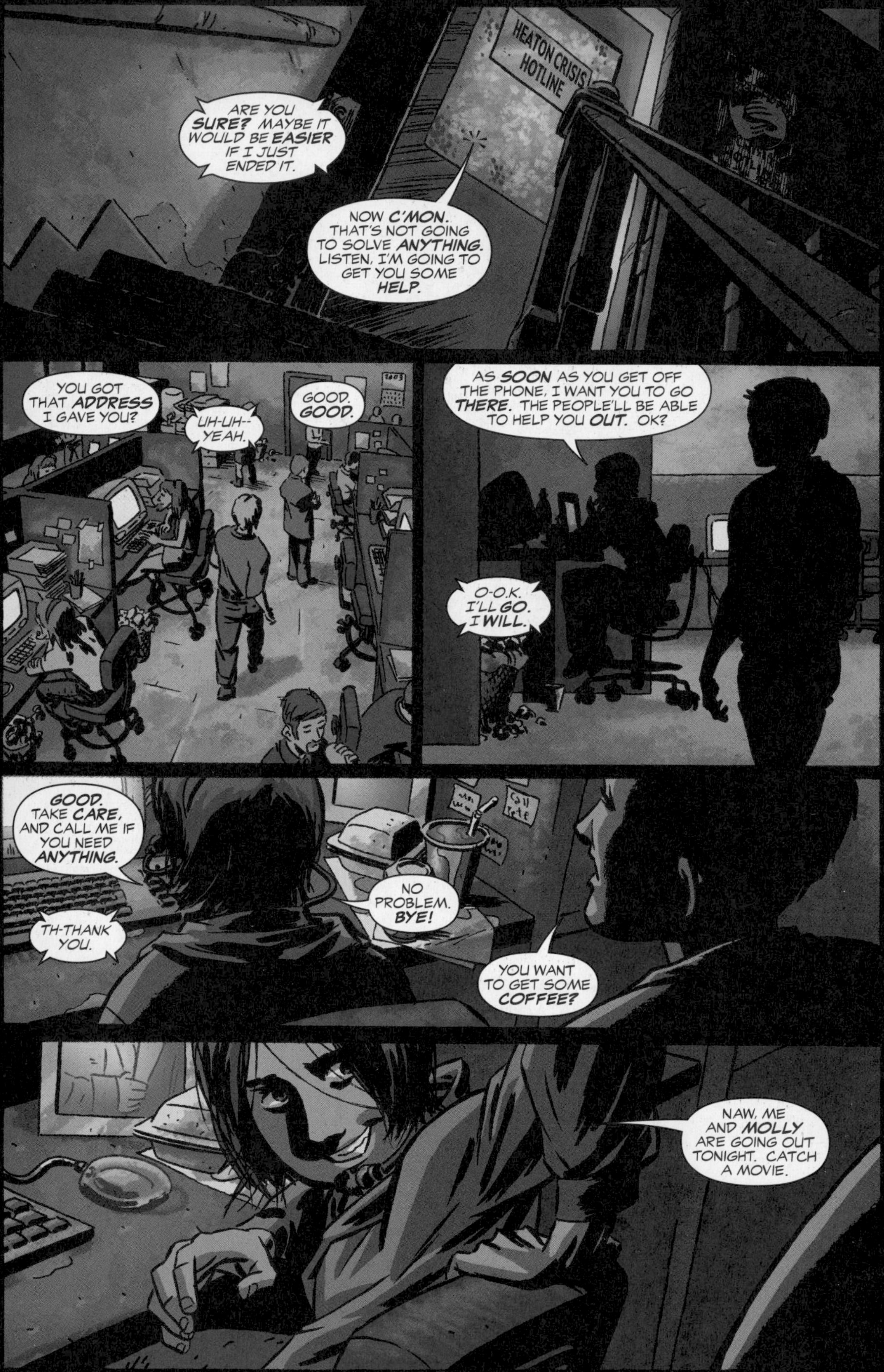
HEATON CRISIS HOTLINE
ARE YOU SURE? MAYBE IT WOULD BE EASIER IF I JUST ENDED IT.
NOW C'MON. THAT'S NOT GOING TO SOLVE ANYTHING. LISTEN, I'M GOING TO GET YOU SOME HELP.
YOU GOT THAT ADDRESS I GAVE YOU?
UH-UH-- YEAH.
GOOD. GOOD.
AS SOON AS YOU GET OFF THE PHONE, I WANT YOU TO GO THERE. THE PEOPLE'LL BE ABLE TO HELP YOU OUT. OK?
O-O.K. I'LL GO. I WILL.
GOOD. TAKE CARE, AND CALL ME IF YOU NEED ANYTHING.
TH-THANK YOU.
NO PROBLEM. BYE!
YOU WANT TO GET SOME COFFEE?
NAW, ME AND MOLLY ARE GOING OUT TONIGHT. CATCH A MOVIE.

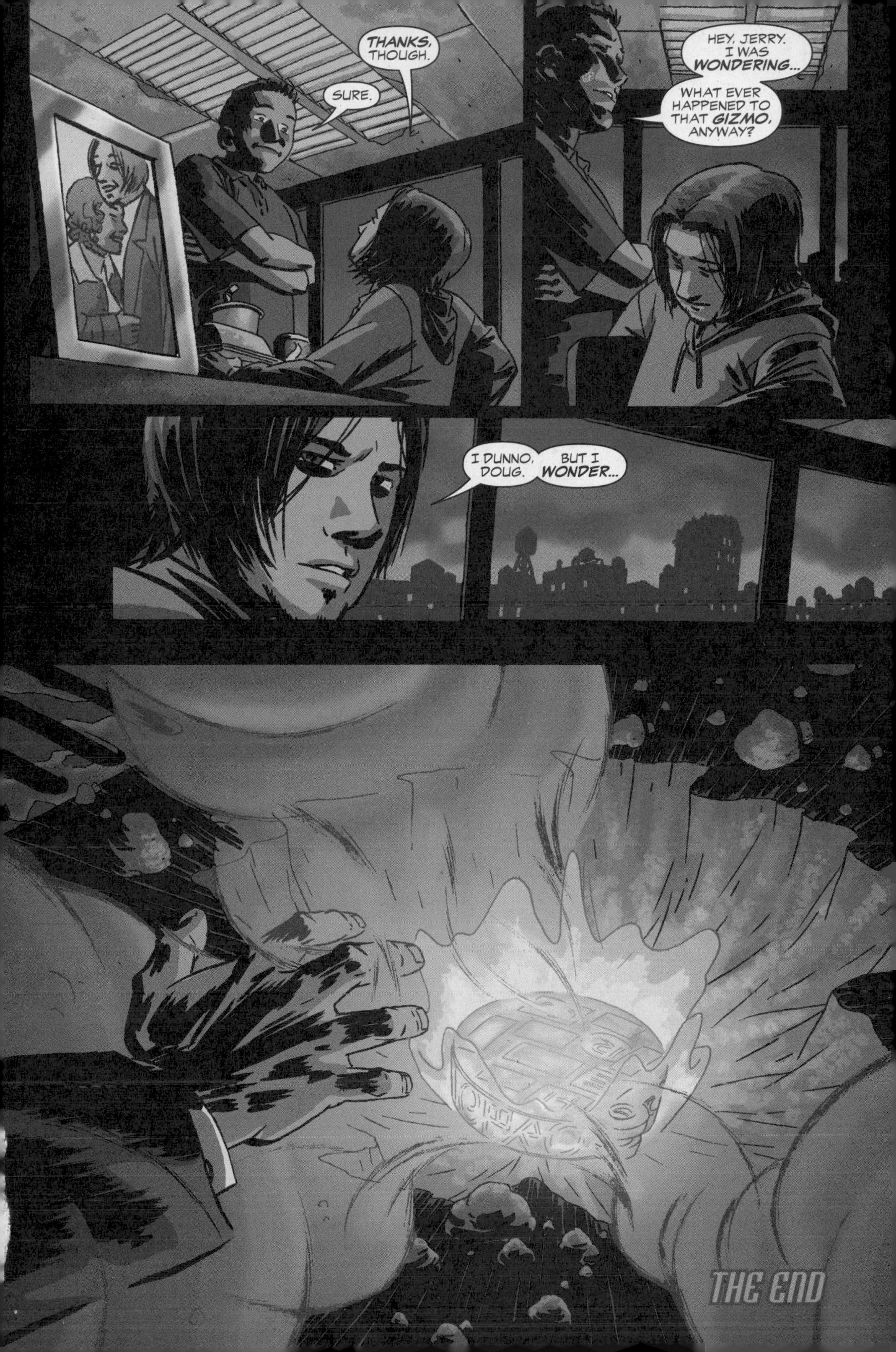
THANKS, THOUGH.
SURE.
HEY, JERRY. I WAS WONDERING...
WHAT EVER HAPPENED TO THAT GIZMO, ANYWAY?
I DUNNO, DOUG.
BUT I WONDER...
THE END

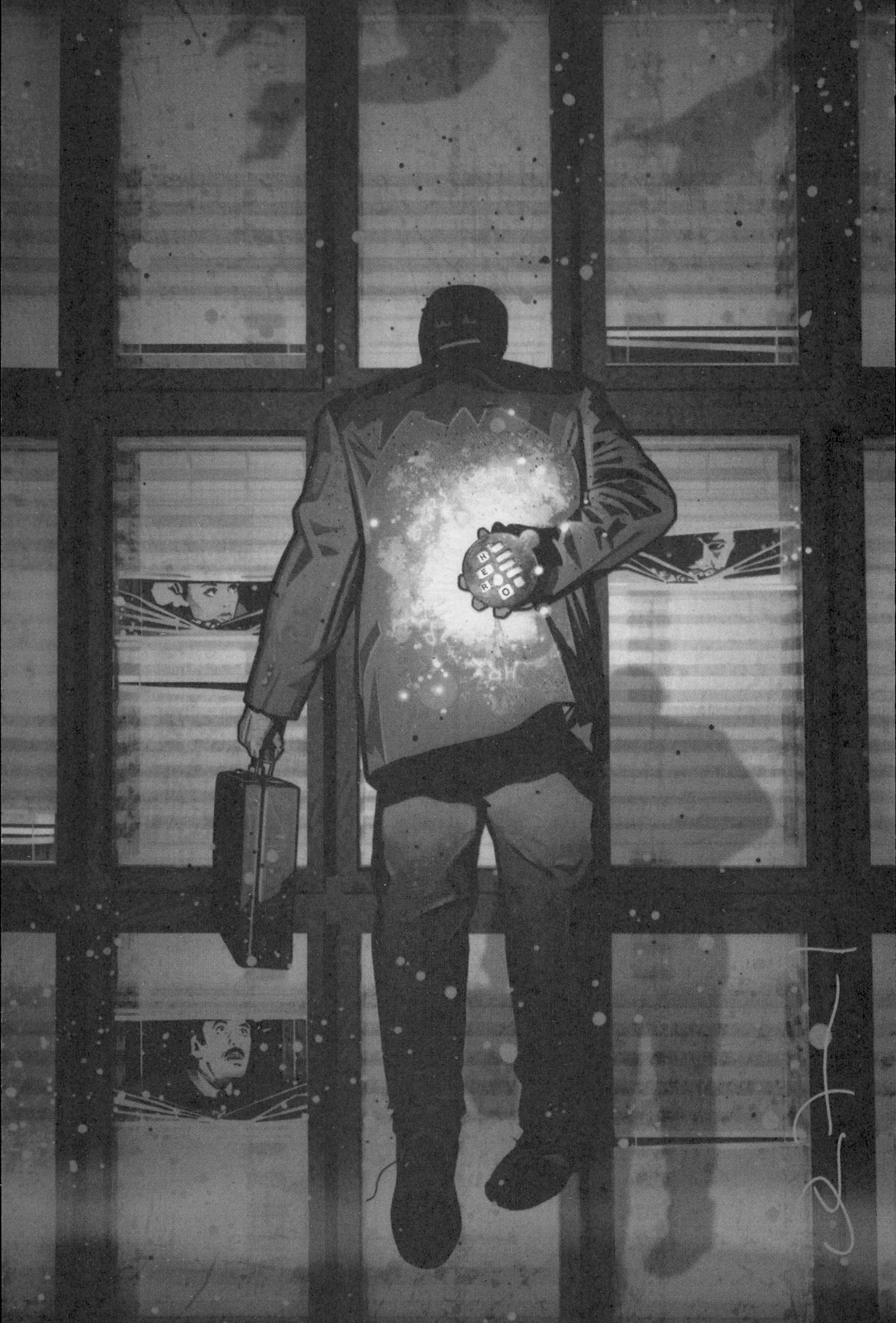

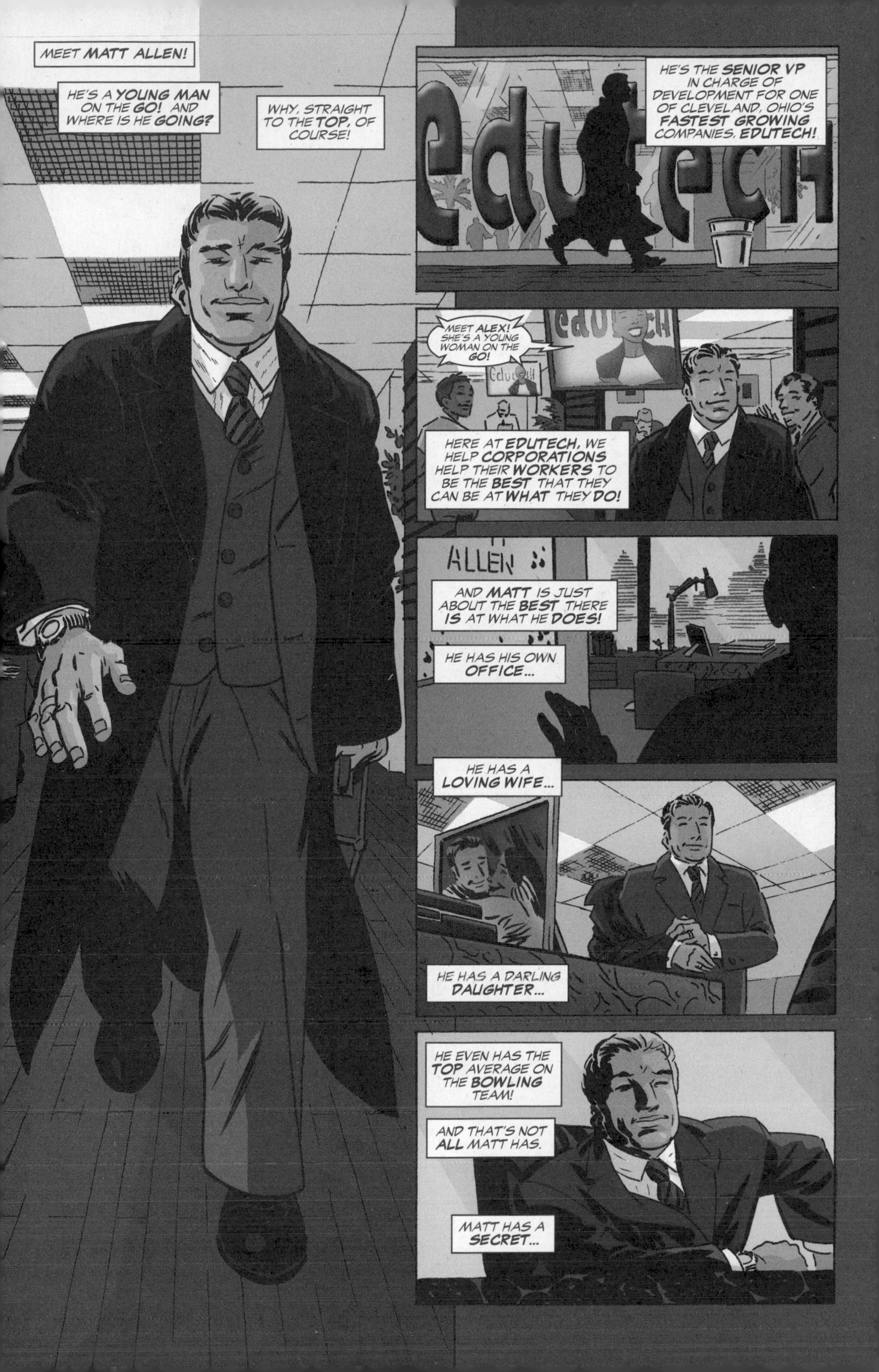
MEET MATT ALLEN!
HE'S A YOUNG MAN ON THE GO! AND WHERE IS HE GOING?
WHY, STRAIGHT TO THE TOP, OF COURSE!
HE'S THE SENIOR VP IN CHARGE OF DEVELOPMENT FOR ONE OF CLEVELAND, OHIO'S FASTEST GROWING COMPANIES, EDUTECH!
MEET ALEX! SHE'S A YOUNG WOMAN ON THE GO!
HERE AT EDUTECH, WE HELP CORPORATIONS HELP THEIR WORKERS TO BE THE BEST THAT THEY CAN BE AT WHAT THEY DO!
ALLEN
AND MATT IS JUST ABOUT THE BEST THERE IS AT WHAT HE DOES!
HE HAS HIS OWN OFFICE...
HE HAS A LOVING WIFE...
HE HAS A DARLING DAUGHTER...
HE EVEN HAS THE TOP AVERAGE ON THE BOWLING TEAM!
AND THAT'S NOT ALL MATT HAS.
MATT HAS A SECRET...

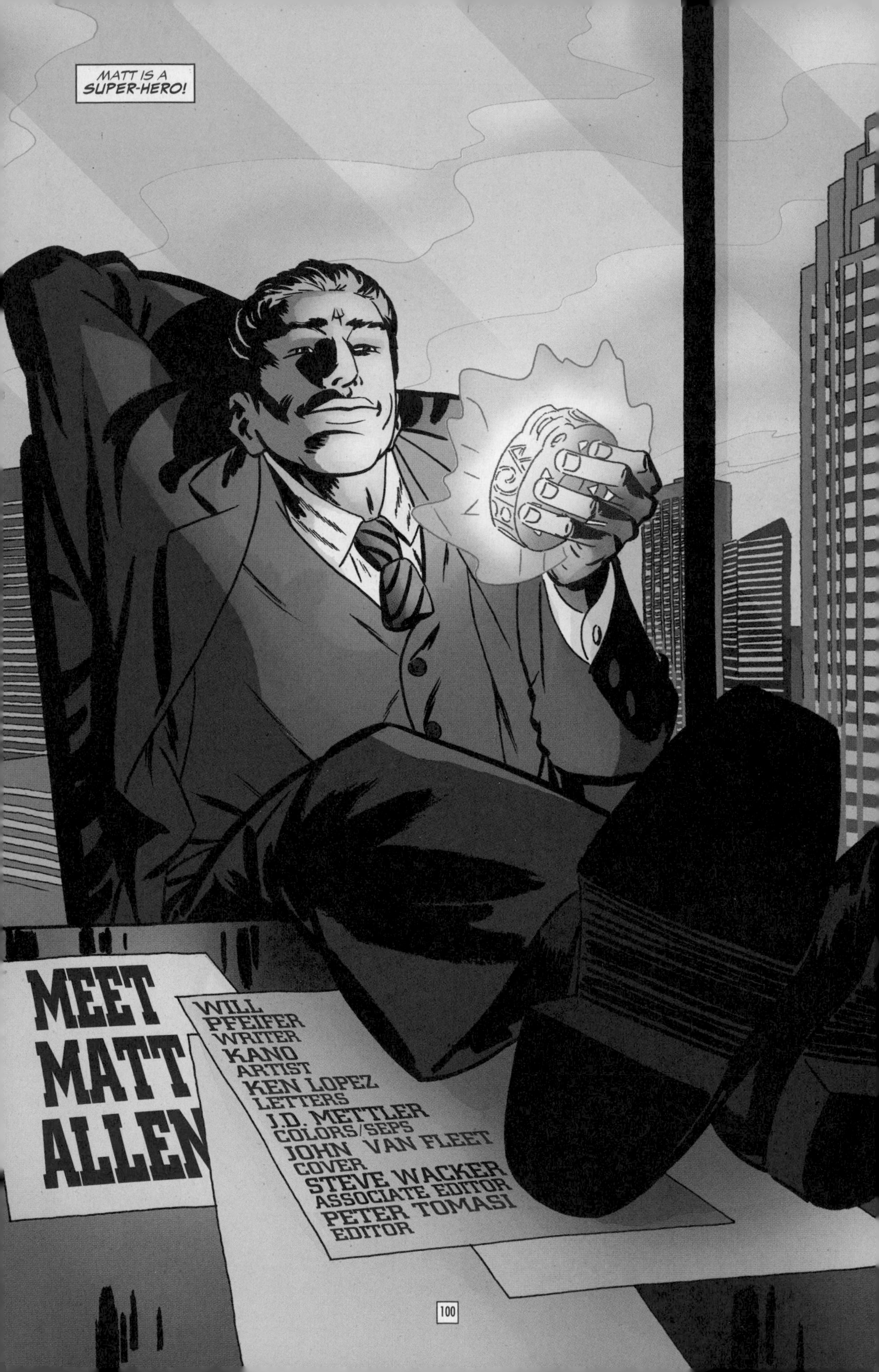
MATT IS A SUPER-HERO!
MEET MATT ALLEN
WILL PFEIFER WRITER
KANO ARTIST
KEN LOPEZ LETTERS
J.D. METTLER COLORS/SEPS
JOHN VAN FLEET COVER
STEVE WACKER ASSOCIATE EDITOR
PETER TOMASI EDITOR

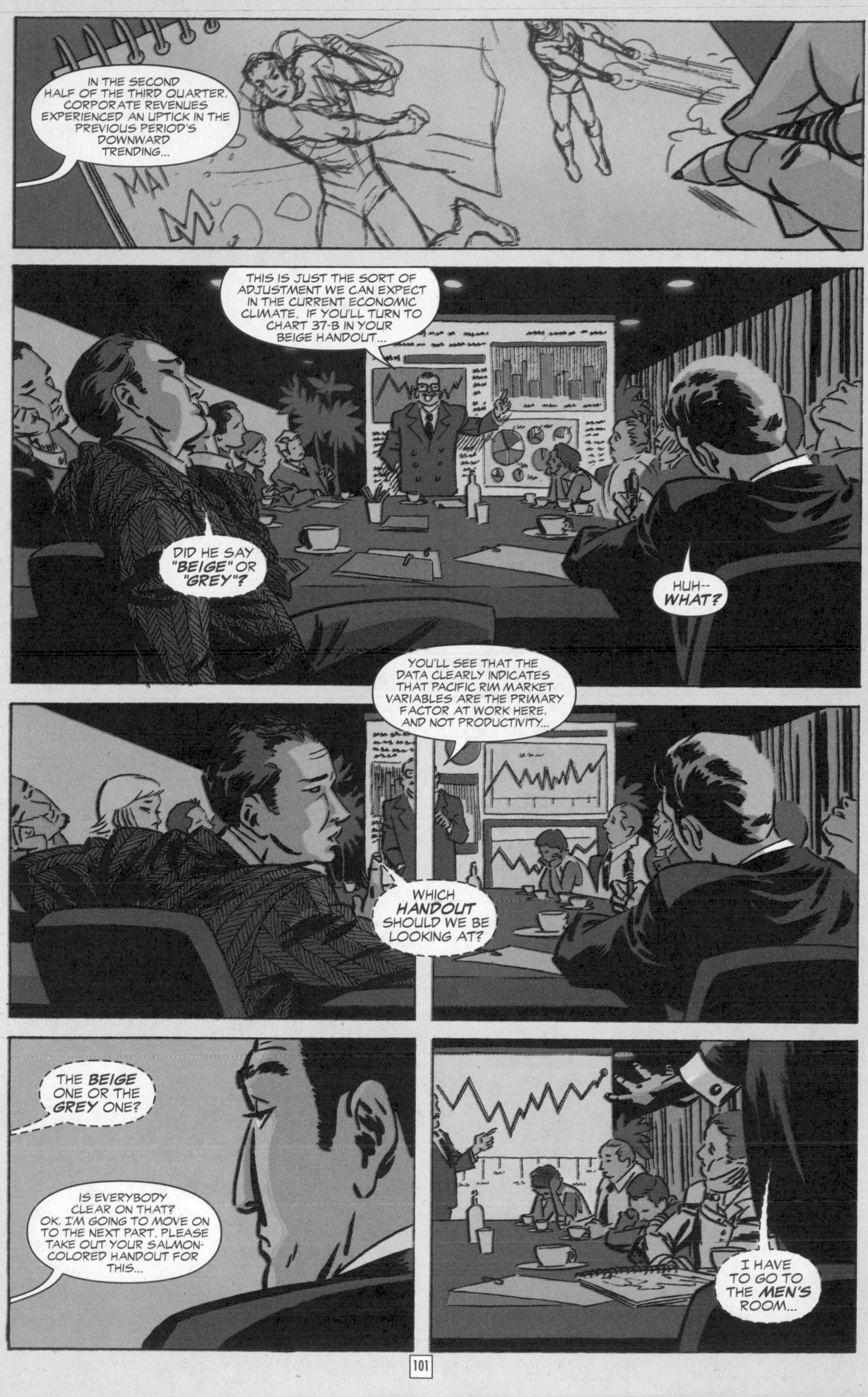
IN THE SECOND HALF OF THE THIRD QUARTER, CORPORATE REVENUES EXPERIENCED AN UPTICK IN THE PREVIOUS PERIOD'S DOWNWARD TRENDING...
THIS IS JUST THE SORT OF ADJUSTMENT WE CAN EXPECT IN THE CURRENT ECONOMIC CLIMATE. IF YOU'LL TURN TO CHART 37-B IN YOUR BEIGE HANDOUT...
DID HE SAY "BEIGE" OR "GREY"?
HUH-- WHAT?
YOU'LL SEE THAT THE DATA CLEARLY INDICATES THAT PACIFIC RIM MARKET VARIABLES ARE THE PRIMARY FACTOR AT WORK HERE, AND NOT PRODUCTIVITY...
WHICH HANDOUT SHOULD WE BE LOOKING AT?
THE BEIGE ONE OR THE GREY ONE?
IS EVERYBODY CLEAR ON THAT? OK. I'M GOING TO MOVE ON TO THE NEXT PART. PLEASE TAKE OUT YOUR SALMON-COLORED HANDOUT FOR THIS...
I HAVE TO GO TO THE MEN'S ROOM...

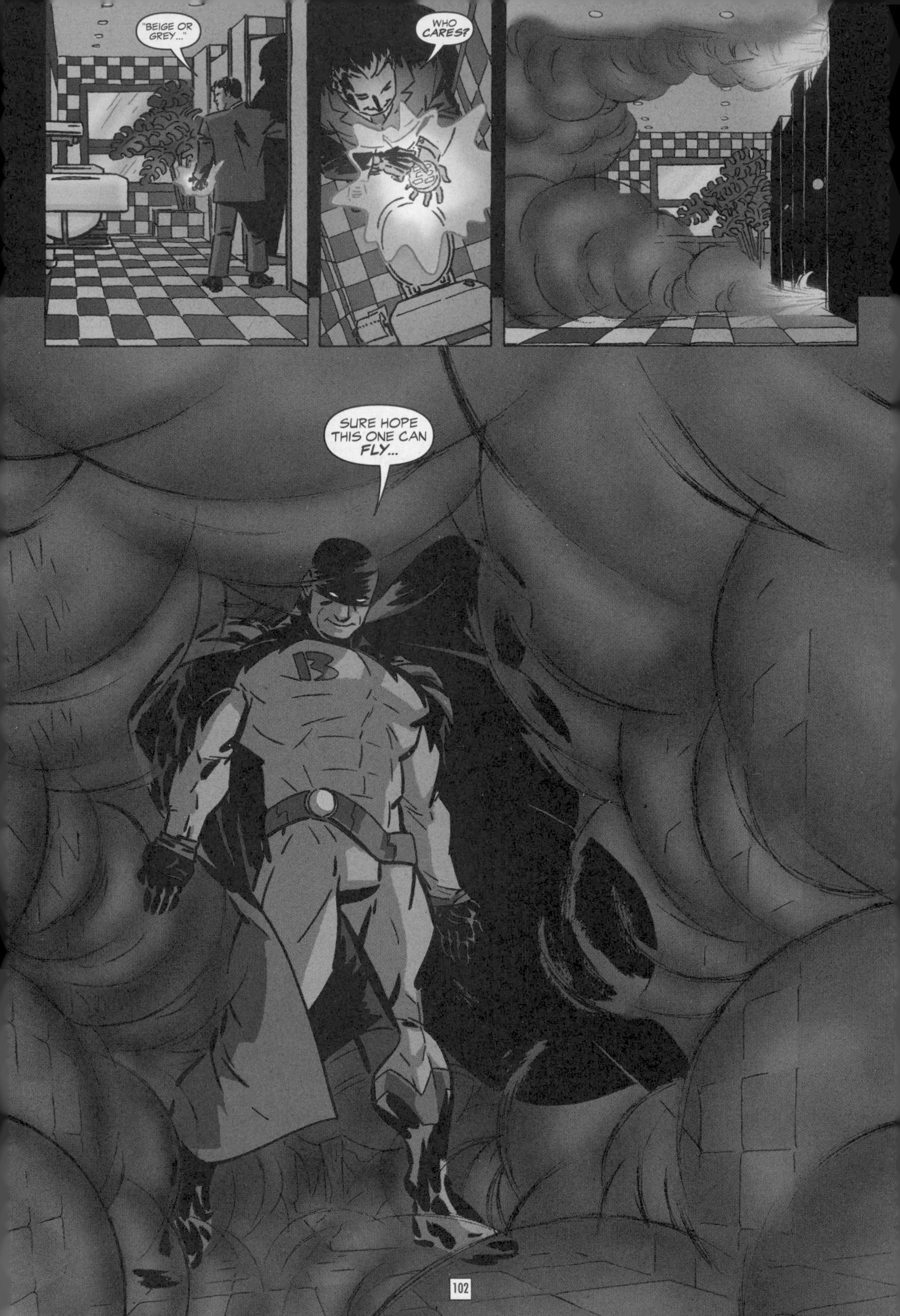
"BEIGE OR GREY..."
WHO CARES?
SURE HOPE THIS ONE CAN FLY...

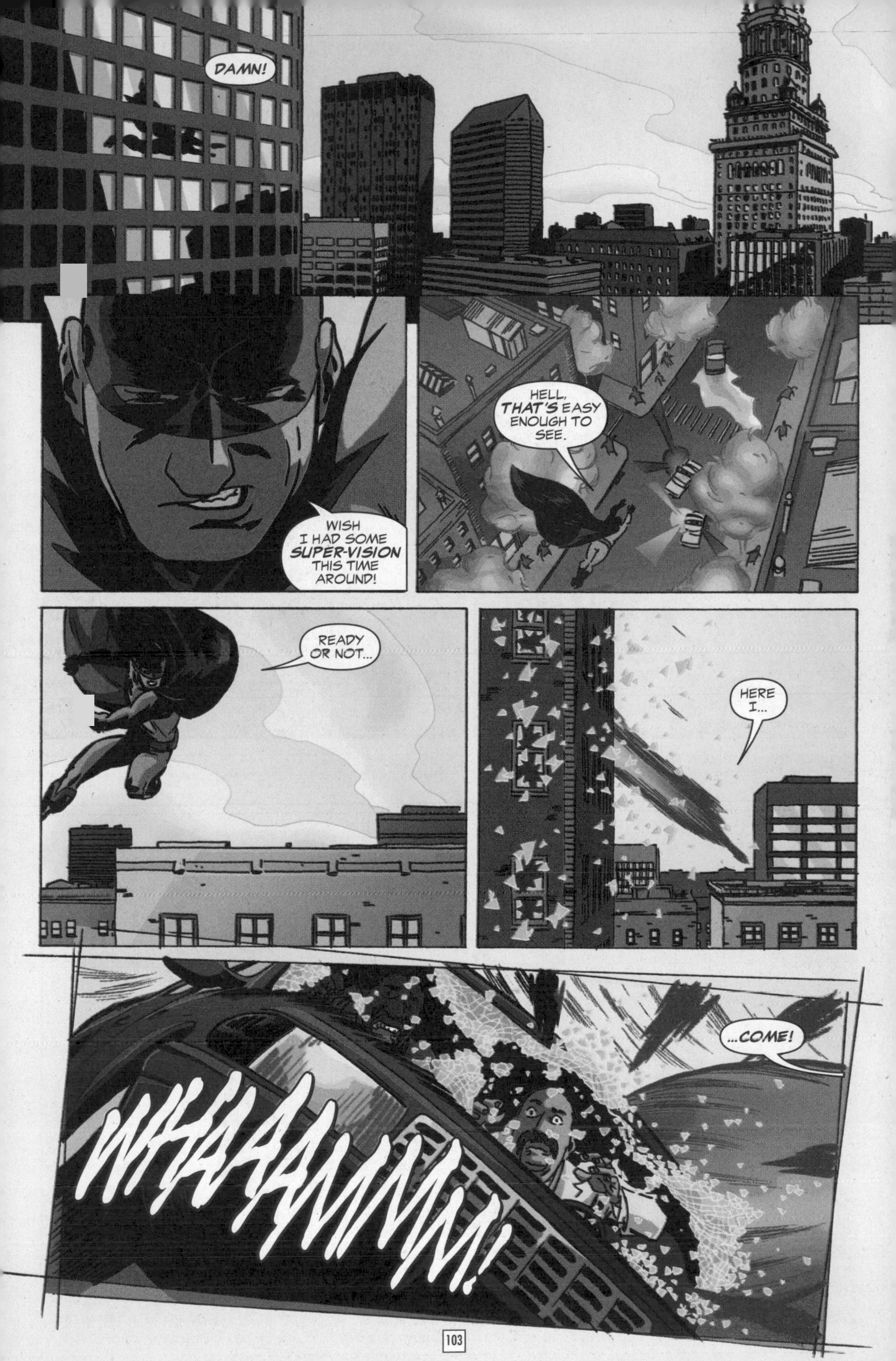
DAMN!
WISH I HAD SOME SUPER-VISION THIS TIME AROUND!
HELL, THAT'S EASY ENOUGH TO SEE.
READY OR NOT...
HERE I...
...COME!
WHAAAMMMM!

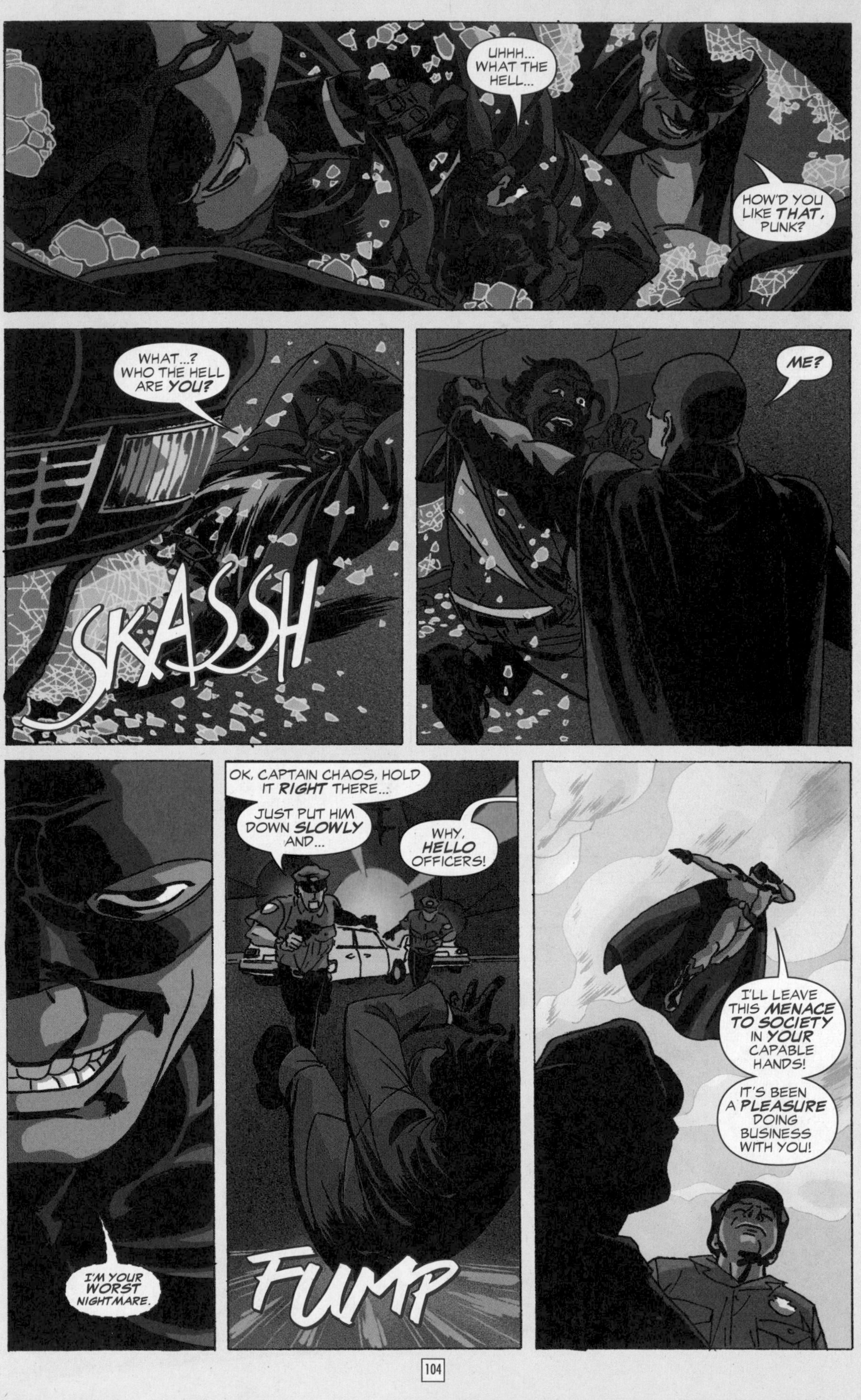
UHHH... WHAT THE HELL...
HOW'D YOU LIKE THAT, PUNK?
WHAT...? WHO THE HELL ARE YOU?
SKASSH
ME?
I'M YOUR WORST NIGHTMARE.
OK, CAPTAIN CHAOS, HOLD IT RIGHT THERE...
JUST PUT HIM DOWN SLOWLY AND...
WHY, HELLO OFFICERS!
FUMP
I'LL LEAVE THIS MENACE TO SOCIETY IN YOUR CAPABLE HANDS!
IT'S BEEN A PLEASURE DOING BUSINESS WITH YOU!

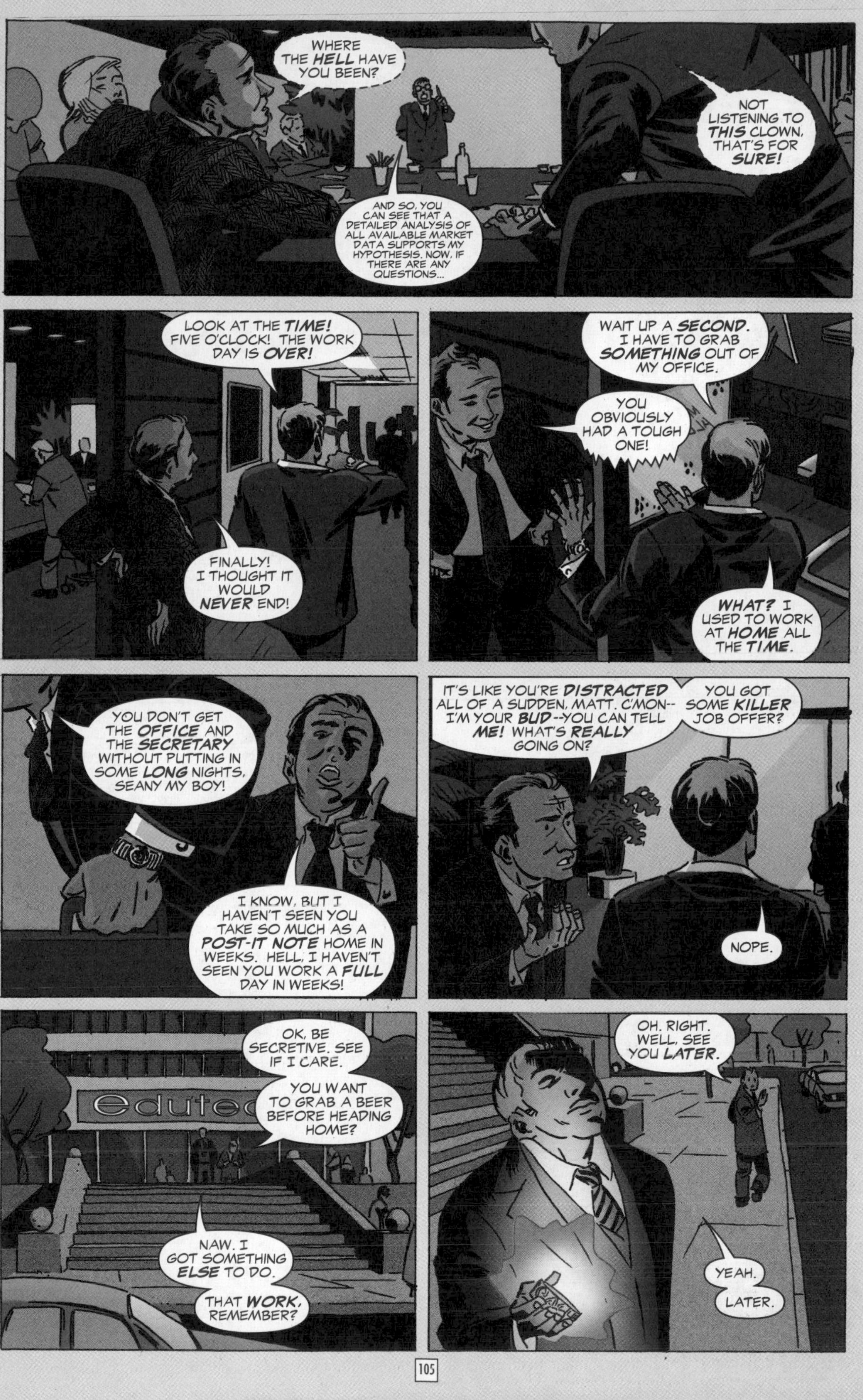
WHERE THE HELL HAVE YOU BEEN?
NOT LISTENING TO THIS CLOWN, THAT'S FOR SURE!
AND SO, YOU CAN SEE THAT A DETAILED ANALYSIS OF ALL AVAILABLE MARKET DATA SUPPORTS MY HYPOTHESIS. NOW, IF THERE ARE ANY QUESTIONS...
LOOK AT THE TIME! FIVE O'CLOCK! THE WORK DAY IS OVER!
FINALLY! I THOUGHT IT WOULD NEVER END!
WAIT UP A SECOND. I HAVE TO GRAB SOMETHING OUT OF MY OFFICE.
YOU OBVIOUSLY HAD A TOUGH ONE!
WHAT? I USED TO WORK AT HOME ALL THE TIME.
YOU DON'T GET THE OFFICE AND THE SECRETARY WITHOUT PUTTING IN SOME LONG NIGHTS, SEANY MY BOY!
I KNOW, BUT I HAVEN'T SEEN YOU TAKE SO MUCH AS A POST-IT NOTE HOME IN WEEKS. HELL, I HAVEN'T SEEN YOU WORK A FULL DAY IN WEEKS!
IT'S LIKE YOU'RE DISTRACTED ALL OF A SUDDEN, MATT. C'MON-- I'M YOUR BUD--YOU CAN TELL ME! WHAT'S REALLY GOING ON?
YOU GOT SOME KILLER JOB OFFER?
NOPE.
OK, BE SECRETIVE. SEE IF I CARE.
YOU WANT TO GRAB A BEER BEFORE HEADING HOME?
NAW. I GOT SOMETHING ELSE TO DO.
THAT WORK, REMEMBER?
OH. RIGHT. WELL, SEE YOU LATER.
YEAH.
LATER.

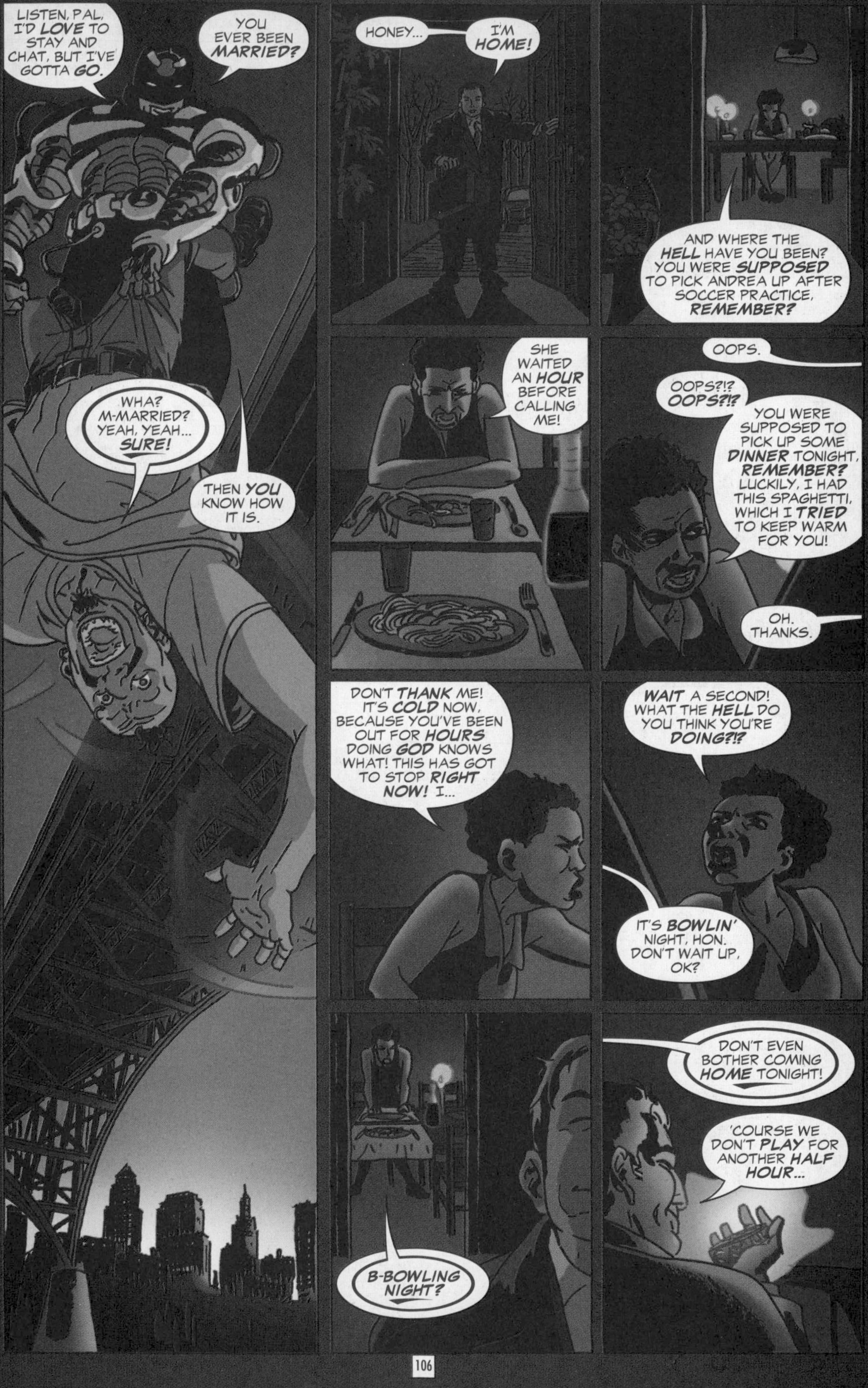
LISTEN, PAL, I'D LOVE TO STAY AND CHAT, BUT I'VE GOTTA GO.
YOU EVER BEEN MARRIED?
WHA? M-MARRIED? YEAH, YEAH... SURE!
THEN YOU KNOW HOW IT IS.
HONEY...
I'M HOME!
AND WHERE THE HELL HAVE YOU BEEN? YOU WERE SUPPOSED TO PICK ANDREA UP AFTER SOCCER PRACTICE, REMEMBER?
SHE WAITED AN HOUR BEFORE CALLING ME!
OOPS.
OOPS?!? OOPS?!?
YOU WERE SUPPOSED TO PICK UP SOME DINNER TONIGHT, REMEMBER? LUCKILY, I HAD THIS SPAGHETTI, WHICH I TRIED TO KEEP WARM FOR YOU!
OH. THANKS.
DON'T THANK ME! IT'S COLD NOW, BECAUSE YOU'VE BEEN OUT FOR HOURS DOING GOD KNOWS WHAT! THIS HAS GOT TO STOP RIGHT NOW! I...
WAIT A SECOND! WHAT THE HELL DO YOU THINK YOU'RE DOING?!?
IT'S BOWLIN' NIGHT, HON. DON'T WAIT UP, OK?
B-BOWLING NIGHT?
DON'T EVEN BOTHER COMING HOME TONIGHT!
'COURSE WE DON'T PLAY FOR ANOTHER HALF HOUR...

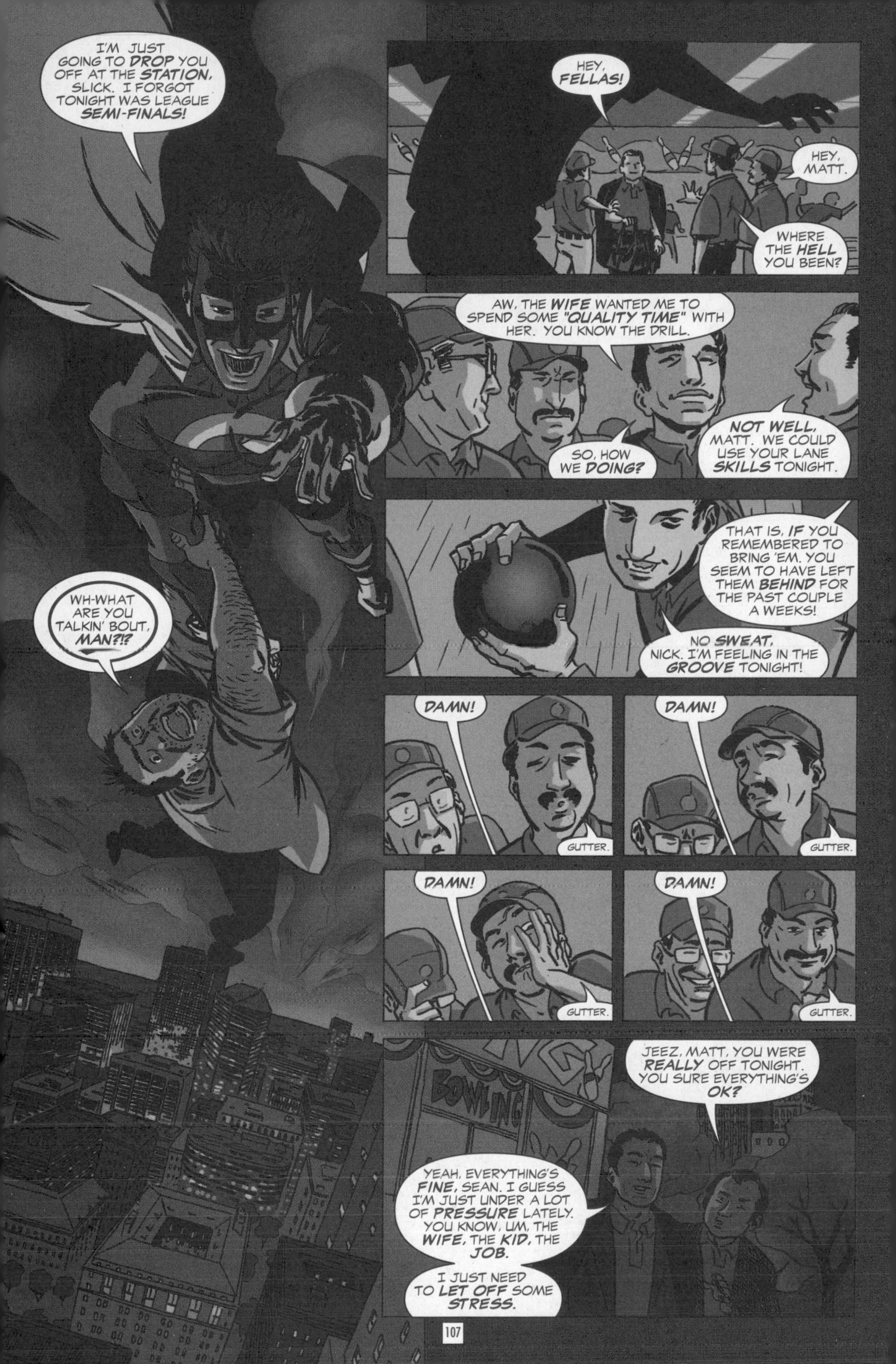
I'M JUST GOING TO DROP YOU OFF AT THE STATION, SLICK. I FORGOT TONIGHT WAS LEAGUE SEMI-FINALS!
WH-WHAT ARE YOU TALKIN' BOUT, MAN?!?
HEY, FELLAS!
HEY, MATT.
WHERE THE HELL YOU BEEN?
AW, THE WIFE WANTED ME TO SPEND SOME "QUALITY TIME" WITH HER. YOU KNOW THE DRILL.
SO, HOW WE DOING?
NOT WELL, MATT. WE COULD USE YOUR LANE SKILLS TONIGHT.
THAT IS, IF YOU REMEMBERED TO BRING 'EM. YOU SEEM TO HAVE LEFT THEM BEHIND FOR THE PAST COUPLE A WEEKS!
NO SWEAT, NICK. I'M FEELING IN THE GROOVE TONIGHT!
DAMN!
GUTTER.
DAMN!
GUTTER.
DAMN!
GUTTER.
DAMN!
GUTTER.
BOWLING
JEEZ, MATT, YOU WERE REALLY OFF TONIGHT. YOU SURE EVERYTHING'S OK?
YEAH, EVERYTHING'S FINE, SEAN. I GUESS I'M JUST UNDER A LOT OF PRESSURE LATELY. YOU KNOW, UM, THE WIFE, THE KID, THE JOB.
I JUST NEED TO LET OFF SOME STRESS.

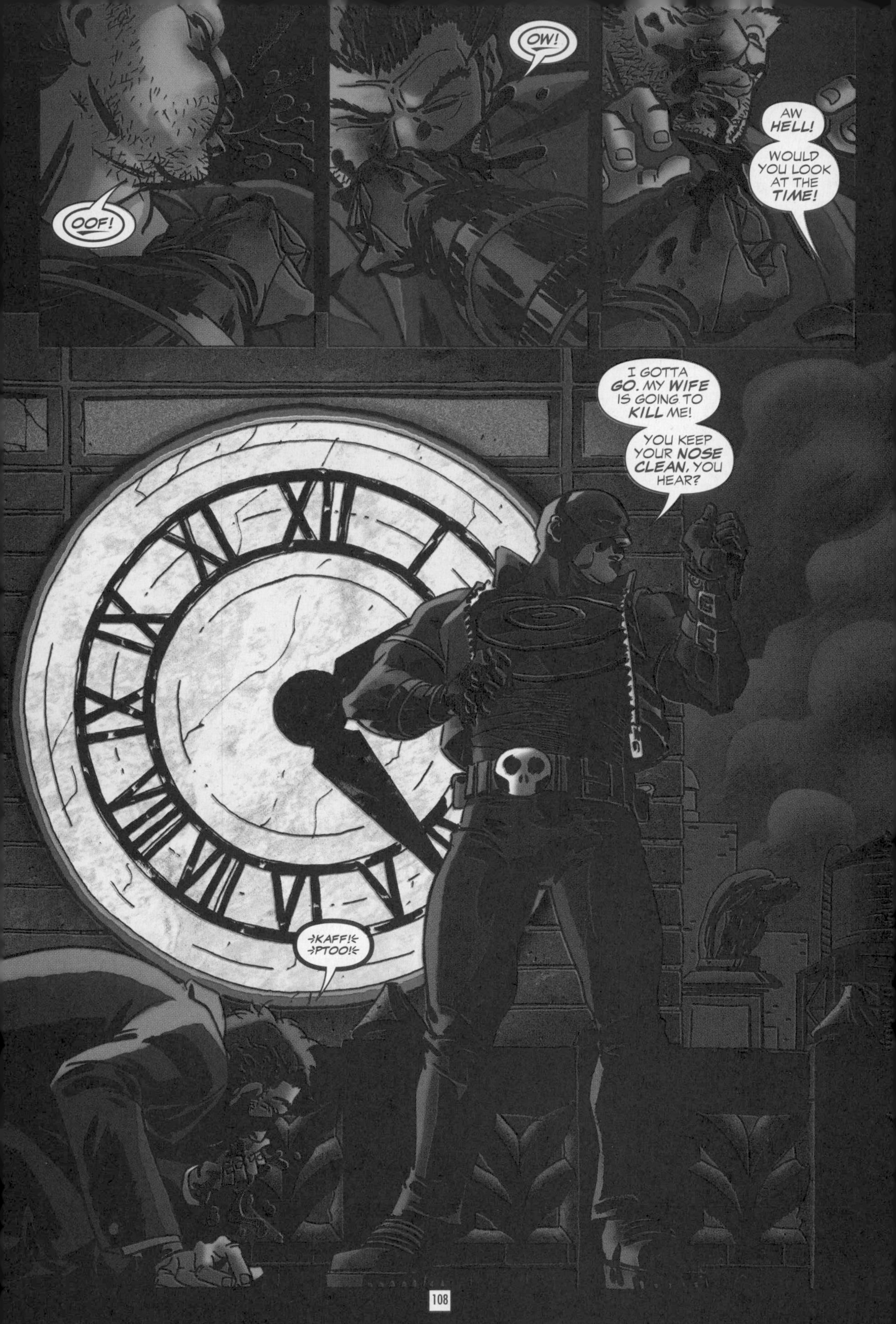
OOF!
OW!
AW HELL!
WOULD YOU LOOK AT THE TIME!
I GOTTA GO. MY WIFE IS GOING TO KILL ME!
YOU KEEP YOUR NOSE CLEAN, YOU HEAR?
KAFF! PTOO!

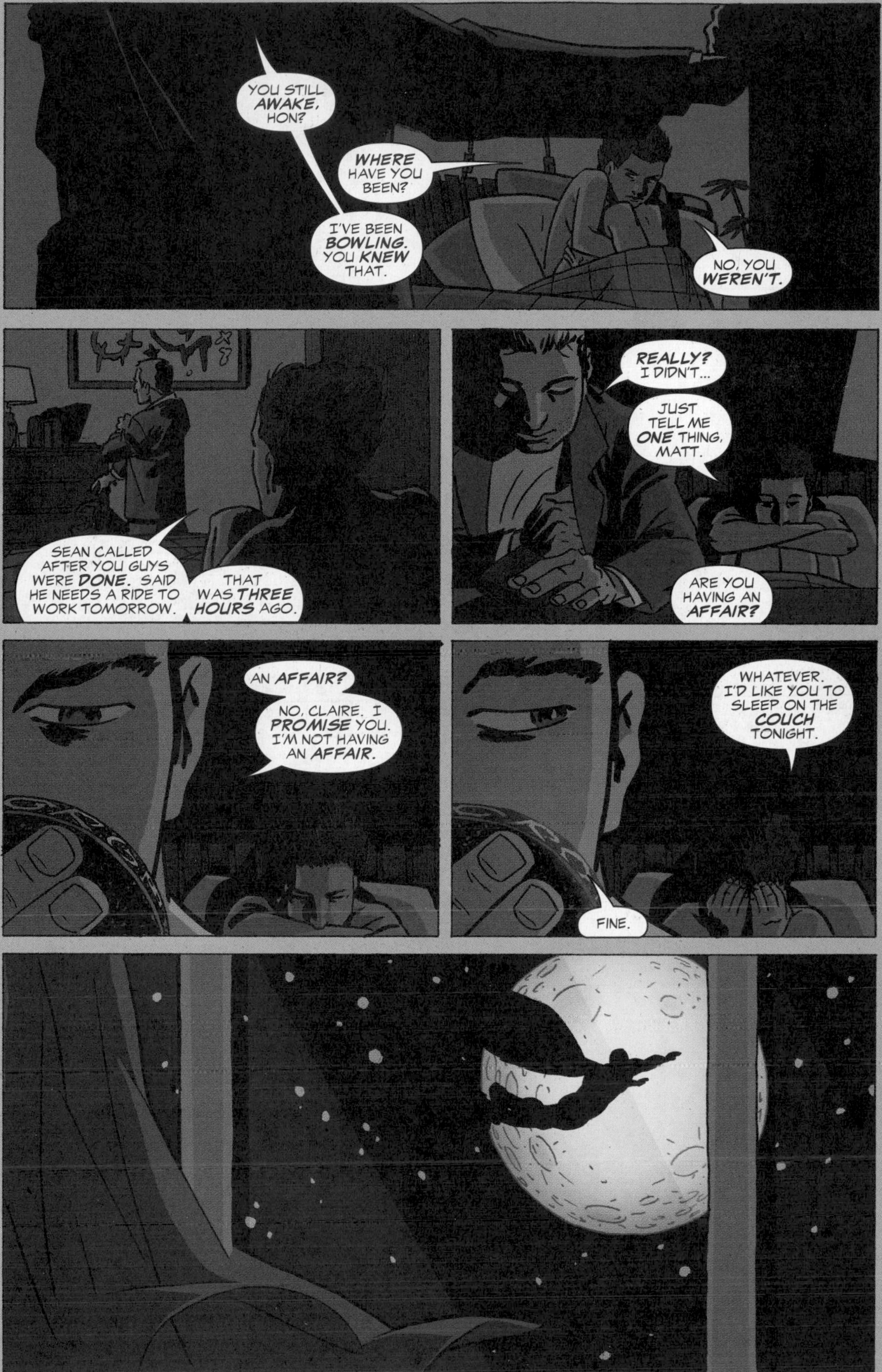
YOU STILL AWAKE, HON?
WHERE HAVE YOU BEEN?
I'VE BEEN BOWLING. YOU KNEW THAT.
NO, YOU WEREN'T.
SEAN CALLED AFTER YOU GUYS WERE DONE. SAID HE NEEDS A RIDE TO WORK TOMORROW.
THAT WAS THREE HOURS AGO.
REALLY? I DIDN'T...
JUST TELL ME ONE THING, MATT.
ARE YOU HAVING AN AFFAIR?
AN AFFAIR?
NO, CLAIRE. I PROMISE YOU. I'M NOT HAVING AN AFFAIR.
WHATEVER. I'D LIKE YOU TO SLEEP ON THE COUCH TONIGHT.
FINE.

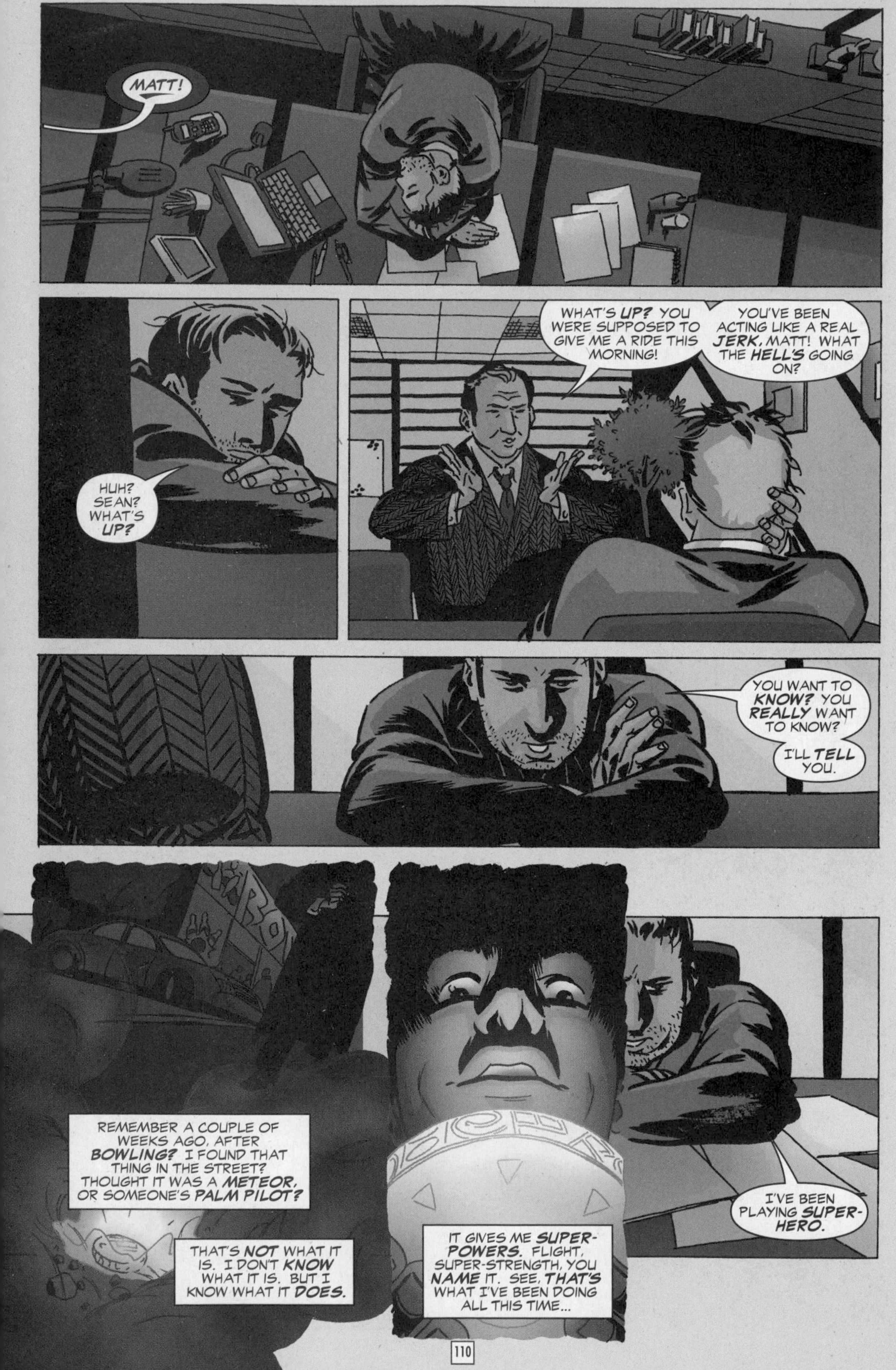
MATT!
HUH? SEAN? WHAT'S UP?
WHAT'S UP? YOU WERE SUPPOSED TO GIVE ME A RIDE THIS MORNING!
YOU'VE BEEN ACTING LIKE A REAL JERK, MATT! WHAT THE HELL'S GOING ON?
YOU WANT TO KNOW? YOU REALLY WANT TO KNOW?
I'LL TELL YOU.
REMEMBER A COUPLE OF WEEKS AGO, AFTER BOWLING? I FOUND THAT THING IN THE STREET? THOUGHT IT WAS A METEOR, OR SOMEONE'S PALM PILOT?
THAT'S NOT WHAT IT IS. I DON'T KNOW WHAT IT IS. BUT I KNOW WHAT IT DOES.
IT GIVES ME SUPER-POWERS. FLIGHT, SUPER-STRENGTH, YOU NAME IT. SEE, THAT'S WHAT I'VE BEEN DOING ALL THIS TIME...
I'VE BEEN PLAYING SUPER-HERO.

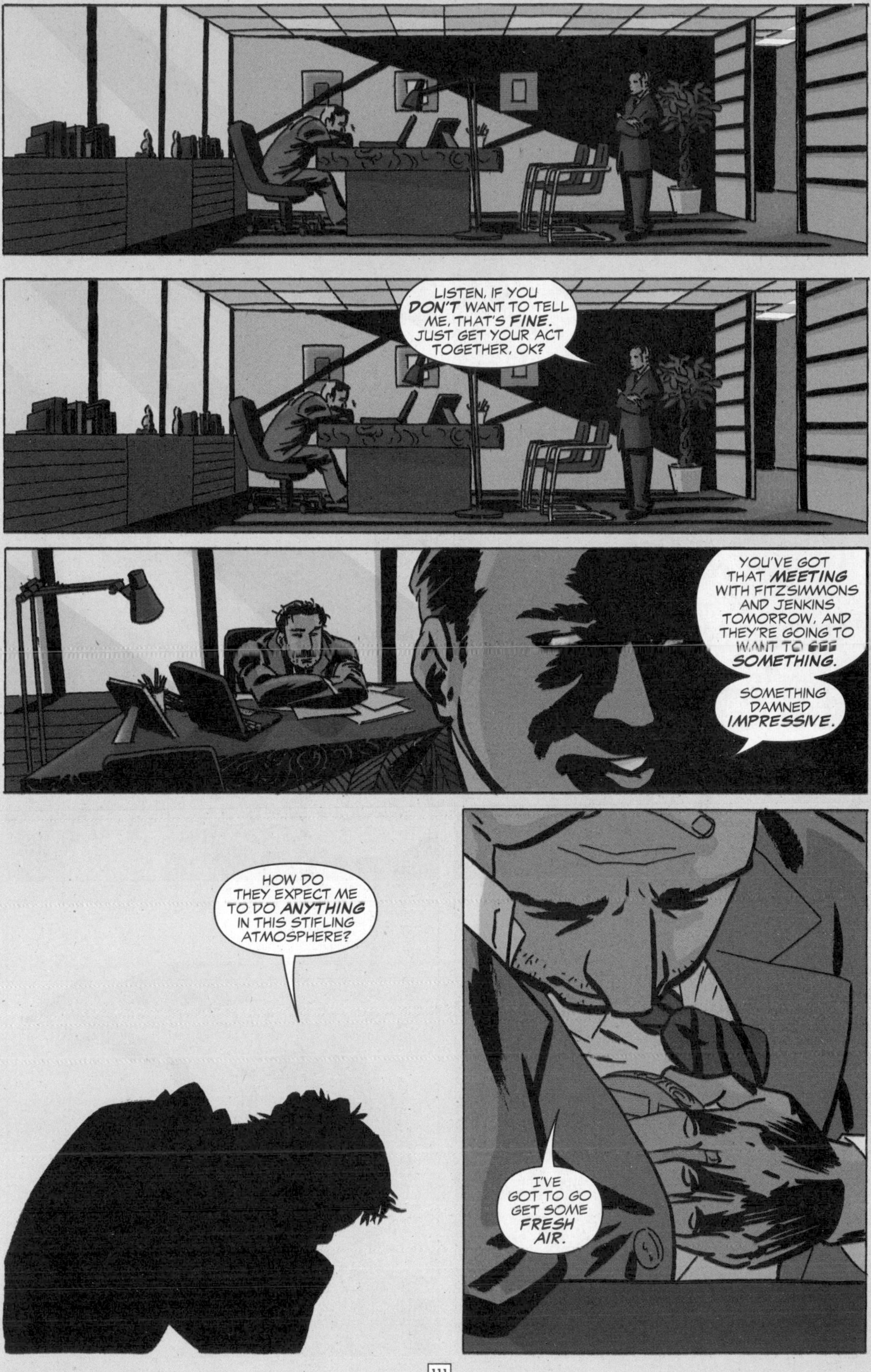
LISTEN, IF YOU DON'T WANT TO TELL ME, THAT'S FINE. JUST GET YOUR ACT TOGETHER, OK?
YOU'VE GOT THAT MEETING WITH FITZSIMMONS AND JENKINS TOMORROW, AND THEY'RE GOING TO WANT TO SEE SOMETHING.
SOMETHING DAMNED IMPRESSIVE.
HOW DO THEY EXPECT ME TO DO ANYTHING IN THIS STIFLING ATMOSPHERE?
I'VE GOT TO GO GET SOME FRESH AIR.

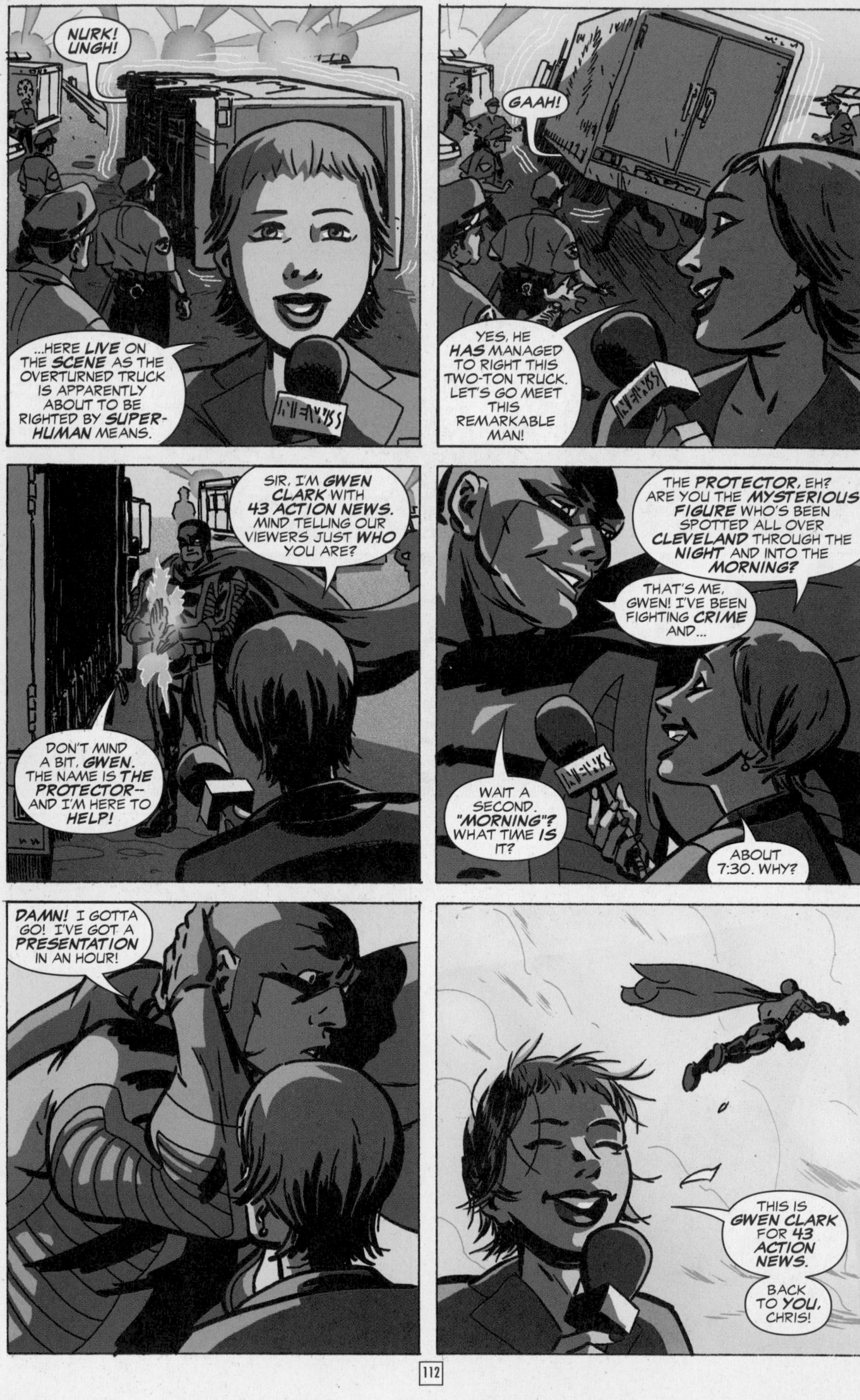
NURK! UNGH!
...HERE LIVE ON THE SCENE AS THE OVERTURNED TRUCK IS APPARENTLY ABOUT TO BE RIGHTED BY SUPER-HUMAN MEANS.
GAAH!
YES, HE HAS MANAGED TO RIGHT THIS TWO-TON TRUCK. LET'S GO MEET THIS REMARKABLE MAN!
SIR, I'M GWEN CLARK WITH 43 ACTION NEWS. MIND TELLING OUR VIEWERS JUST WHO YOU ARE?
DON'T MIND A BIT, GWEN. THE NAME IS THE PROTECTOR-- AND I'M HERE TO HELP!
THE PROTECTOR, EH? ARE YOU THE MYSTERIOUS FIGURE WHO'S BEEN SPOTTED ALL OVER CLEVELAND THROUGH THE NIGHT AND INTO THE MORNING?
THAT'S ME, GWEN! I'VE BEEN FIGHTING CRIME AND...
WAIT A SECOND. "MORNING"? WHAT TIME IS IT?
ABOUT 7:30. WHY?
DAMN! I GOTTA GO! I'VE GOT A PRESENTATION IN AN HOUR!
THIS IS GWEN CLARK FOR 43 ACTION NEWS.
BACK TO YOU, CHRIS!

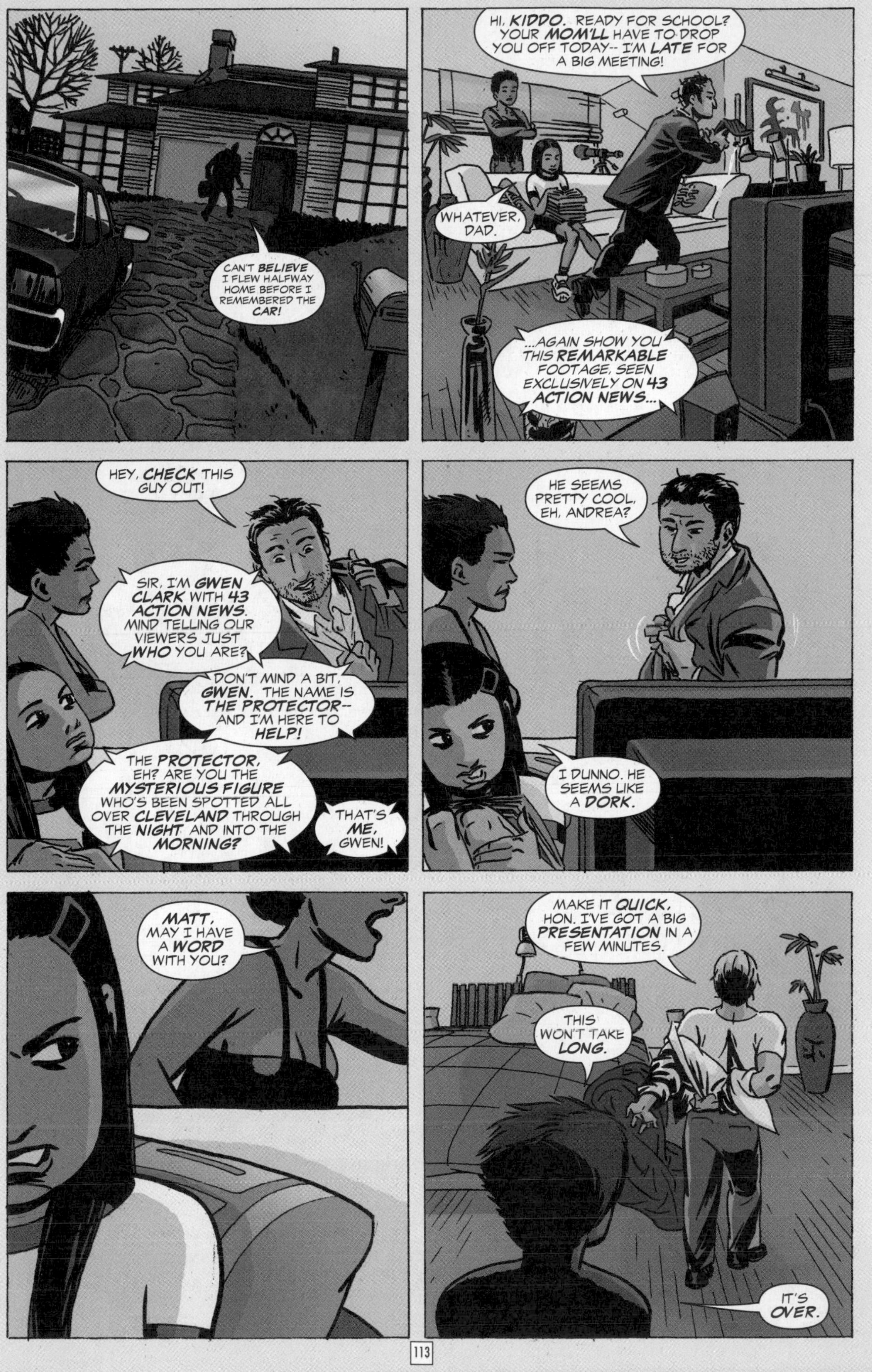
CAN'T BELIEVE I FLEW HALFWAY HOME BEFORE I REMEMBERED THE CAR!
HI, KIDDO. READY FOR SCHOOL? YOUR MOM'LL HAVE TO DROP YOU OFF TODAY-- I'M LATE FOR A BIG MEETING!
WHATEVER, DAD.
...AGAIN SHOW YOU THIS REMARKABLE FOOTAGE, SEEN EXCLUSIVELY ON 43 ACTION NEWS...
HEY, CHECK THIS GUY OUT!
SIR, I'M GWEN CLARK WITH 43 ACTION NEWS. MIND TELLING OUR VIEWERS JUST WHO YOU ARE?
DON'T MIND A BIT, GWEN. THE NAME IS THE PROTECTOR-- AND I'M HERE TO HELP!
THE PROTECTOR, EH? ARE YOU THE MYSTERIOUS FIGURE WHO'S BEEN SPOTTED ALL OVER CLEVELAND THROUGH THE NIGHT AND INTO THE MORNING?
THAT'S ME, GWEN!
HE SEEMS PRETTY COOL, EH, ANDREA?
I DUNNO. HE SEEMS LIKE A DORK.
MATT, MAY I HAVE A WORD WITH YOU?
MAKE IT QUICK, HON. I'VE GOT A BIG PRESENTATION IN A FEW MINUTES.
THIS WON'T TAKE LONG.
IT'S OVER.

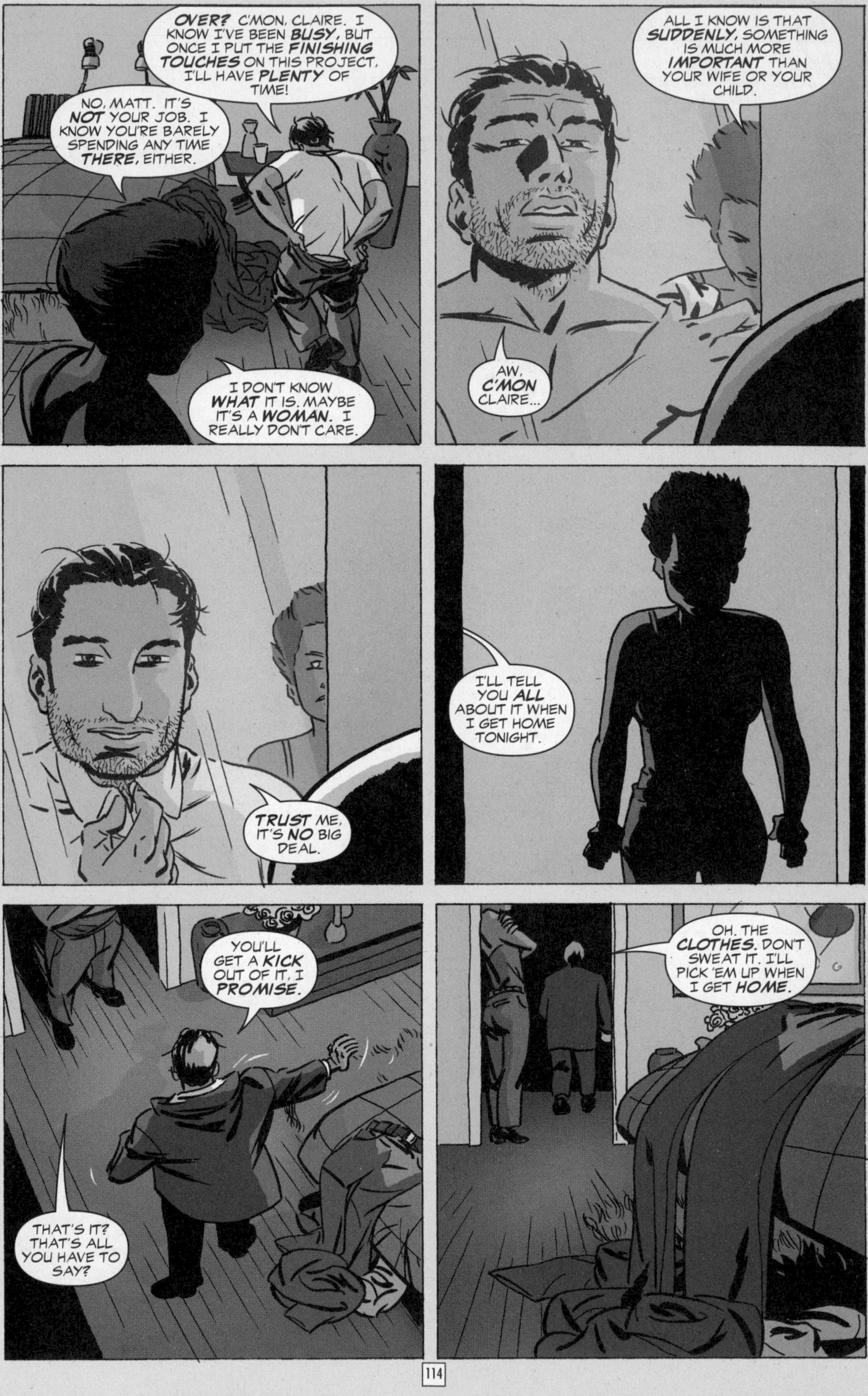
OVER? C'MON, CLAIRE. I KNOW I'VE BEEN BUSY, BUT ONCE I PUT THE FINISHING TOUCHES ON THIS PROJECT, I'LL HAVE PLENTY OF TIME!
NO, MATT. IT'S NOT YOUR JOB. I KNOW YOU'RE BARELY SPENDING ANY TIME THERE, EITHER.
I DON'T KNOW WHAT IT IS. MAYBE IT'S A WOMAN. I REALLY DON'T CARE.
ALL I KNOW IS THAT SUDDENLY, SOMETHING IS MUCH MORE IMPORTANT THAN YOUR WIFE OR YOUR CHILD.
AW, C'MON CLAIRE...
TRUST ME, IT'S NO BIG DEAL.
I'LL TELL YOU ALL ABOUT IT WHEN I GET HOME TONIGHT.
YOU'LL GET A KICK OUT OF IT, I PROMISE.
THAT'S IT? THAT'S ALL YOU HAVE TO SAY?
OH. THE CLOTHES. DON'T SWEAT IT. I'LL PICK 'EM UP WHEN I GET HOME.

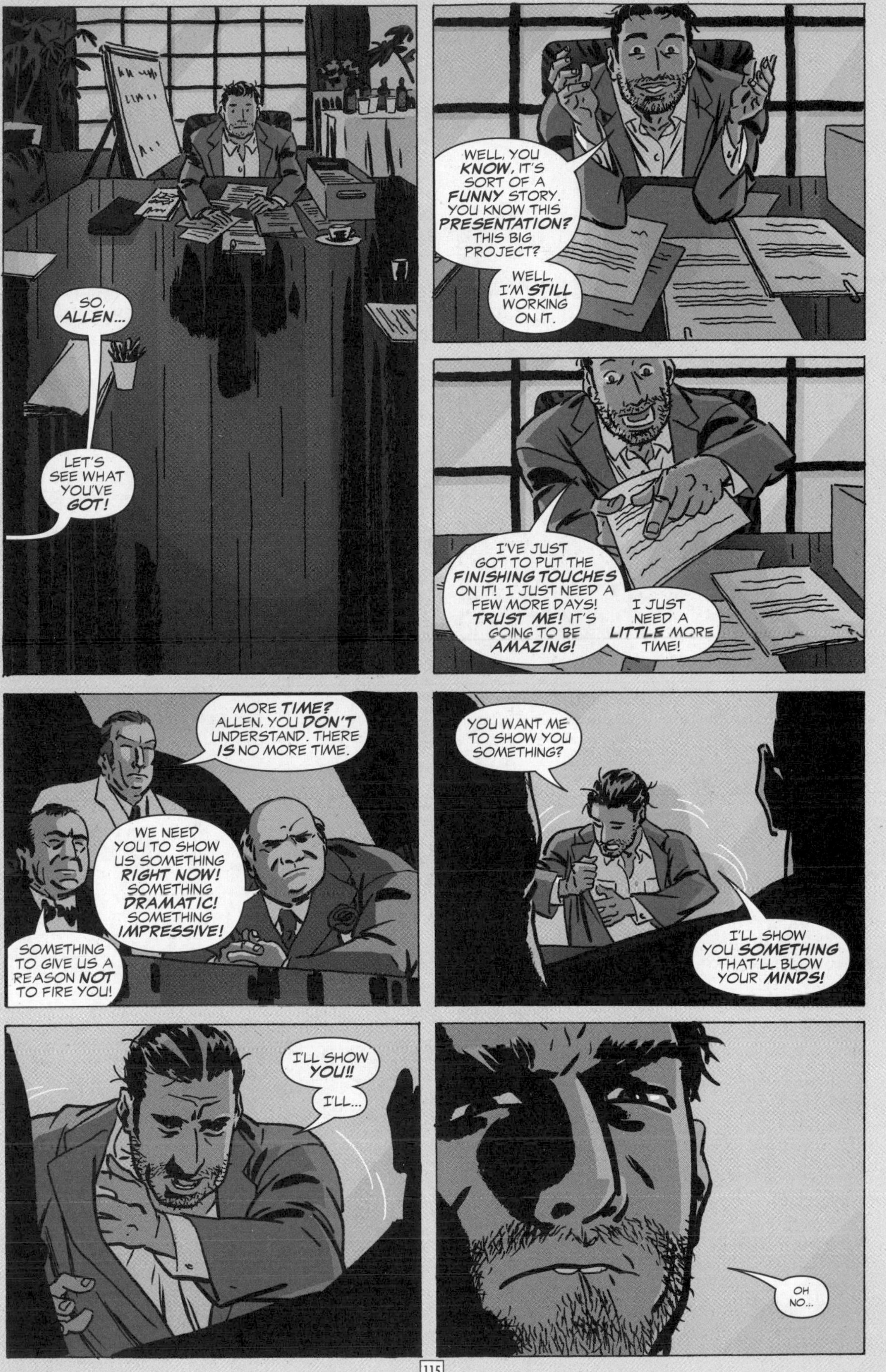
SO, ALLEN...
LET'S SEE WHAT YOU'VE GOT!
WELL, YOU KNOW, IT'S SORT OF A FUNNY STORY. YOU KNOW THIS PRESENTATION? THIS BIG PROJECT?
WELL, I'M STILL WORKING ON IT.
I'VE JUST GOT TO PUT THE FINISHING TOUCHES ON IT! I JUST NEED A FEW MORE DAYS! TRUST ME! IT'S GOING TO BE AMAZING!
I JUST NEED A LITTLE MORE TIME!
MORE TIME? ALLEN, YOU DON'T UNDERSTAND. THERE IS NO MORE TIME.
WE NEED YOU TO SHOW US SOMETHING RIGHT NOW! SOMETHING DRAMATIC! SOMETHING IMPRESSIVE!
SOMETHING TO GIVE US A REASON NOT TO FIRE YOU!
YOU WANT ME TO SHOW YOU SOMETHING?
I'LL SHOW YOU SOMETHING THAT'LL BLOW YOUR MINDS!
I'LL SHOW YOU!!
I'LL...
OH NO...

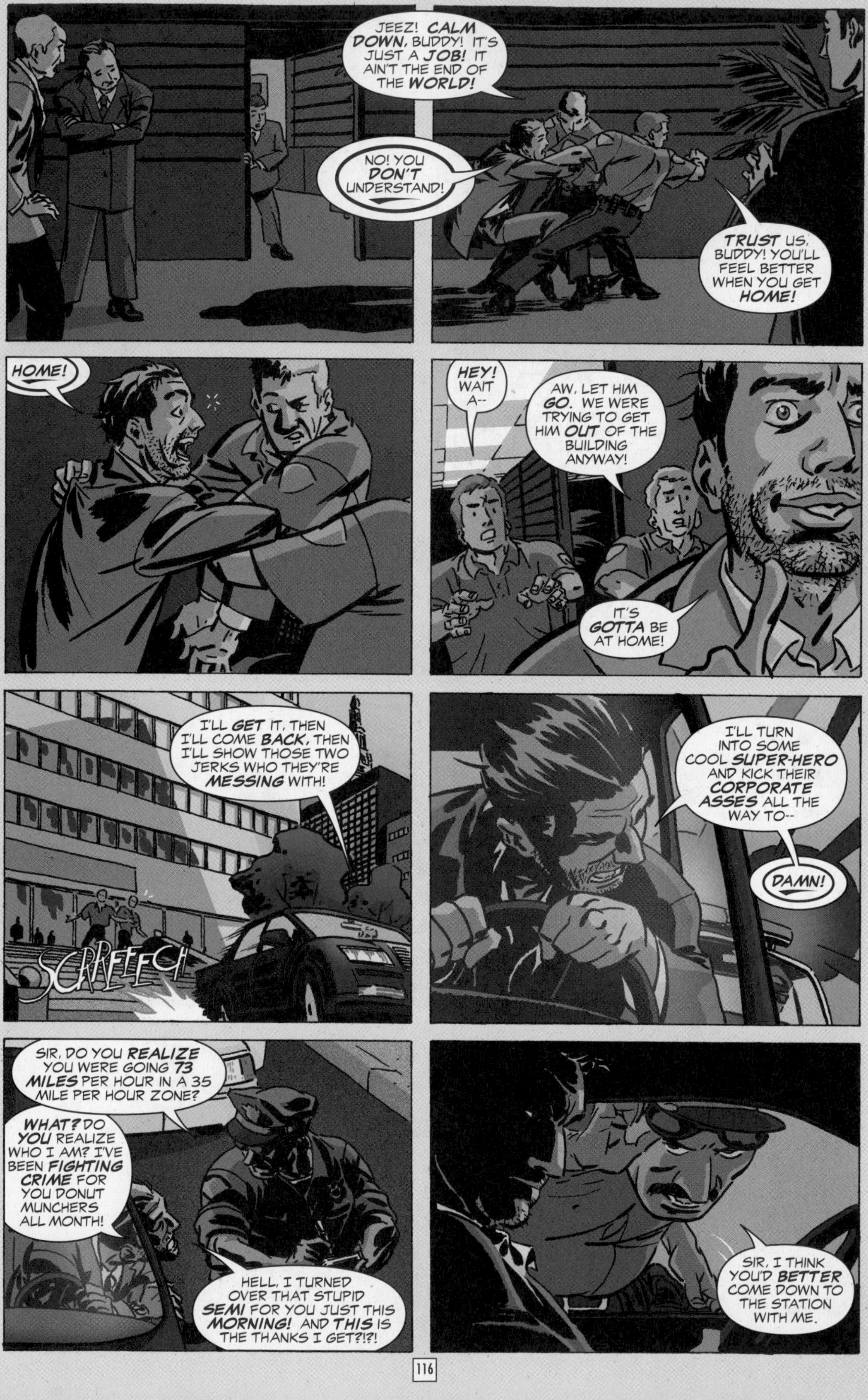
JEEZ! CALM DOWN, BUDDY! IT'S JUST A JOB! IT AIN'T THE END OF THE WORLD!
NO! YOU DON'T UNDERSTAND!
TRUST US, BUDDY! YOU'LL FEEL BETTER WHEN YOU GET HOME!
HOME!
HEY! WAIT A--
AW, LET HIM GO. WE WERE TRYING TO GET HIM OUT OF THE BUILDING ANYWAY!
IT'S GOTTA BE AT HOME!
I'LL GET IT, THEN I'LL COME BACK, THEN I'LL SHOW THOSE TWO JERKS WHO THEY'RE MESSING WITH!
SCREEECH
I'LL TURN INTO SOME COOL SUPER-HERO AND KICK THEIR CORPORATE ASSES ALL THE WAY TO--
DAMN!
SIR, DO YOU REALIZE YOU WERE GOING 73 MILES PER HOUR IN A 35 MILE PER HOUR ZONE?
WHAT? DO YOU REALIZE WHO I AM? I'VE BEEN FIGHTING CRIME FOR YOU DONUT MUNCHERS ALL MONTH!
HELL, I TURNED OVER THAT STUPID SEMI FOR YOU JUST THIS MORNING! AND THIS IS THE THANKS I GET?!?!
SIR, I THINK YOU'D BETTER COME DOWN TO THE STATION WITH ME.

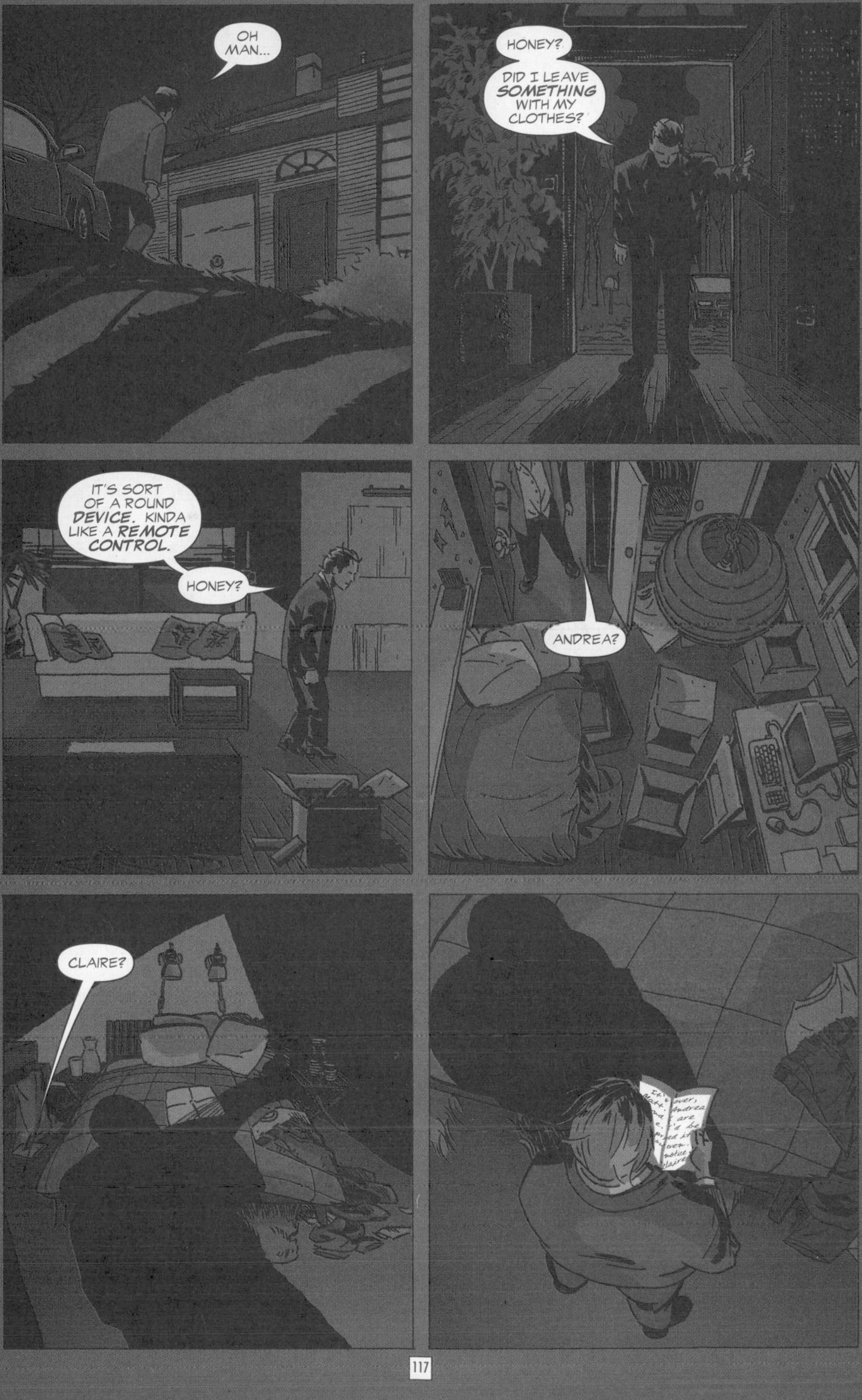
OH MAN...
HONEY?
DID I LEAVE SOMETHING WITH MY CLOTHES?
IT'S SORT OF A ROUND DEVICE. KINDA LIKE A REMOTE CONTROL.
HONEY?
ANDREA?
CLAIRE?

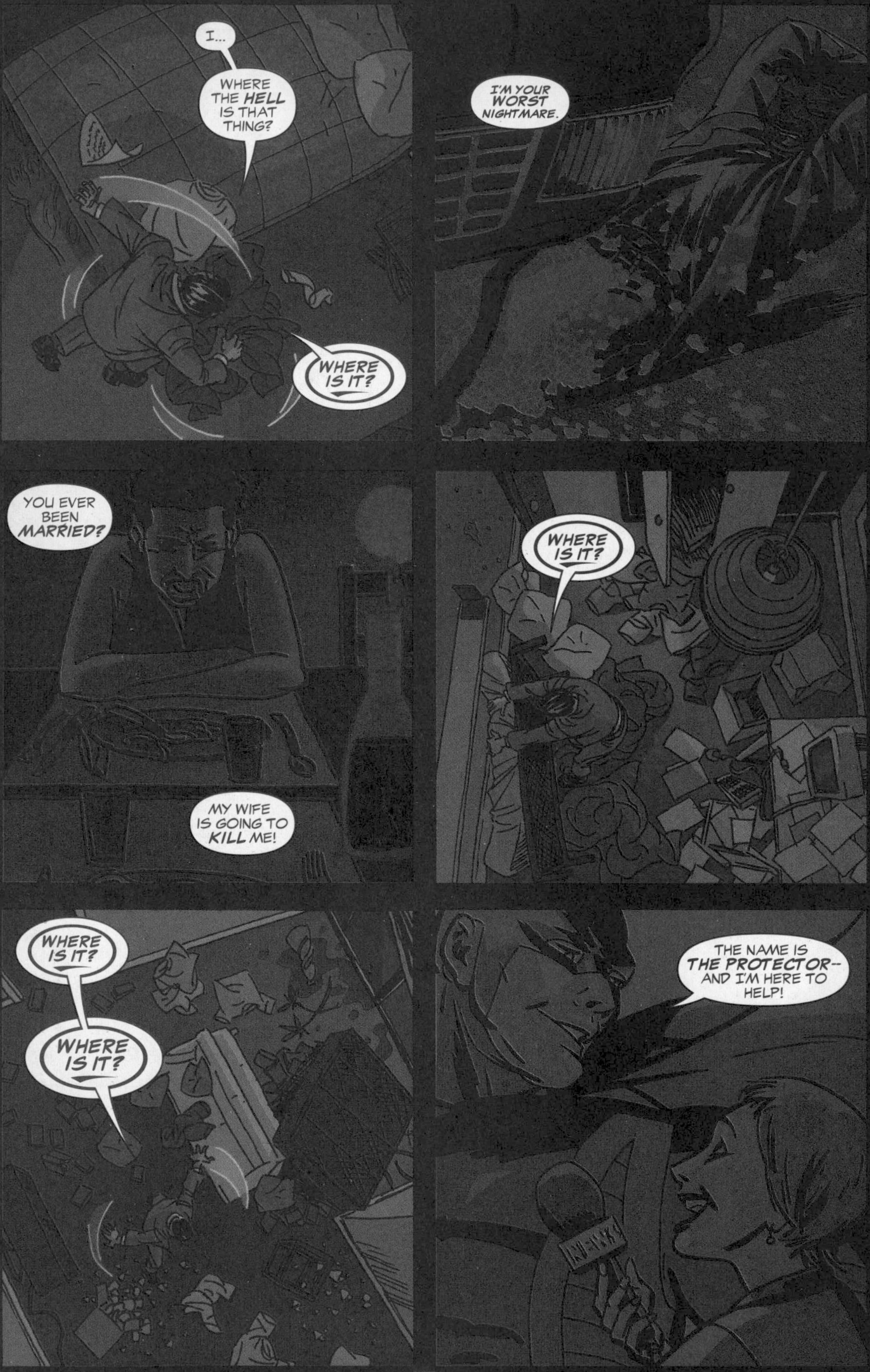
I...
WHERE THE HELL IS THAT THING?
WHERE IS IT?
I'M YOUR WORST NIGHTMARE.
YOU EVER BEEN MARRIED?
MY WIFE IS GOING TO KILL ME!
WHERE IS IT?
WHERE IS IT?
WHERE IS IT?
THE NAME IS THE PROTECTOR-- AND I'M HERE TO HELP!

MEET MATT ALLEN!
HE'S A YOUNG MAN ON THE GO!
DAMN IT...
WHERE IS IT?
It's over, Matt. Andrea and I are gone. I'd be surprised if you ever notice.
Claire

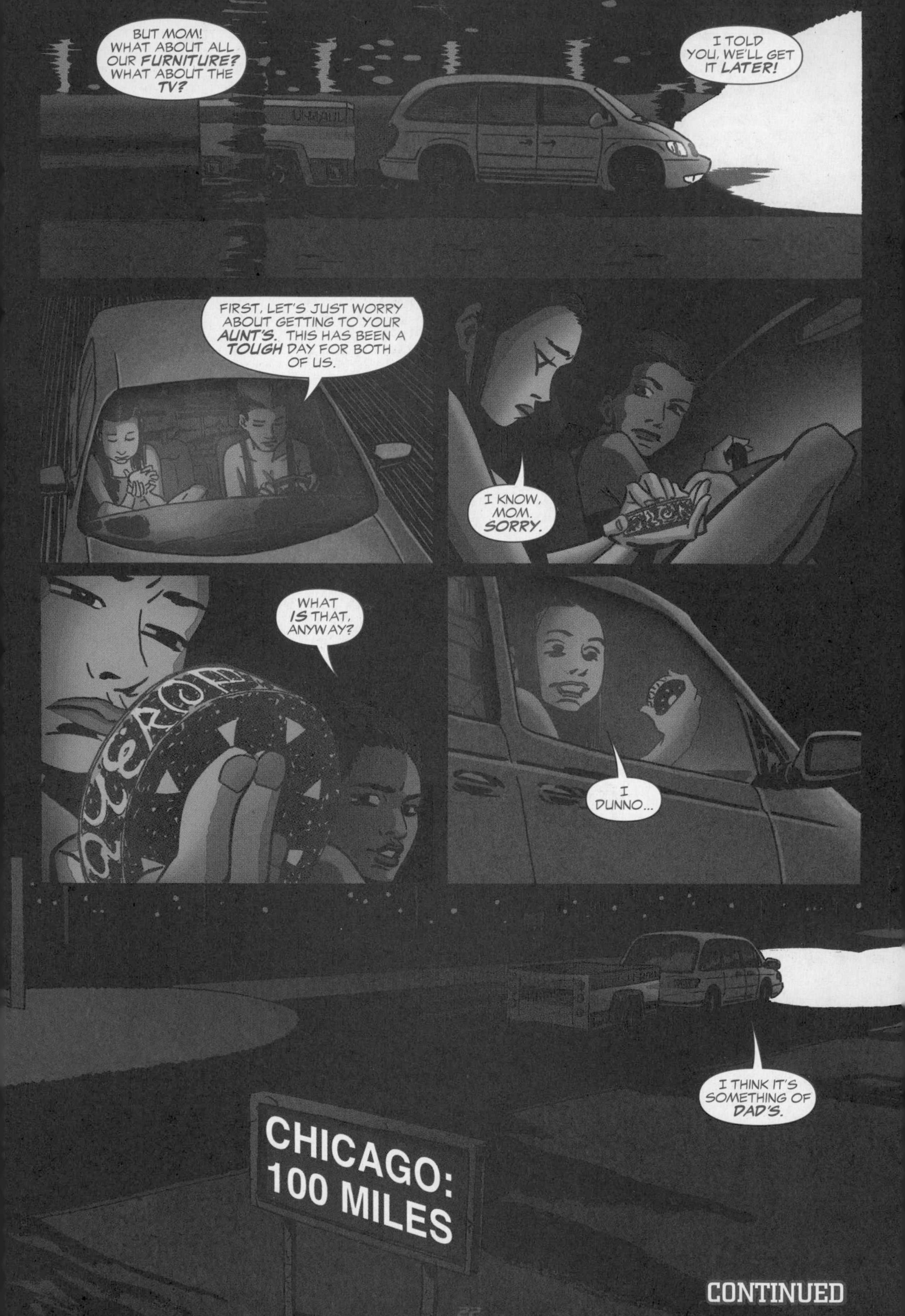
BUT MOM! WHAT ABOUT ALL OUR FURNITURE? WHAT ABOUT THE TV?
I TOLD YOU, WE'LL GET IT LATER!
FIRST, LET'S JUST WORRY ABOUT GETTING TO YOUR AUNT'S. THIS HAS BEEN A TOUGH DAY FOR BOTH OF US.
I KNOW, MOM. SORRY.
WHAT IS THAT, ANYWAY?
I DUNNO...
I THINK IT'S SOMETHING OF DAD'S.
CHICAGO: 100 MILES
CONTINUED

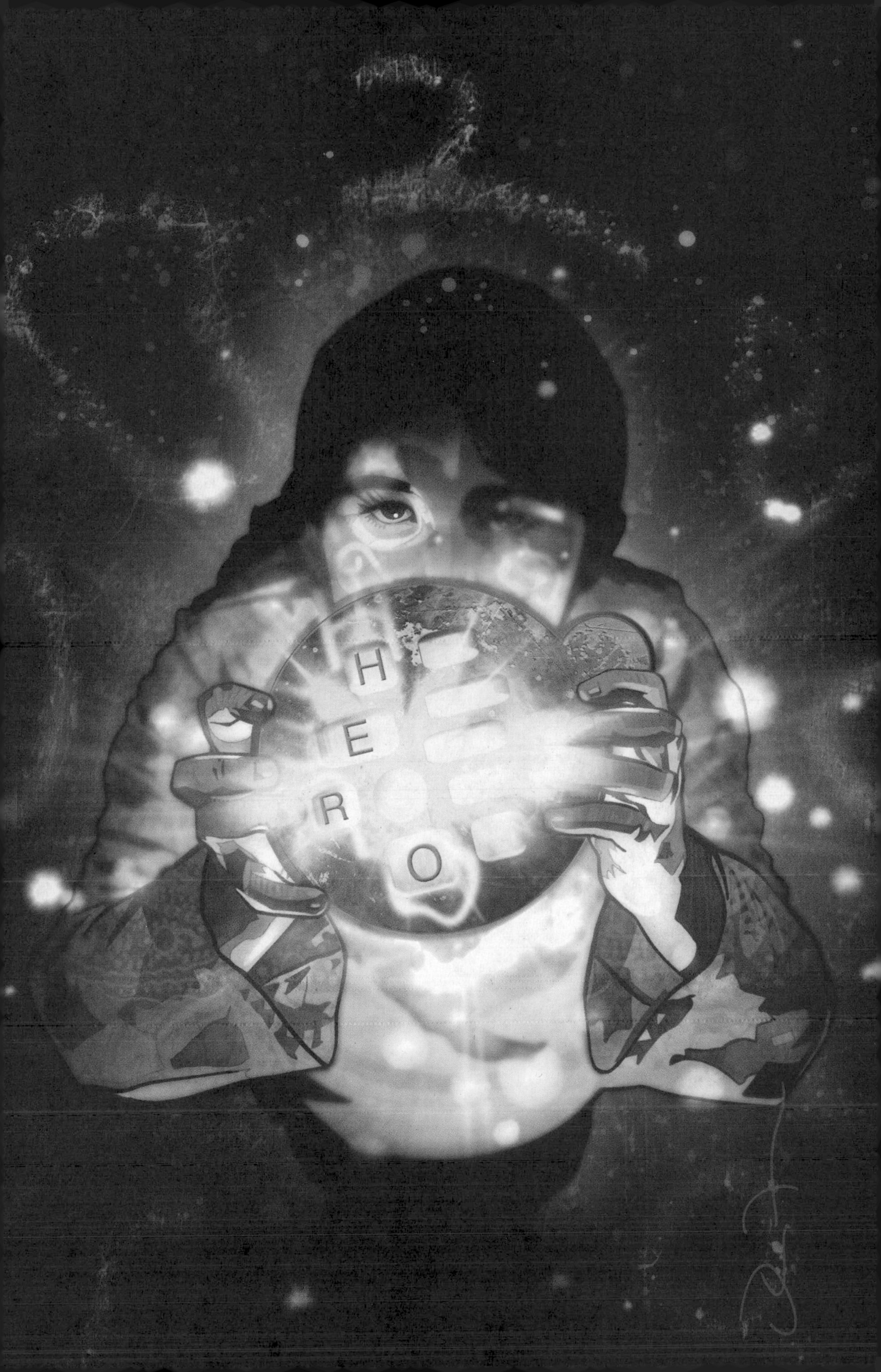
H
E
R
O

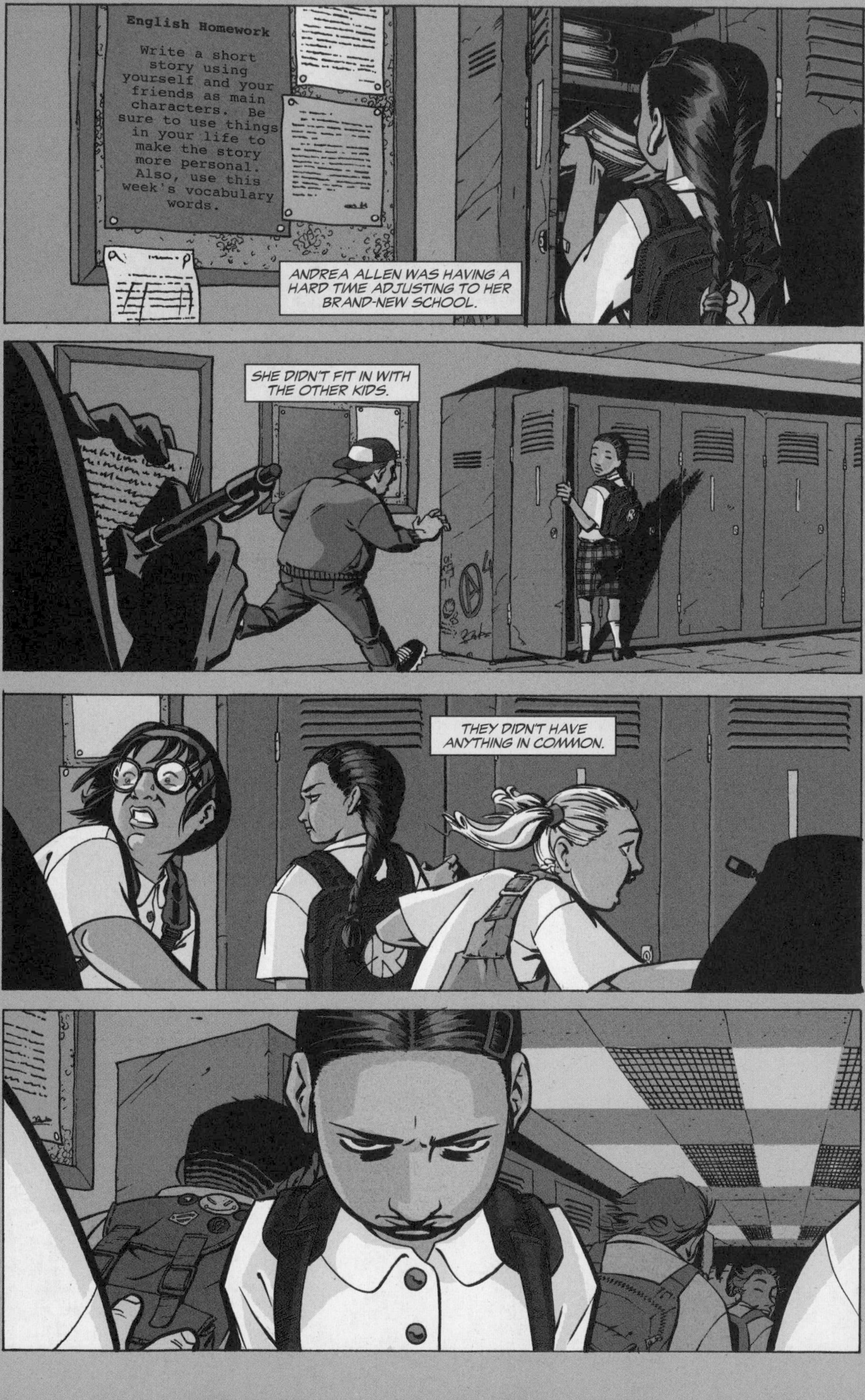
English Homework
Write a short story using yourself and your friends as main characters. Be sure to use things in your life to make the story more personal. Also, use this week's vocabulary words.
ANDREA ALLEN WAS HAVING A HARD TIME ADJUSTING TO HER BRAND-NEW SCHOOL.
SHE DIDN'T FIT IN WITH THE OTHER KIDS.
THEY DIDN'T HAVE ANYTHING IN COMMON.

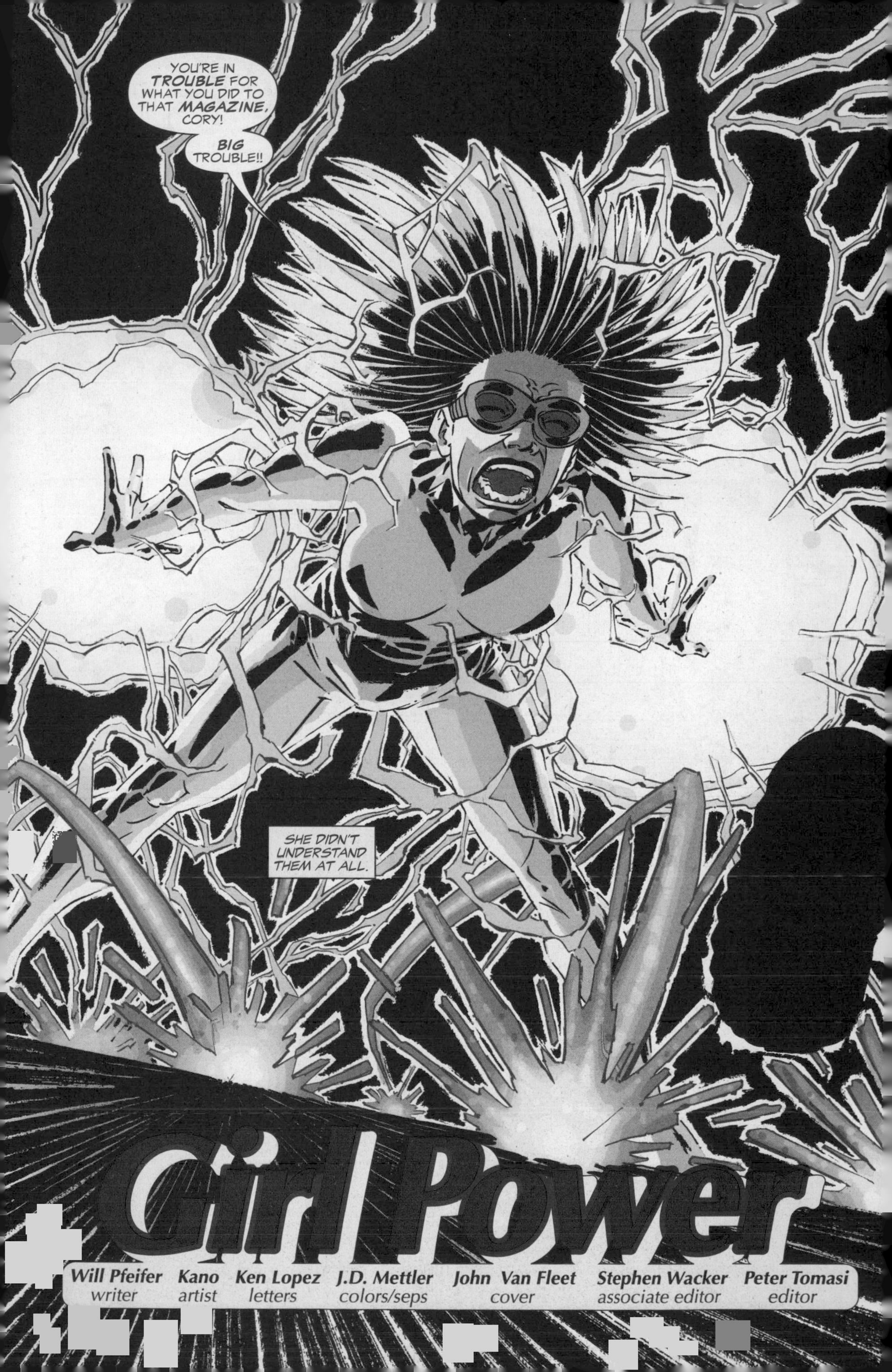
YOU'RE IN TROUBLE FOR WHAT YOU DID TO THAT MAGAZINE, CORY!
BIG TROUBLE!!
SHE DIDN'T UNDERSTAND THEM AT ALL.
Girl Power
Will Pfeifer writer
Kano artist
Ken Lopez letters
J.D. Mettler colors/seps
John Van Fleet cover
Stephen Wacker associate editor
Peter Tomasi editor

SHE'S THE ONE WHO'S GONNA BE IN *TROUBLE*...

WHERE DID SHE GO?

D-DOWN THE HALL...

GRRRRR!

HEY!

A-ANDREA!

WHAT DO *YOU* WANT?

YOU KNOW WHAT I *WANT!*

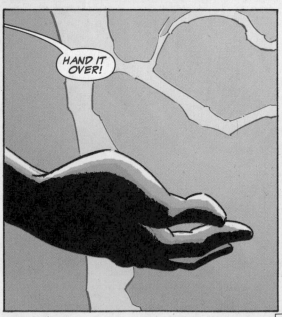

HAND IT OVER!

SHE DIDN'T THINK THIS WOULD BE SO HARD...

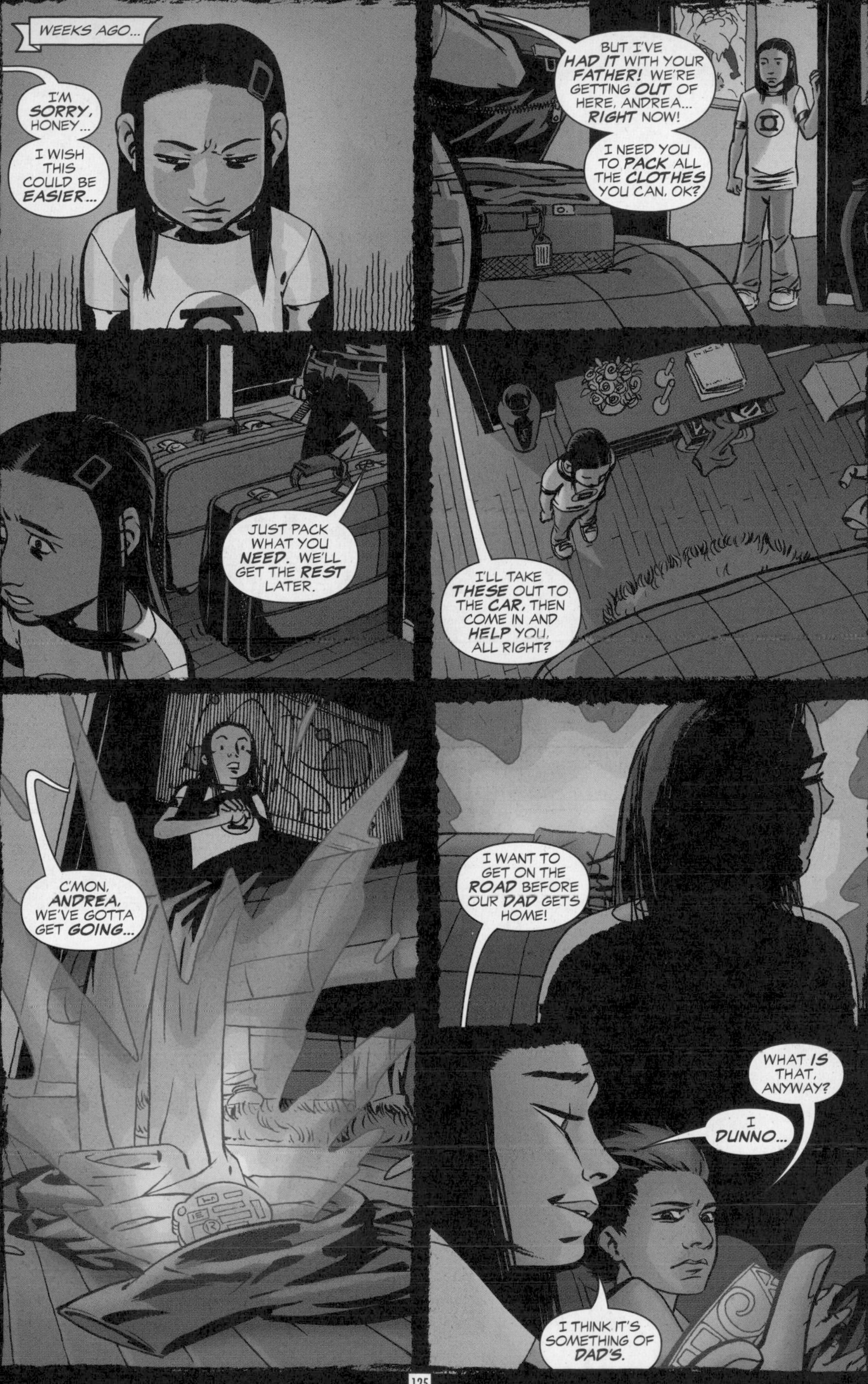
WEEKS AGO...
I'M SORRY, HONEY...
I WISH THIS COULD BE EASIER...
BUT I'VE HAD IT WITH YOUR FATHER! WE'RE GETTING OUT OF HERE, ANDREA... RIGHT NOW!
I NEED YOU TO PACK ALL THE CLOTHES YOU CAN, OK?
JUST PACK WHAT YOU NEED. WE'LL GET THE REST LATER.
I'LL TAKE THESE OUT TO THE CAR, THEN COME IN AND HELP YOU, ALL RIGHT?
C'MON, ANDREA, WE'VE GOTTA GET GOING...
I WANT TO GET ON THE ROAD BEFORE OUR DAD GETS HOME!
WHAT IS THAT, ANYWAY?
I DUNNO...
I THINK IT'S SOMETHING OF DAD'S.

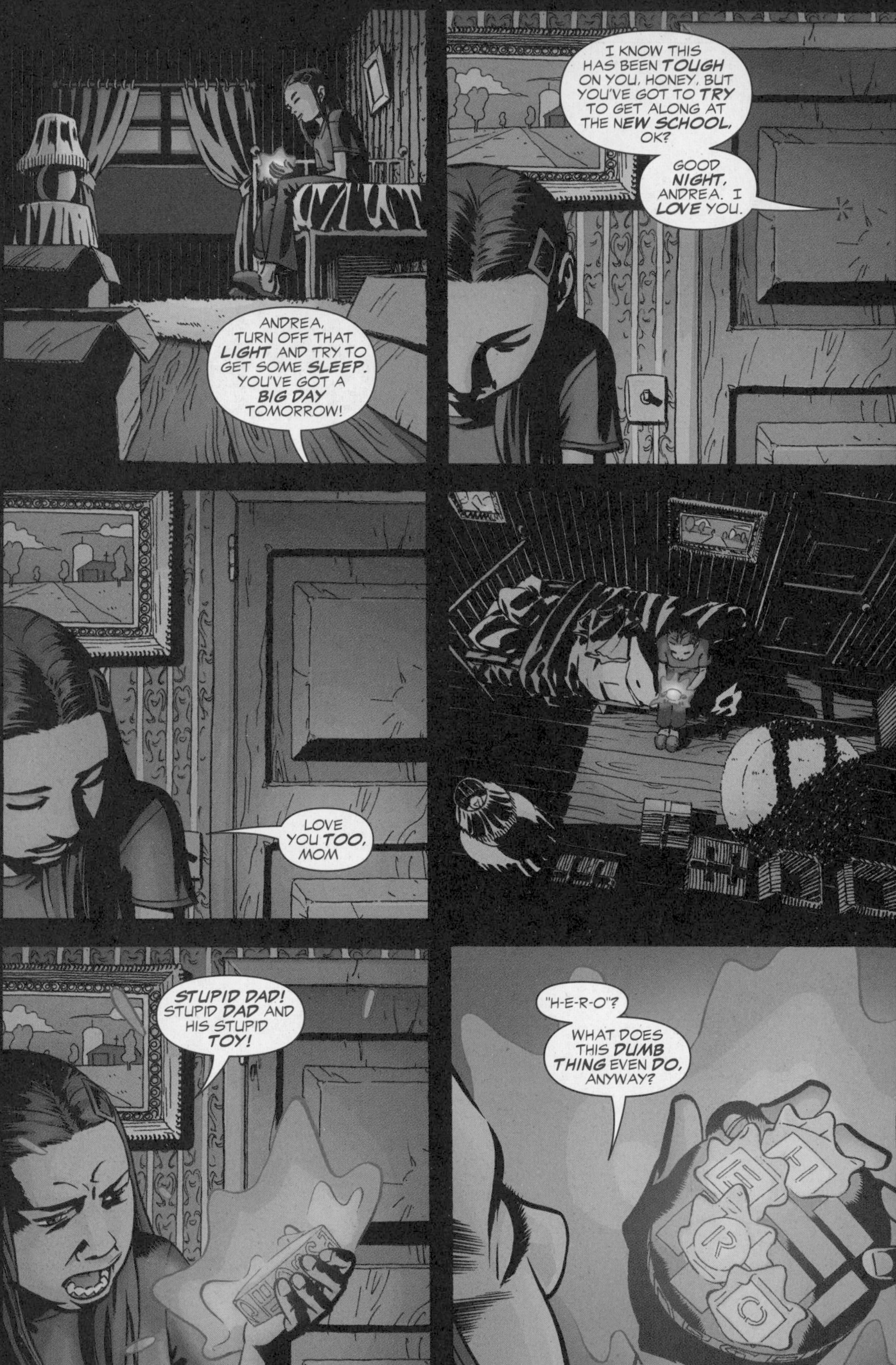
ANDREA, TURN OFF THAT LIGHT AND TRY TO GET SOME SLEEP. YOU'VE GOT A BIG DAY TOMORROW!
I KNOW THIS HAS BEEN TOUGH ON YOU, HONEY, BUT YOU'VE GOT TO TRY TO GET ALONG AT THE NEW SCHOOL, OK?
GOOD NIGHT, ANDREA. I LOVE YOU.
LOVE YOU TOO, MOM
STUPID DAD! STUPID DAD AND HIS STUPID TOY!
"H-E-R-O"?
WHAT DOES THIS DUMB THING EVEN DO, ANYWAY?

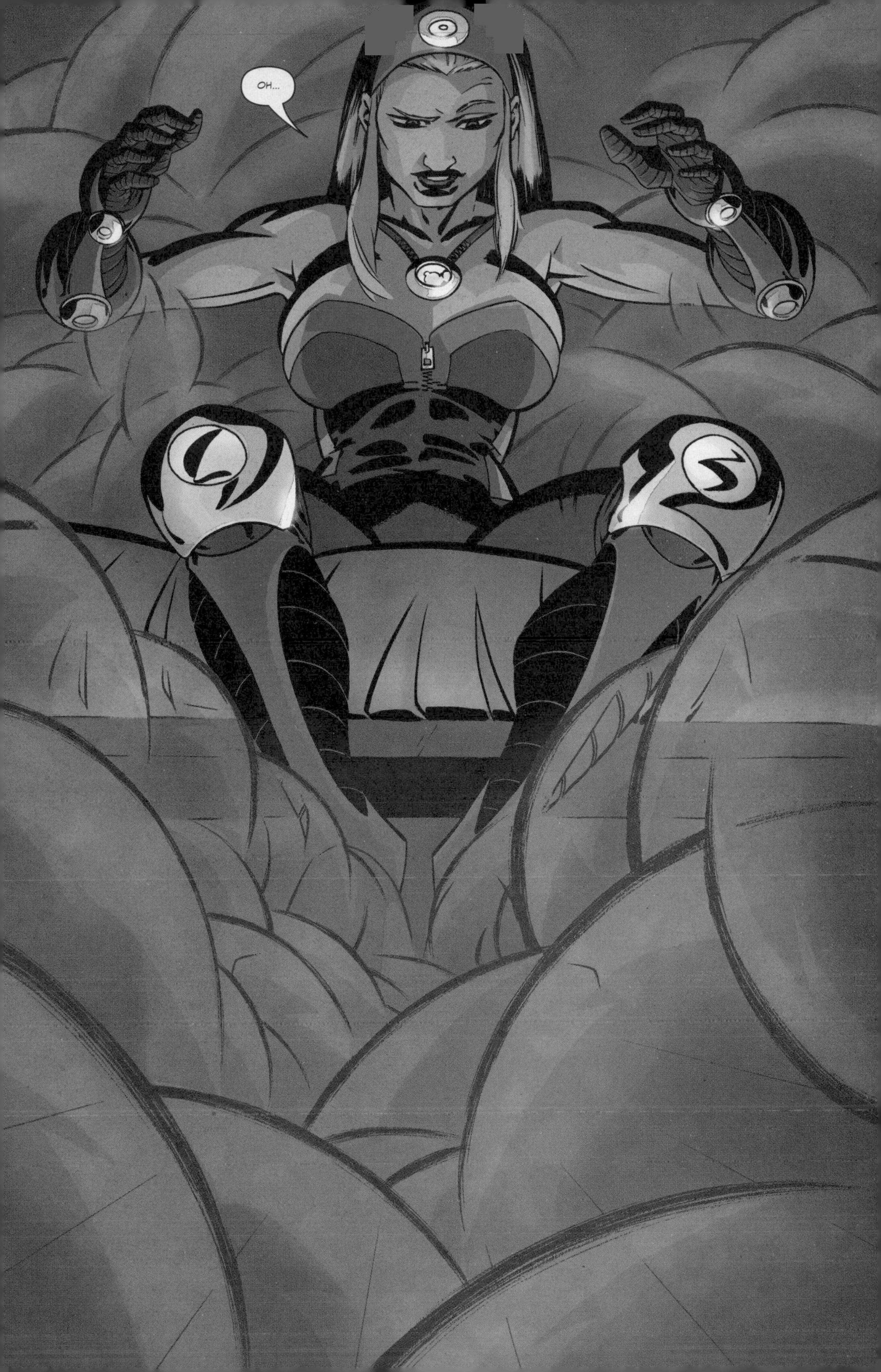
OH...

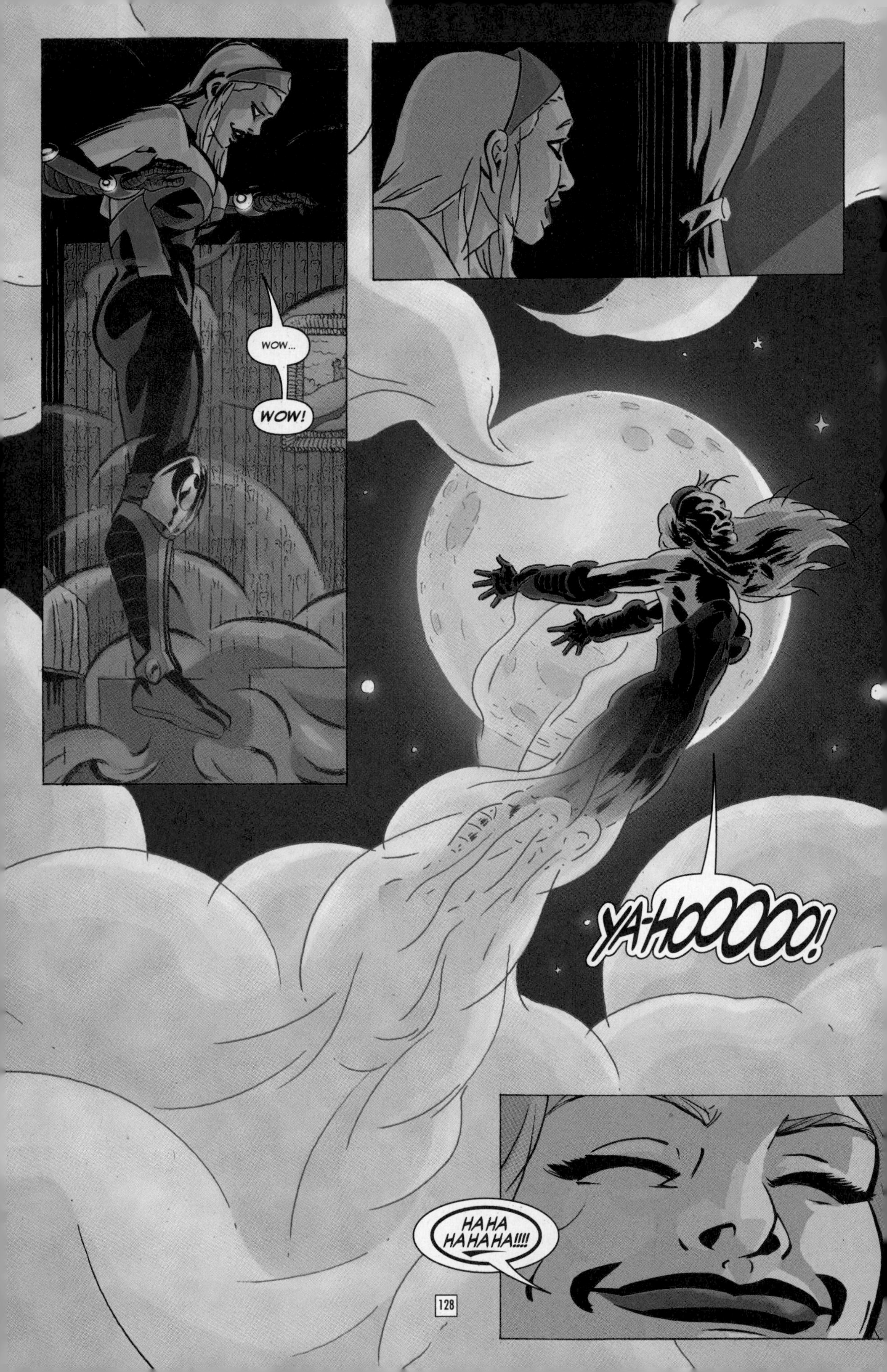
WOW...
WOW!
YA-HOOOOOO!
HAHA HAHAHA!!!!

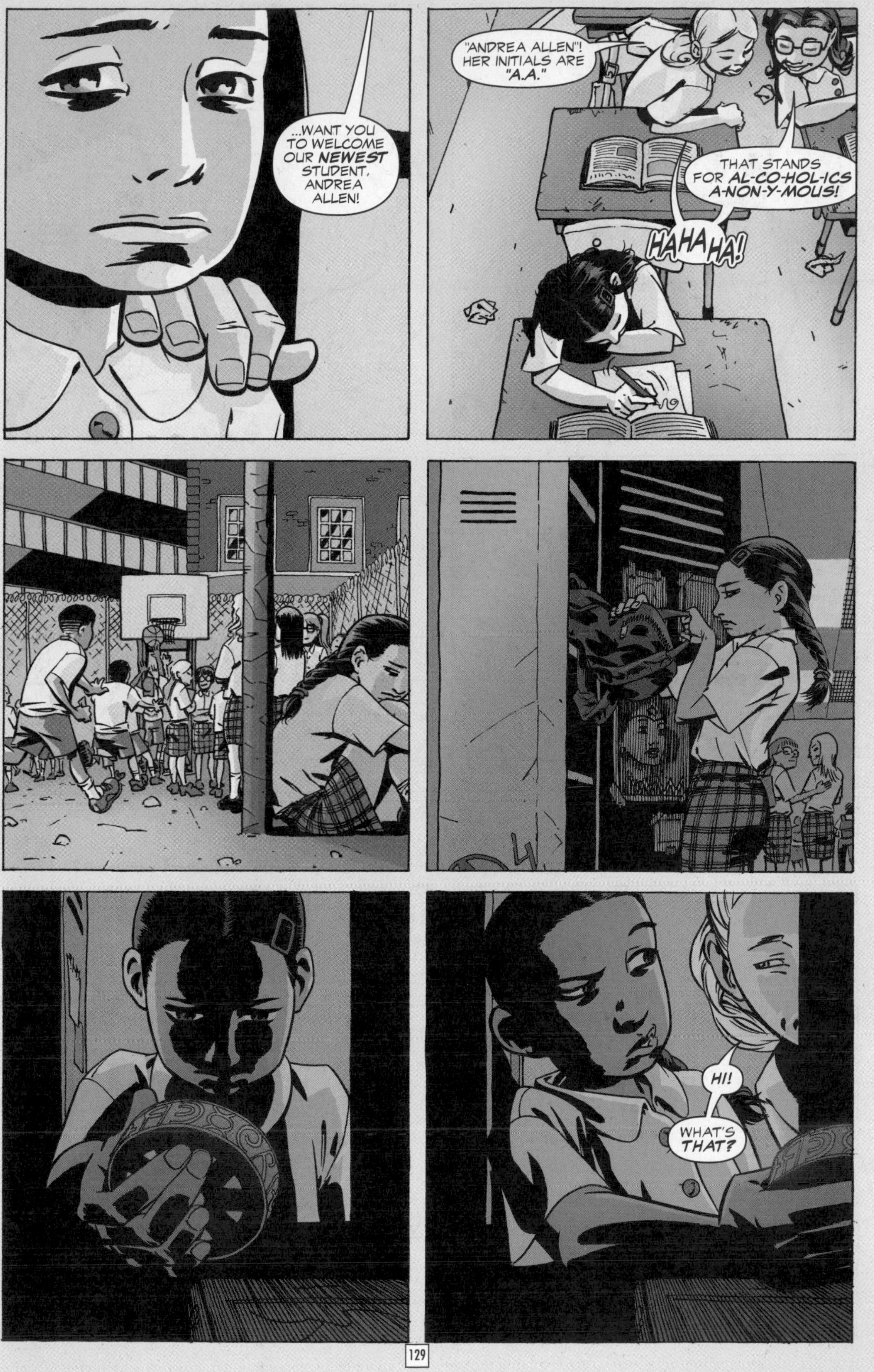
...WANT YOU TO WELCOME OUR NEWEST STUDENT, ANDREA ALLEN!
"ANDREA ALLEN"! HER INITIALS ARE "A.A."
THAT STANDS FOR AL-CO-HOL-ICS A-NON-Y-MOUS!
HAHAHA!
HI!
WHAT'S THAT?

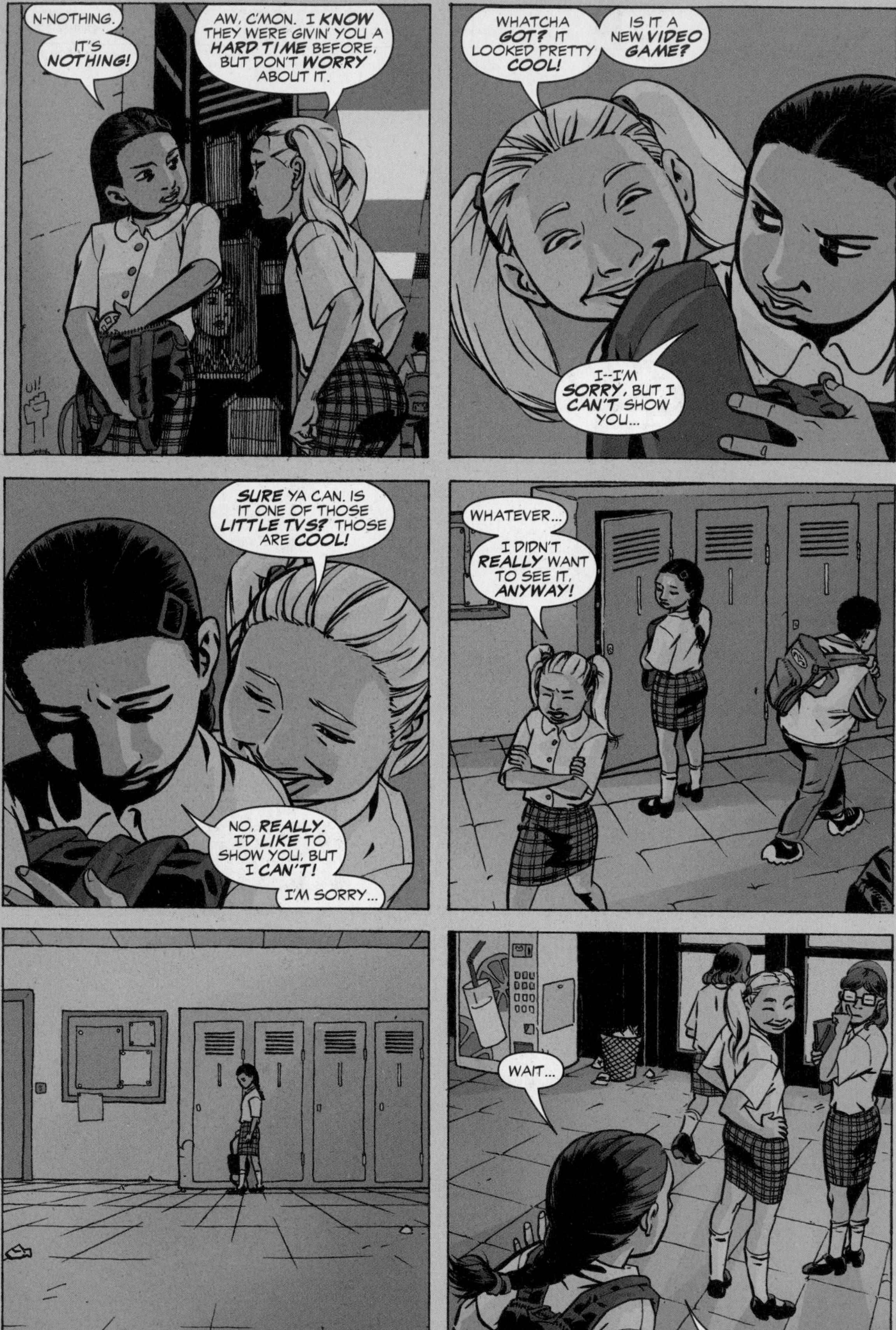
N-NOTHING.
IT'S NOTHING!
AW, C'MON. I KNOW THEY WERE GIVIN' YOU A HARD TIME BEFORE, BUT DON'T WORRY ABOUT IT.
WHATCHA GOT? IT LOOKED PRETTY COOL!
IS IT A NEW VIDEO GAME?
I--I'M SORRY, BUT I CAN'T SHOW YOU...
SURE YA CAN. IS IT ONE OF THOSE LITTLE TVS? THOSE ARE COOL!
NO, REALLY. I'D LIKE TO SHOW YOU, BUT I CAN'T!
I'M SORRY...
WHATEVER...
I DIDN'T REALLY WANT TO SEE IT, ANYWAY!
WAIT...
CAN YOU KEEP A SECRET?

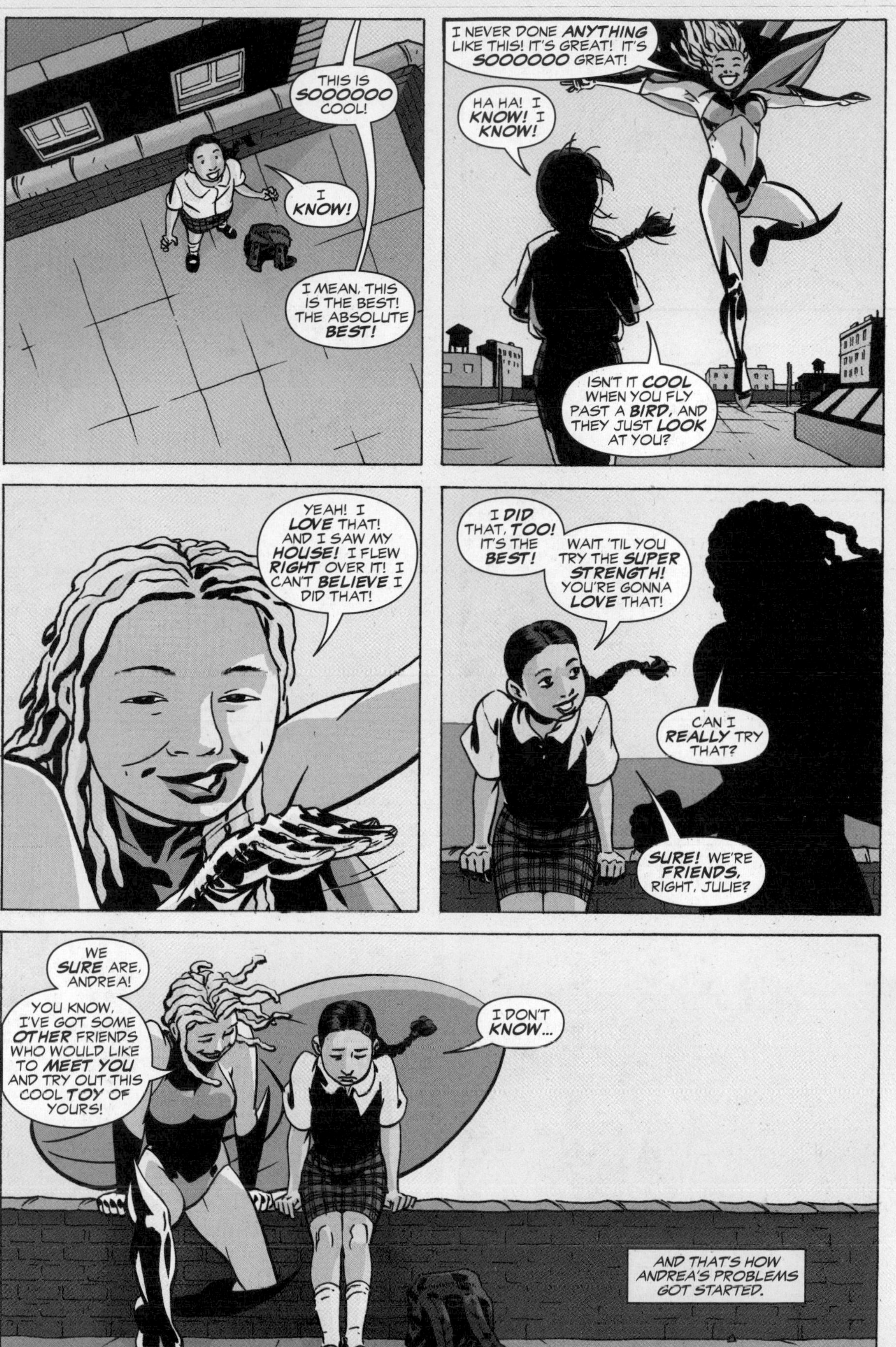

THIS IS SOOOOOO COOL!
I KNOW!
I MEAN, THIS IS THE BEST! THE ABSOLUTE BEST!
I NEVER DONE ANYTHING LIKE THIS! IT'S GREAT! IT'S SOOOOOO GREAT!
HA HA! I KNOW! I KNOW!
ISN'T IT COOL WHEN YOU FLY PAST A BIRD, AND THEY JUST LOOK AT YOU?
YEAH! I LOVE THAT! AND I SAW MY HOUSE! I FLEW RIGHT OVER IT! I CAN'T BELIEVE I DID THAT!
I DID THAT, TOO! IT'S THE BEST!
WAIT 'TIL YOU TRY THE SUPER STRENGTH! YOU'RE GONNA LOVE THAT!
CAN I REALLY TRY THAT?
SURE! WE'RE FRIENDS, RIGHT, JULIE?
WE SURE ARE, ANDREA!
YOU KNOW, I'VE GOT SOME OTHER FRIENDS WHO WOULD LIKE TO MEET YOU AND TRY OUT THIS COOL TOY OF YOURS!
I DON'T KNOW...
AND THAT'S HOW ANDREA'S PROBLEMS GOT STARTED.

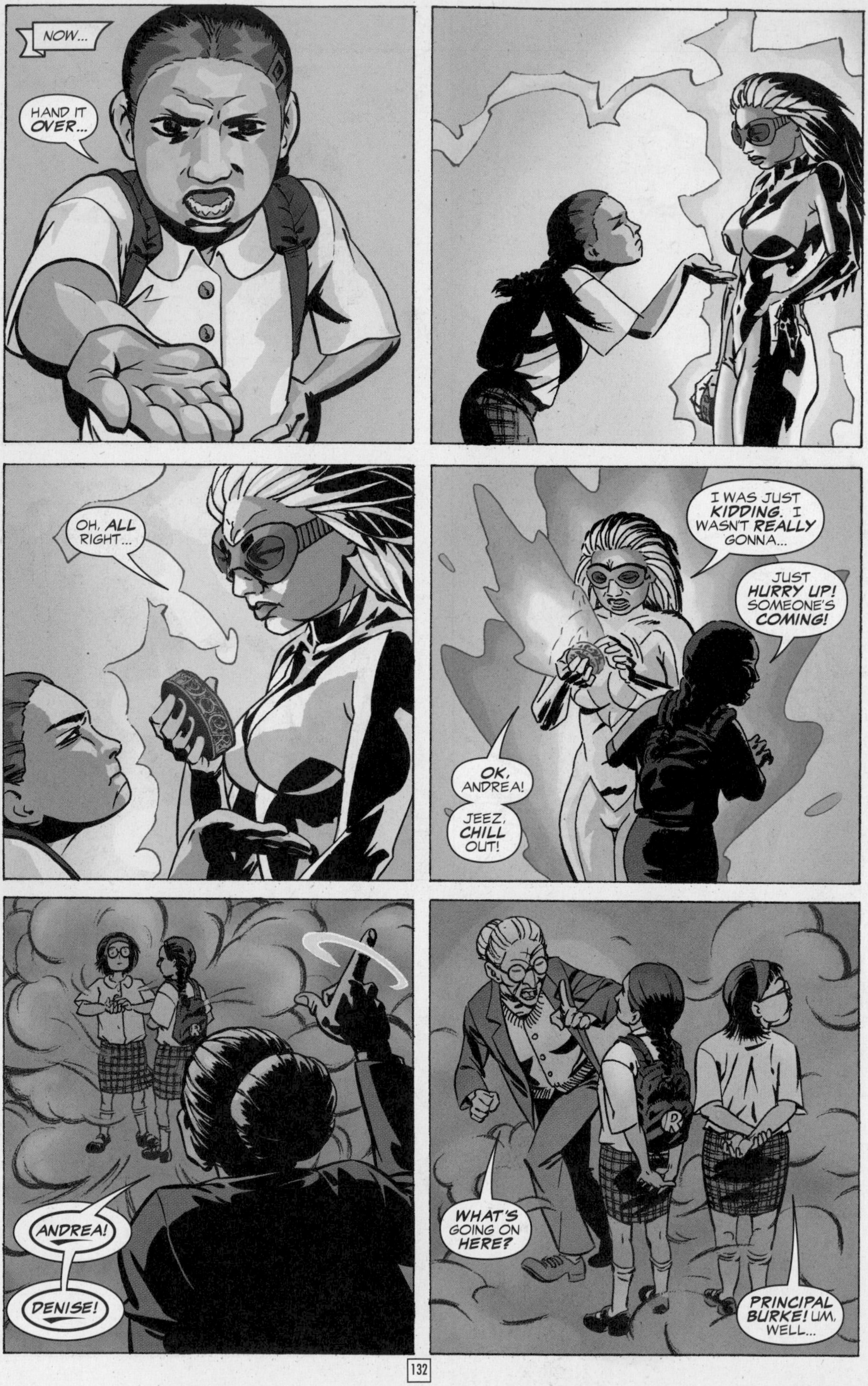
NOW...
HAND IT OVER...
OH, ALL RIGHT...
I WAS JUST KIDDING. I WASN'T REALLY GONNA...
JUST HURRY UP! SOMEONE'S COMING!
OK, ANDREA!
JEEZ, CHILL OUT!
ANDREA!
DENISE!
WHAT'S GOING ON HERE?
PRINCIPAL BURKE! UM, WELL...

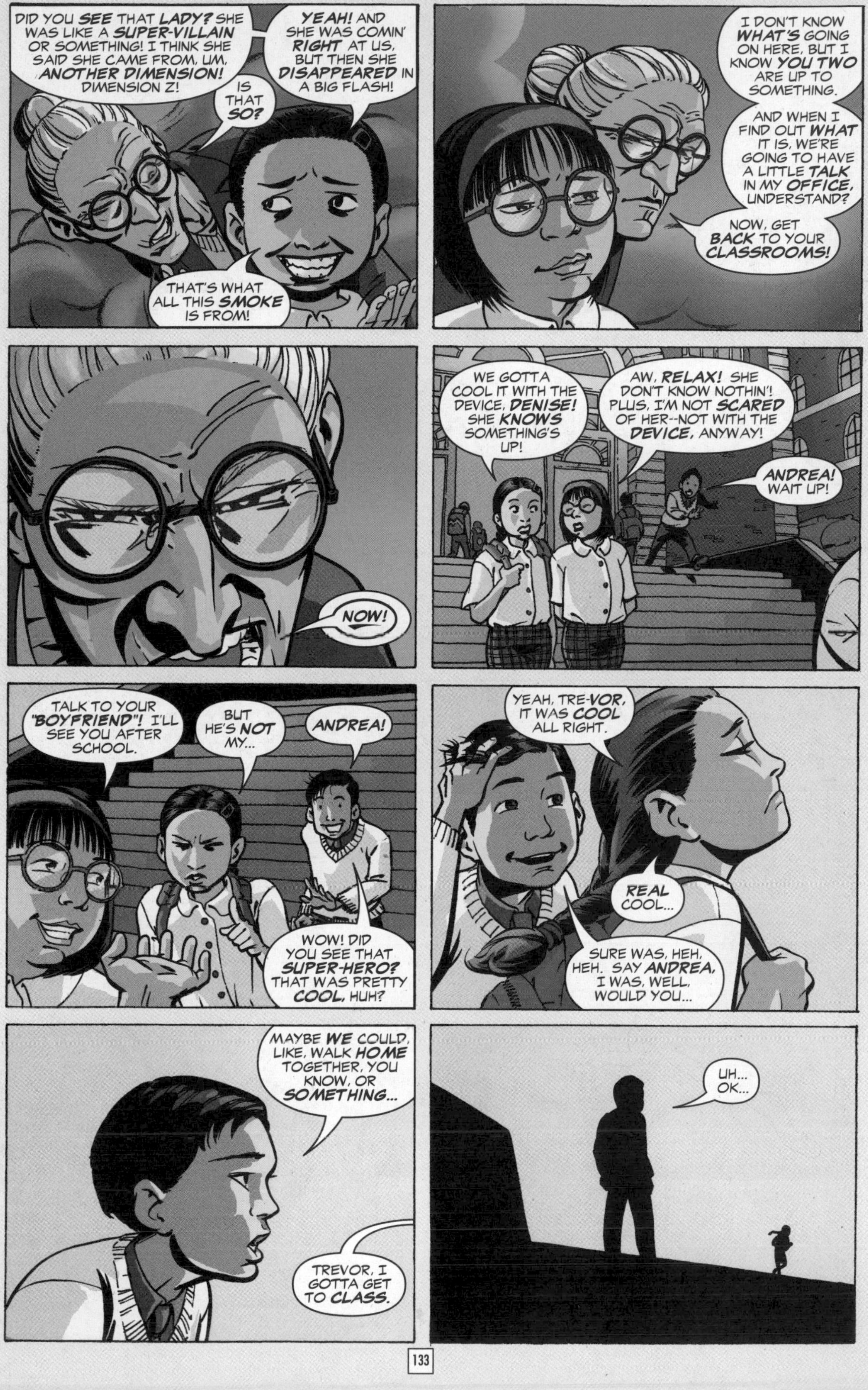
DID YOU SEE THAT LADY? SHE WAS LIKE A SUPER-VILLAIN OR SOMETHING! I THINK SHE SAID SHE CAME FROM, UM, ANOTHER DIMENSION! DIMENSION Z!
YEAH! AND SHE WAS COMIN' RIGHT AT US, BUT THEN SHE DISAPPEARED IN A BIG FLASH!
IS THAT SO?
THAT'S WHAT ALL THIS SMOKE IS FROM!
I DON'T KNOW WHAT'S GOING ON HERE, BUT I KNOW YOU TWO ARE UP TO SOMETHING.
AND WHEN I FIND OUT WHAT IT IS, WE'RE GOING TO HAVE A LITTLE TALK IN MY OFFICE, UNDERSTAND?
NOW, GET BACK TO YOUR CLASSROOMS!
NOW!
WE GOTTA COOL IT WITH THE DEVICE, DENISE! SHE KNOWS SOMETHING'S UP!
AW, RELAX! SHE DON'T KNOW NOTHIN'! PLUS, I'M NOT SCARED OF HER--NOT WITH THE DEVICE, ANYWAY!
ANDREA! WAIT UP!
TALK TO YOUR "BOYFRIEND"! I'LL SEE YOU AFTER SCHOOL.
BUT HE'S NOT MY...
ANDREA!
WOW! DID YOU SEE THAT SUPER-HERO? THAT WAS PRETTY COOL, HUH?
YEAH, TRE-VOR, IT WAS COOL ALL RIGHT.
REAL COOL...
SURE WAS, HEH, HEH. SAY ANDREA, I WAS, WELL, WOULD YOU...
MAYBE WE COULD, LIKE, WALK HOME TOGETHER, YOU KNOW, OR SOMETHING...
TREVOR, I GOTTA GET TO CLASS.
UH... OK...

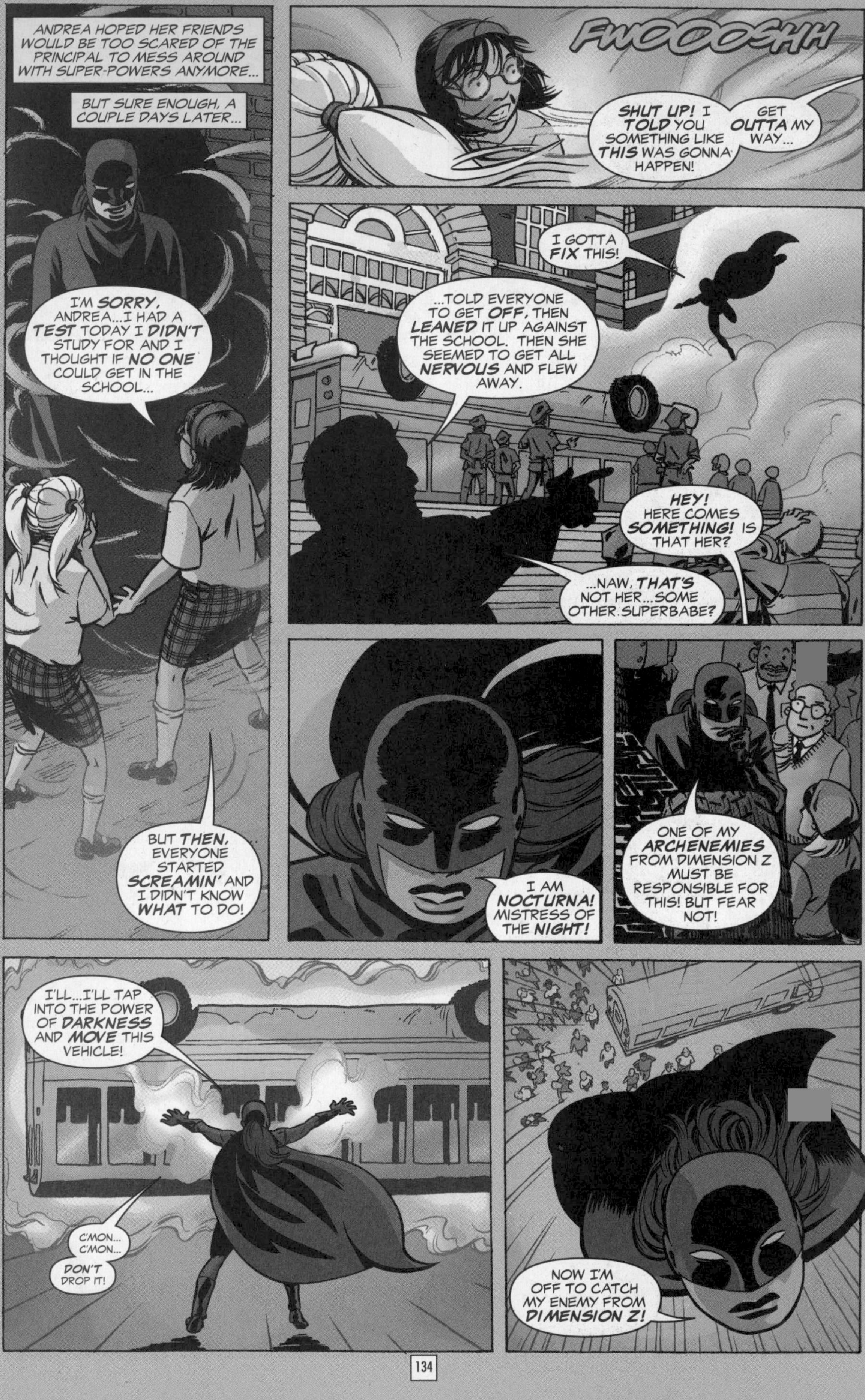
ANDREA HOPED HER FRIENDS WOULD BE TOO SCARED OF THE PRINCIPAL TO MESS AROUND WITH SUPER-POWERS ANYMORE...
BUT SURE ENOUGH, A COUPLE DAYS LATER...
I'M SORRY, ANDREA...I HAD A TEST TODAY I DIDN'T STUDY FOR AND I THOUGHT IF NO ONE COULD GET IN THE SCHOOL...
BUT THEN, EVERYONE STARTED SCREAMIN' AND I DIDN'T KNOW WHAT TO DO!
FWOOOOSHH
SHUT UP! I TOLD YOU SOMETHING LIKE THIS WAS GONNA HAPPEN!
GET OUTTA MY WAY...
I GOTTA FIX THIS!
...TOLD EVERYONE TO GET OFF, THEN LEANED IT UP AGAINST THE SCHOOL. THEN SHE SEEMED TO GET ALL NERVOUS AND FLEW AWAY.
HEY! HERE COMES SOMETHING! IS THAT HER?
...NAW, THAT'S NOT HER...SOME OTHER SUPERBABE?
I AM NOCTURNA! MISTRESS OF THE NIGHT!
ONE OF MY ARCHENEMIES FROM DIMENSION Z MUST BE RESPONSIBLE FOR THIS! BUT FEAR NOT!
I'LL...I'LL TAP INTO THE POWER OF DARKNESS AND MOVE THIS VEHICLE!
C'MON... C'MON...
DON'T DROP IT!
NOW I'M OFF TO CATCH MY ENEMY FROM DIMENSION Z!

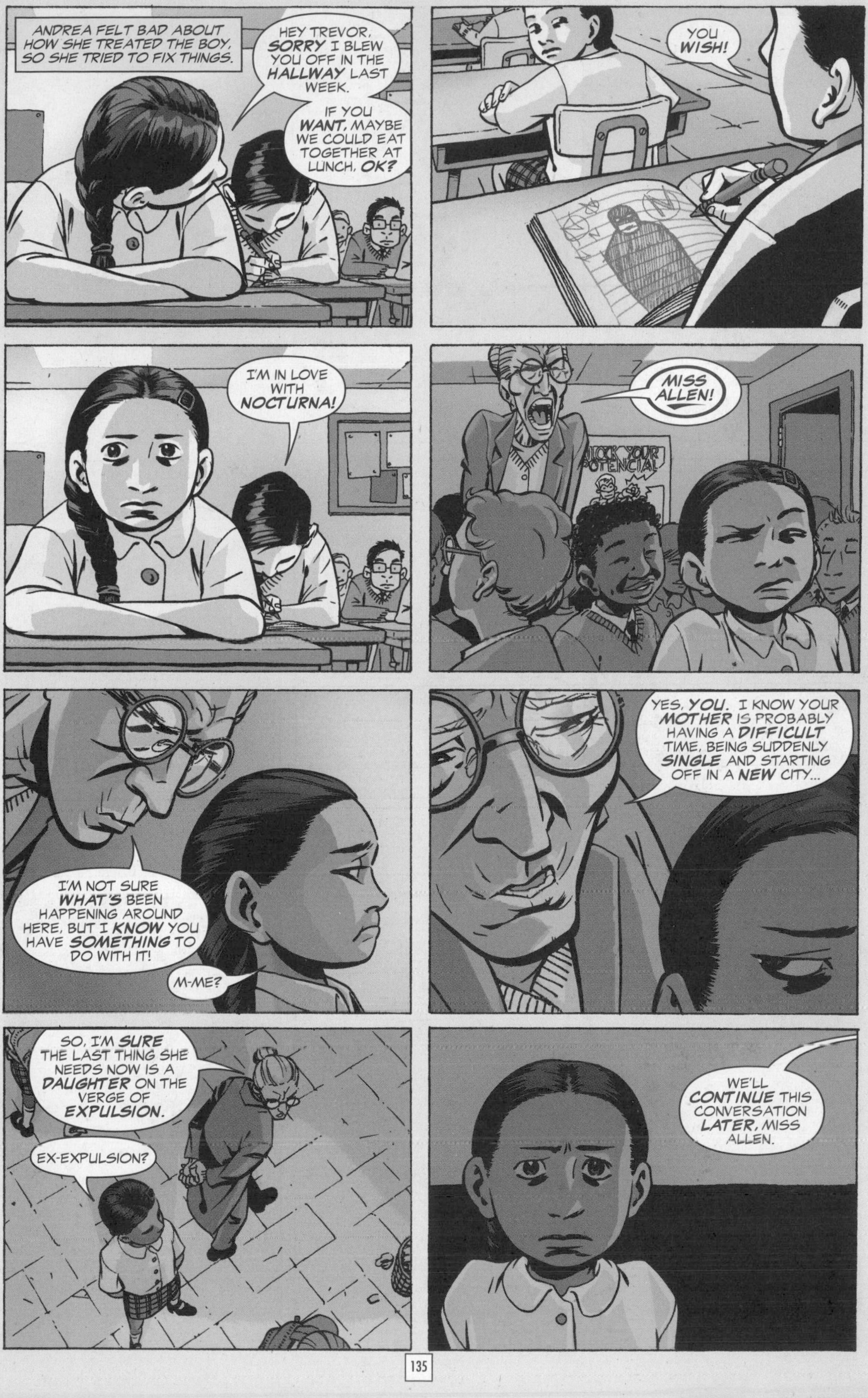
ANDREA FELT BAD ABOUT HOW SHE TREATED THE BOY, SO SHE TRIED TO FIX THINGS.
HEY TREVOR, SORRY I BLEW YOU OFF IN THE HALLWAY LAST WEEK.
IF YOU WANT, MAYBE WE COULD EAT TOGETHER AT LUNCH, OK?
YOU WISH!
I'M IN LOVE WITH NOCTURNA!
MISS ALLEN!
I'M NOT SURE WHAT'S BEEN HAPPENING AROUND HERE, BUT I KNOW YOU HAVE SOMETHING TO DO WITH IT!
M-ME?
YES, YOU. I KNOW YOUR MOTHER IS PROBABLY HAVING A DIFFICULT TIME, BEING SUDDENLY SINGLE AND STARTING OFF IN A NEW CITY...
SO, I'M SURE THE LAST THING SHE NEEDS NOW IS A DAUGHTER ON THE VERGE OF EXPULSION.
EX-EXPULSION?
WE'LL CONTINUE THIS CONVERSATION LATER, MISS ALLEN.

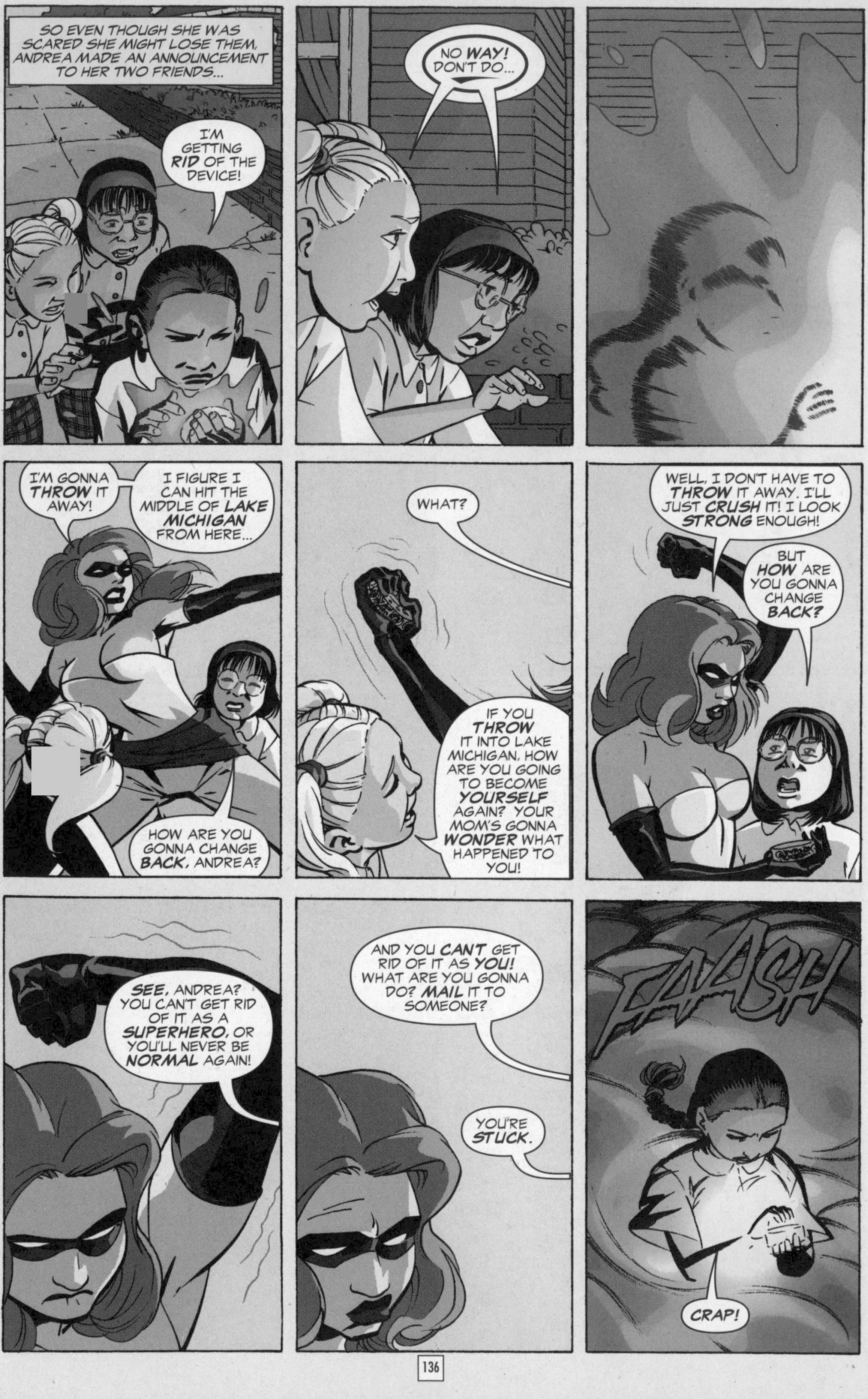
SO EVEN THOUGH SHE WAS SCARED SHE MIGHT LOSE THEM, ANDREA MADE AN ANNOUNCEMENT TO HER TWO FRIENDS...
I'M GETTING RID OF THE DEVICE!
NO WAY! DON'T DO...
I'M GONNA THROW IT AWAY!
I FIGURE I CAN HIT THE MIDDLE OF LAKE MICHIGAN FROM HERE...
HOW ARE YOU GONNA CHANGE BACK, ANDREA?
WHAT?
IF YOU THROW IT INTO LAKE MICHIGAN, HOW ARE YOU GOING TO BECOME YOURSELF AGAIN? YOUR MOM'S GONNA WONDER WHAT HAPPENED TO YOU!
WELL, I DON'T HAVE TO THROW IT AWAY. I'LL JUST CRUSH IT! I LOOK STRONG ENOUGH!
BUT HOW ARE YOU GONNA CHANGE BACK?
SEE, ANDREA? YOU CAN'T GET RID OF IT AS A SUPERHERO, OR YOU'LL NEVER BE NORMAL AGAIN!
AND YOU CAN'T GET RID OF IT AS YOU! WHAT ARE YOU GONNA DO? MAIL IT TO SOMEONE?
YOU'RE STUCK.
FAASH
CRAP!

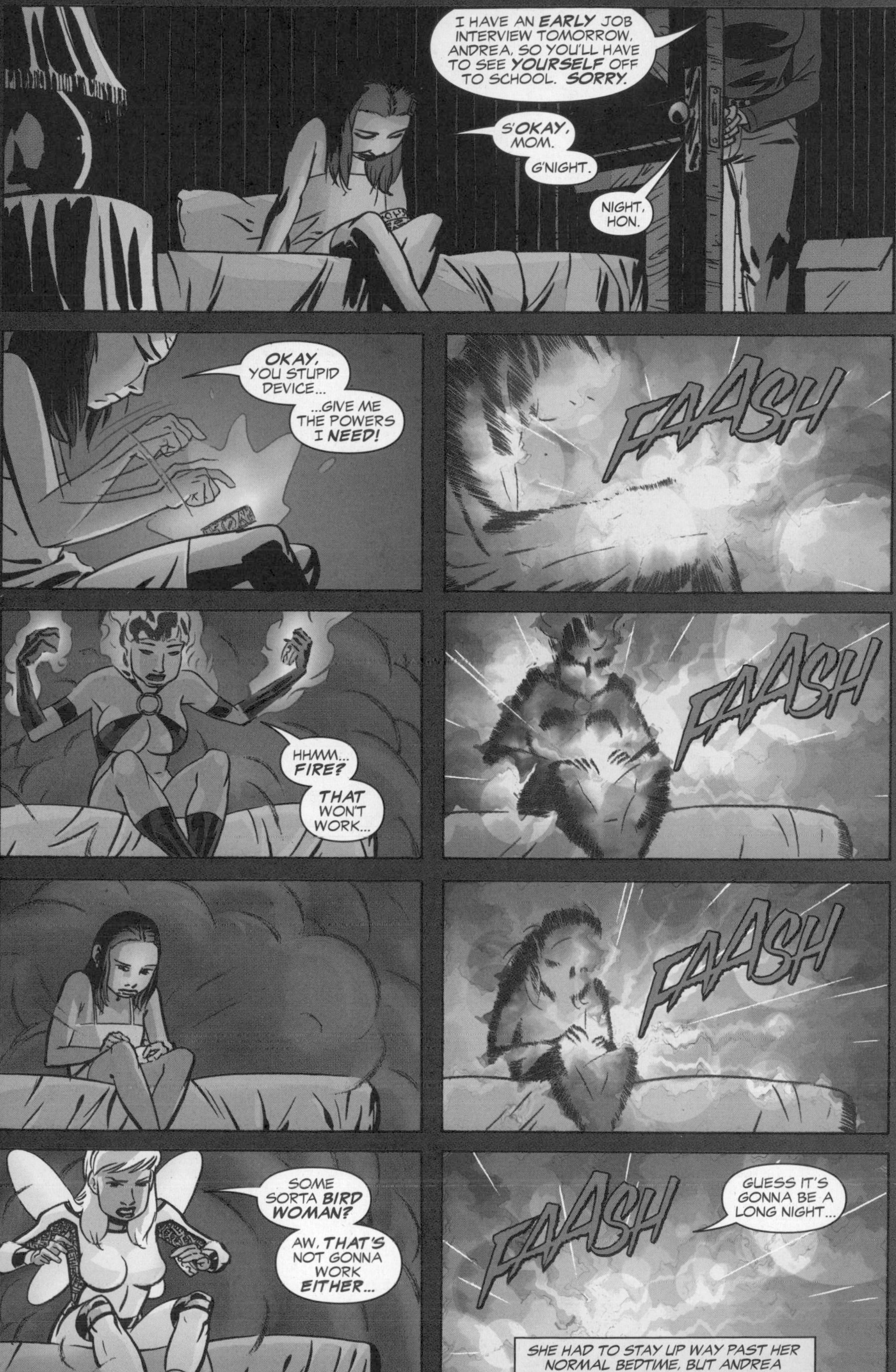
I HAVE AN EARLY JOB INTERVIEW TOMORROW, ANDREA, SO YOU'LL HAVE TO SEE YOURSELF OFF TO SCHOOL. SORRY.
S'OKAY, MOM.
G'NIGHT.
NIGHT, HON.
OKAY, YOU STUPID DEVICE... ...GIVE ME THE POWERS I NEED!
FAASH
HHMM... FIRE?
THAT WON'T WORK...
FAASH
FAASH
SOME SORTA BIRD WOMAN?
AW, THAT'S NOT GONNA WORK EITHER...
FAASH
GUESS IT'S GONNA BE A LONG NIGHT...
SHE HAD TO STAY UP WAY PAST HER NORMAL BEDTIME, BUT ANDREA FINALLY GOT THE HERO SHE NEEDED.

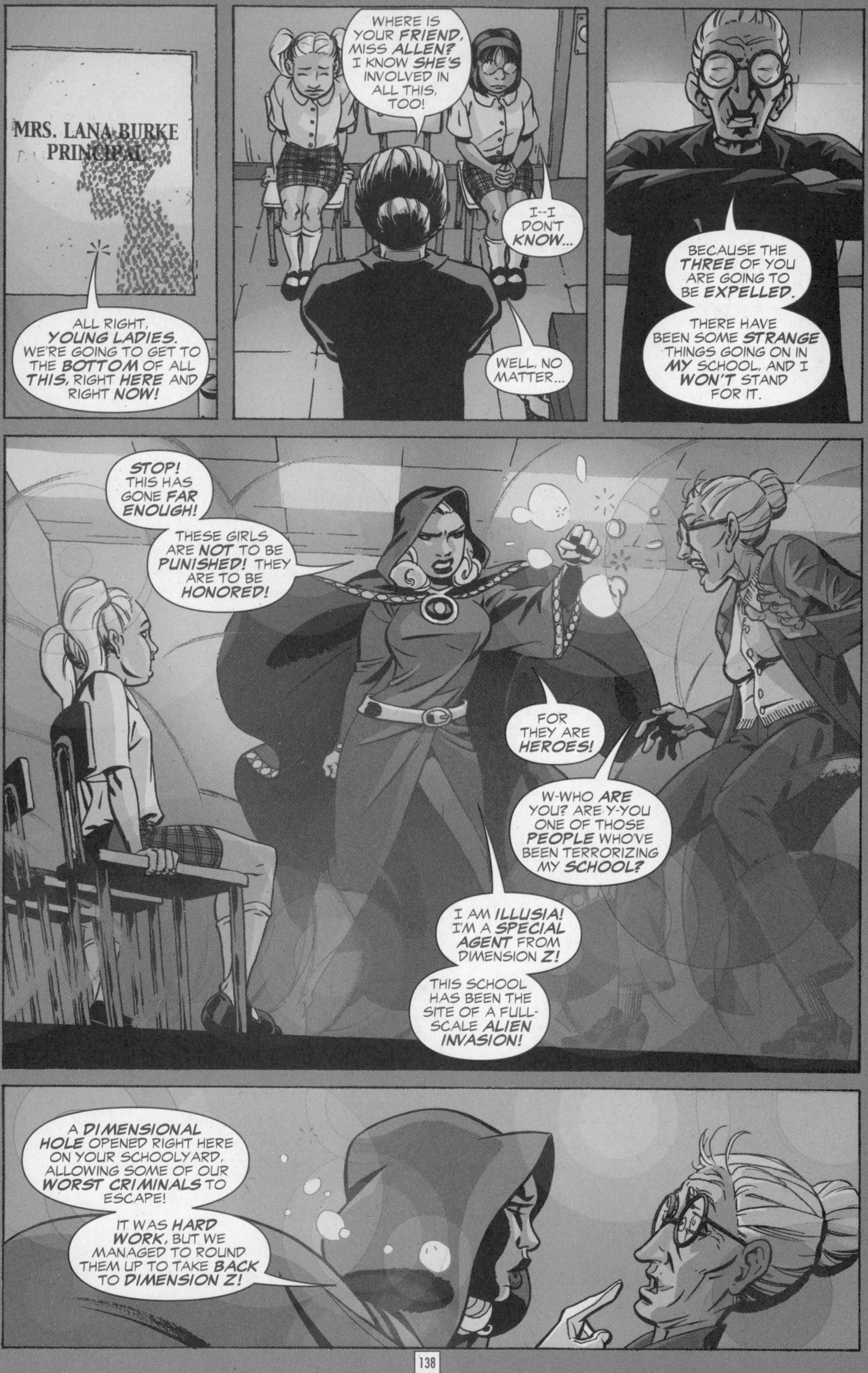
MRS. LANA BURKE
PRINCIPAL
ALL RIGHT, YOUNG LADIES. WE'RE GOING TO GET TO THE BOTTOM OF ALL THIS, RIGHT HERE AND RIGHT NOW!
WHERE IS YOUR FRIEND, MISS ALLEN? I KNOW SHE'S INVOLVED IN ALL THIS, TOO!
I--I DON'T KNOW...
WELL, NO MATTER...
BECAUSE THE THREE OF YOU ARE GOING TO BE EXPELLED.
THERE HAVE BEEN SOME STRANGE THINGS GOING ON IN MY SCHOOL, AND I WON'T STAND FOR IT.
STOP! THIS HAS GONE FAR ENOUGH!
THESE GIRLS ARE NOT TO BE PUNISHED! THEY ARE TO BE HONORED!
FOR THEY ARE HEROES!
W-WHO ARE YOU? ARE Y-YOU ONE OF THOSE PEOPLE WHO'VE BEEN TERRORIZING MY SCHOOL?
I AM ILLUSIA! I'M A SPECIAL AGENT FROM DIMENSION Z!
THIS SCHOOL HAS BEEN THE SITE OF A FULL-SCALE ALIEN INVASION!
A DIMENSIONAL HOLE OPENED RIGHT HERE ON YOUR SCHOOLYARD, ALLOWING SOME OF OUR WORST CRIMINALS TO ESCAPE!
IT WAS HARD WORK, BUT WE MANAGED TO ROUND THEM UP TO TAKE BACK TO DIMENSION Z!

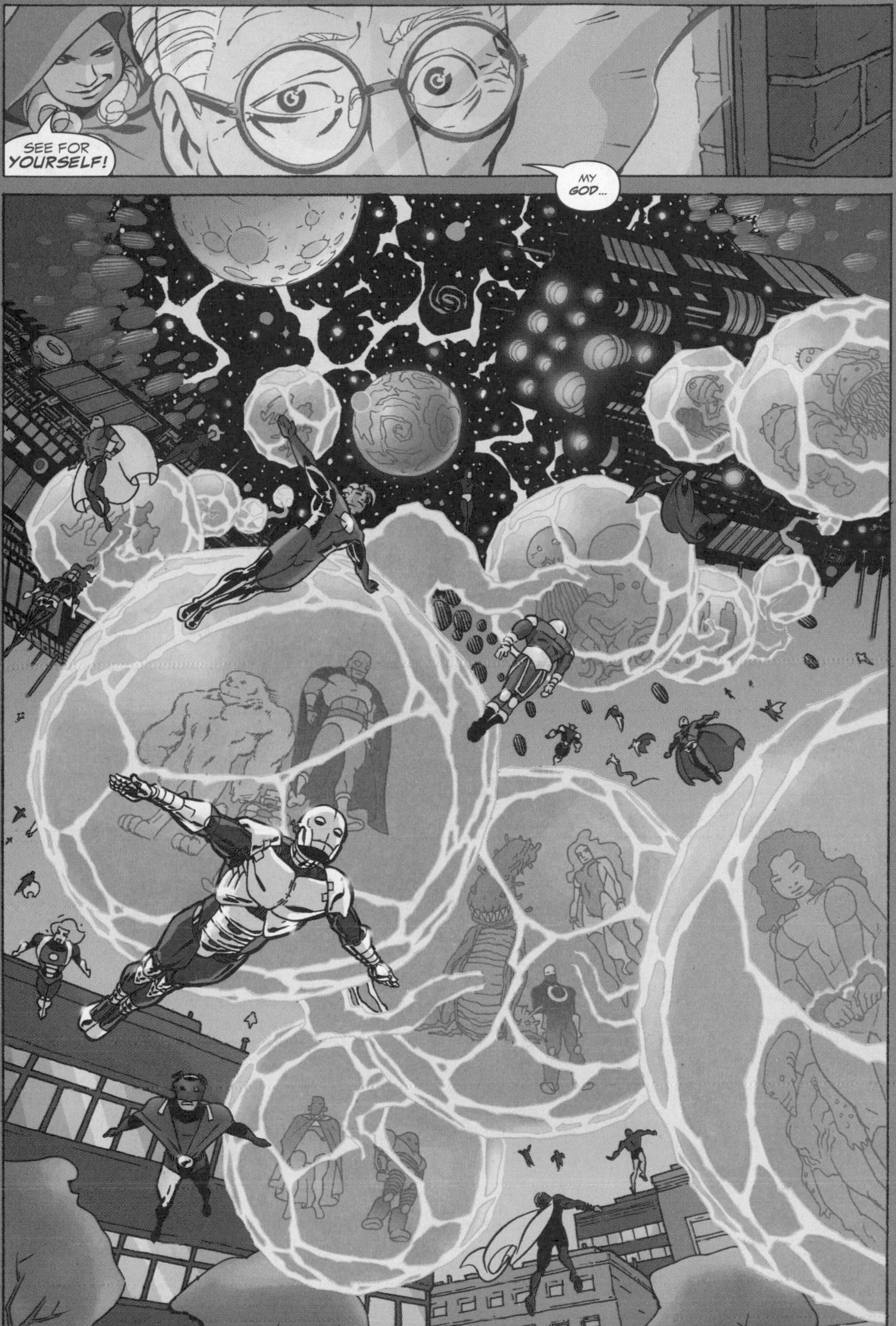
SEE FOR YOURSELF!
MY GOD...

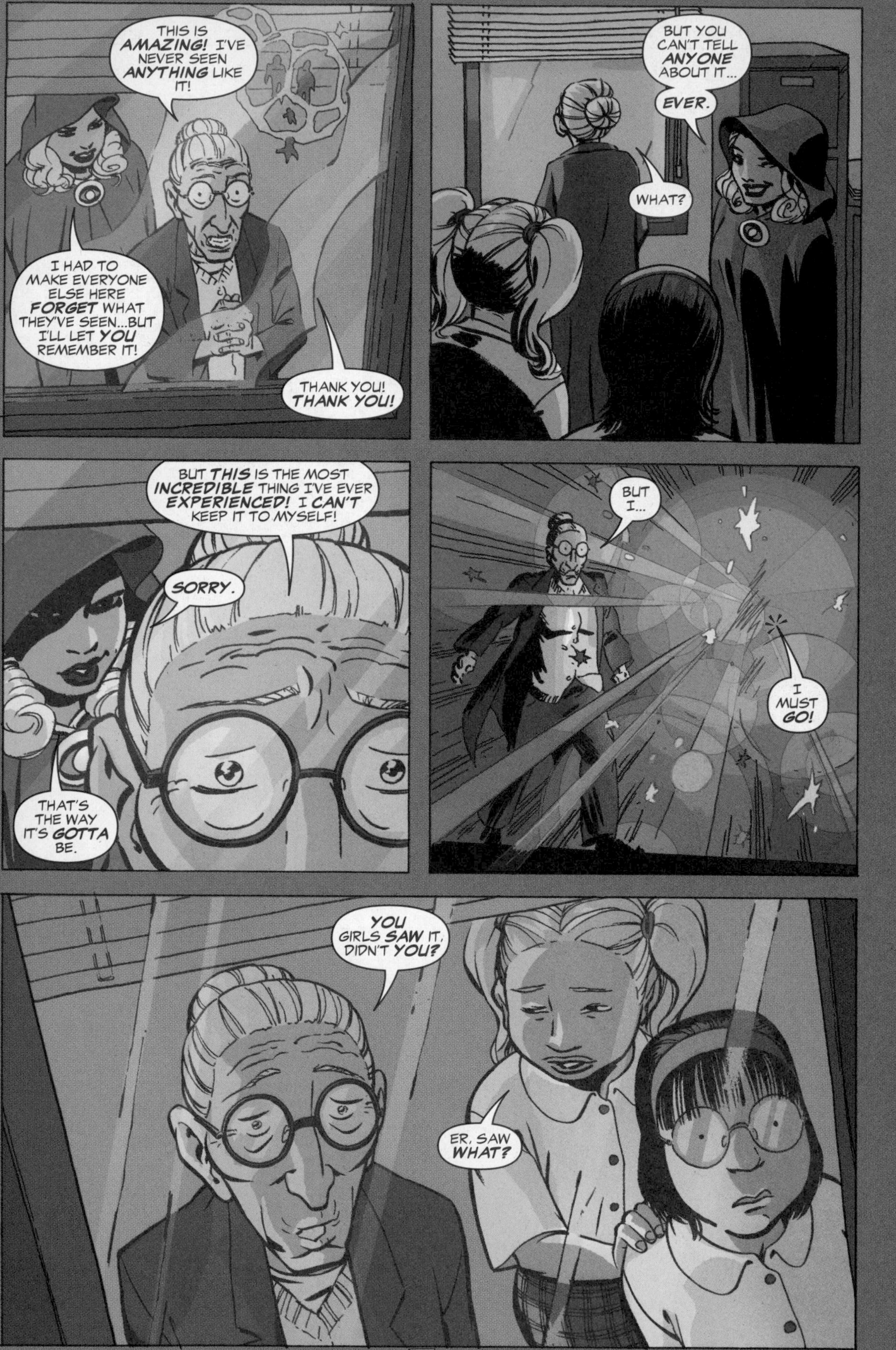
THIS IS AMAZING! I'VE NEVER SEEN ANYTHING LIKE IT!
I HAD TO MAKE EVERYONE ELSE HERE FORGET WHAT THEY'VE SEEN...BUT I'LL LET YOU REMEMBER IT!
THANK YOU! THANK YOU!
BUT YOU CAN'T TELL ANYONE ABOUT IT... EVER.
WHAT?
BUT THIS IS THE MOST INCREDIBLE THING I'VE EVER EXPERIENCED! I CAN'T KEEP IT TO MYSELF!
SORRY.
THAT'S THE WAY IT'S GOTTA BE.
BUT I...
I MUST GO!
YOU GIRLS SAW IT, DIDN'T YOU?
ER, SAW WHAT?

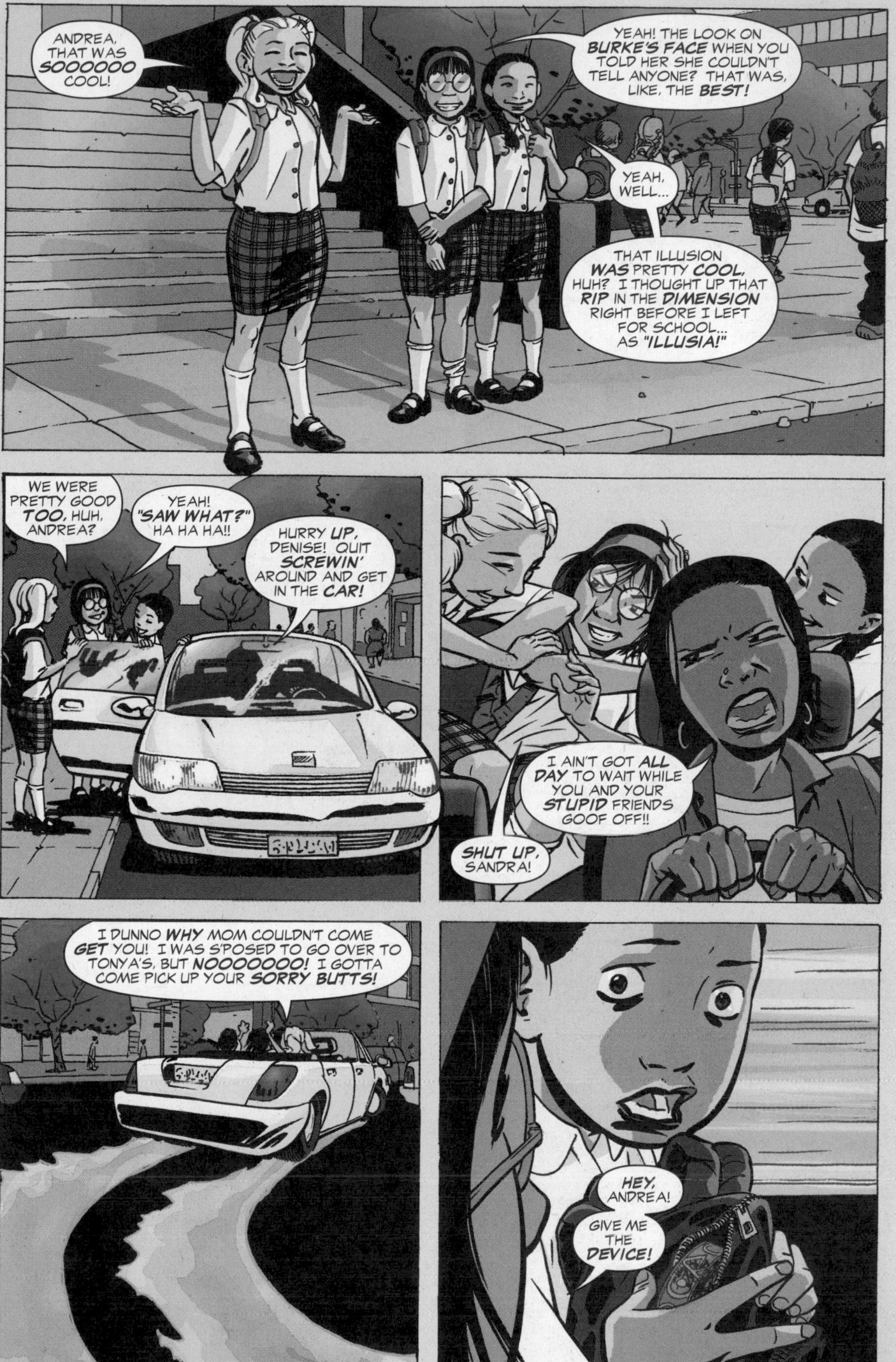

ANDREA, THAT WAS SOOOOOO COOL!
YEAH! THE LOOK ON BURKE'S FACE WHEN YOU TOLD HER SHE COULDN'T TELL ANYONE? THAT WAS, LIKE, THE BEST!
YEAH, WELL...
THAT ILLUSION WAS PRETTY COOL, HUH? I THOUGHT UP THAT RIP IN THE DIMENSION RIGHT BEFORE I LEFT FOR SCHOOL... AS "ILLUSIA!"
WE WERE PRETTY GOOD TOO, HUH, ANDREA?
YEAH! "SAW WHAT?" HA HA HA!!
HURRY UP, DENISE! QUIT SCREWIN' AROUND AND GET IN THE CAR!
I AIN'T GOT ALL DAY TO WAIT WHILE YOU AND YOUR STUPID FRIENDS GOOF OFF!!
SHUT UP, SANDRA!
I DUNNO WHY MOM COULDN'T COME GET YOU! I WAS S'POSED TO GO OVER TO TONYA'S, BUT NOOOOOOO! I GOTTA COME PICK UP YOUR SORRY BUTTS!
HEY, ANDREA!
GIVE ME THE DEVICE!

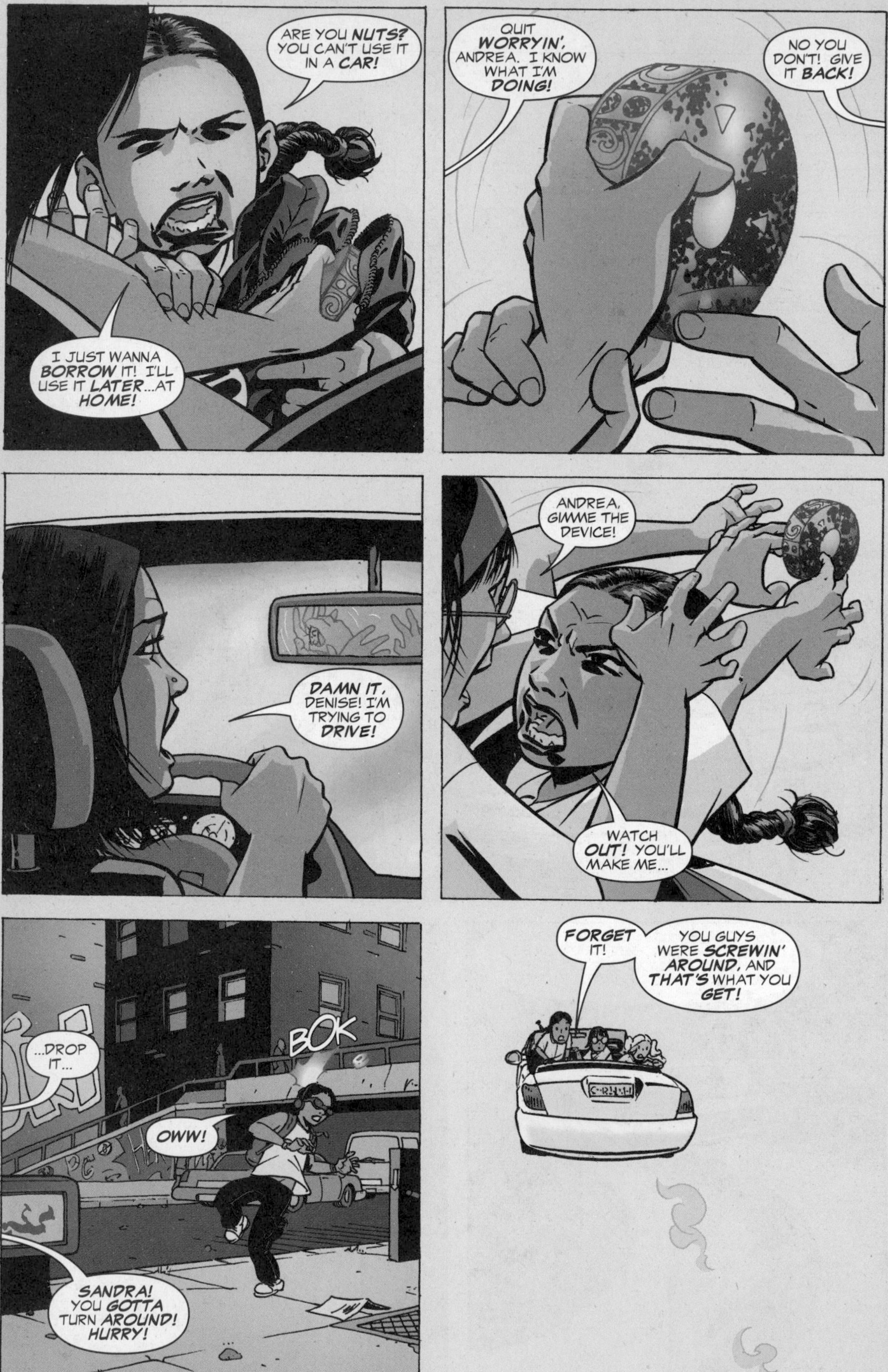
ARE YOU NUTS? YOU CAN'T USE IT IN A CAR!
I JUST WANNA BORROW IT! I'LL USE IT LATER...AT HOME!
QUIT WORRYIN', ANDREA. I KNOW WHAT I'M DOING!
NO YOU DON'T! GIVE IT BACK!
DAMN IT, DENISE! I'M TRYING TO DRIVE!
ANDREA, GIMME THE DEVICE!
WATCH OUT! YOU'LL MAKE ME...
...DROP IT...
BOK
OWW!
SANDRA! YOU GOTTA TURN AROUND! HURRY!
FORGET IT!
YOU GUYS WERE SCREWIN' AROUND, AND THAT'S WHAT YOU GET!

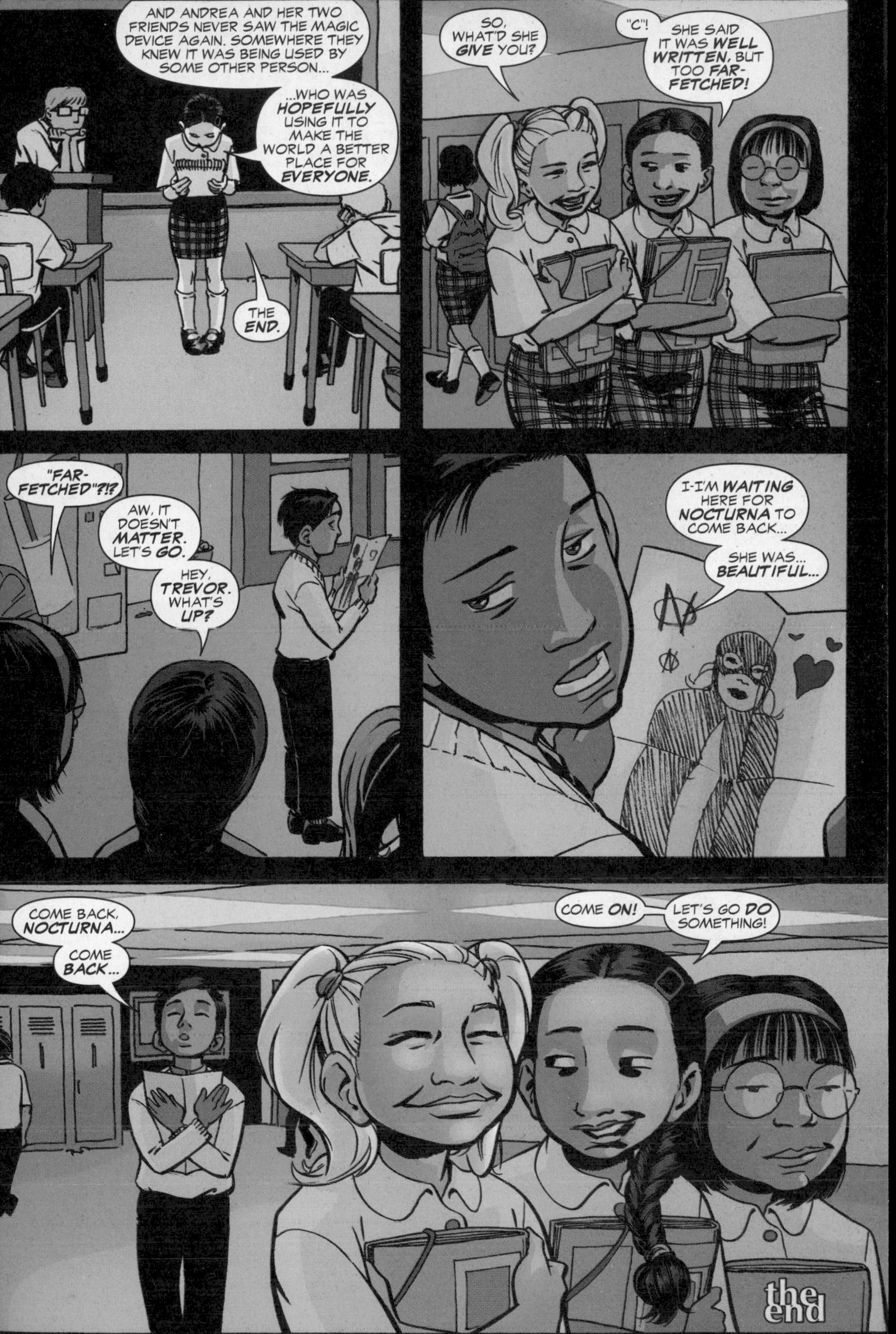
AND ANDREA AND HER TWO FRIENDS NEVER SAW THE MAGIC DEVICE AGAIN. SOMEWHERE THEY KNEW IT WAS BEING USED BY SOME OTHER PERSON...
...WHO WAS HOPEFULLY USING IT TO MAKE THE WORLD A BETTER PLACE FOR EVERYONE.
THE END.
SO, WHAT'D SHE GIVE YOU?
"C"!
SHE SAID IT WAS WELL WRITTEN, BUT TOO FAR-FETCHED!
"FAR-FETCHED"?!?
AW, IT DOESN'T MATTER. LET'S GO.
HEY, TREVOR. WHAT'S UP?
I-I'M WAITING HERE FOR NOCTURNA TO COME BACK...
SHE WAS... BEAUTIFUL...
COME BACK, NOCTURNA...
COME BACK...
COME ON!
LET'S GO DO SOMETHING!
the end

THE STARS OF THE
DC UNIVERSE
CAN ALSO BE FOUND IN THESE BOOKS:

TO FIND MORE COLLECTED EDITIONS AND MONTHLY COMIC BOOKS FROM DC COMICS,
CALL 1-888-COMIC BOOK FOR THE NEAREST COMICS SHOP OR GO TO YOUR LOCAL BOOK STORE.

Visit us at www.dccomics.com

DCU0011